Other books by Susan Noyes Platt PhD.

---

*Art and Politics Now: Cultural Activism in a Time of Crisis*
(Midmarch Arts Press, 2011)

*Art and Politics in the 1930s: Modernism, Marxism, Americanism*
*A History of Cultural Activism during the Depression Years*
(Midmarch Arts Press, 1999)

*Modernism in the 1920s: Interpretations of Modern Art in New*
*York from Expressionism to Constructivism*
(UMI Research Press, 1985)

# BREAKING GROUND

## ART MODERNISMS

### 1920-1950

---

**CLIVE BELL**    **ROGER FRY**

**SHELDON CHENEY**

**JANE HEAP**

**ALFRED H. BARR Jr.**

**ELIZABETH McCAUSLAND**

**BEN SHAHN** AND **BERNARDA BRYSON**

**HOMER SAINT-GAUDENS**

**CLEMENT GREENBERG**

---

## SUSAN NOYES PLATT PHD.

### Collected Writings Vol. 1

*This book is dedicated to my husband, Henry C. Matthews. His intellectual and emotional support is indispensable to my work and my life.*

# CONTENTS



*Original publication formatting retained. All articles published by permission.*

# Introduction

These eight essays range in date from 1985 to 1998, my core years in academia as a professor. They suggest the radical changes in my thinking from an examination of the historiography or even the archeological roots of the theories of modernism to an understanding of the intimate connections of art and politics. During those years, I transformed my practice from archival research to examining the impact of contemporary political events on critics, artists and curators. This dramatic shift is reflected in my three books, *Modernism in the 1920s*, (1985), *Art and Politics in the 1930s, Modernism, Marxism, Americanism*, (1999) and *Art and Politics Now, Cultural Activism in a Time of Crisis*, (2010). The essays in this book, all previously published, address topics included in those books, but in far more detail.

This volume is the first in a planned trilogy of my collected writings. The next two volumes will select from my art criticism. In the past two decades I have focused on reaching out to marginalized artists and ideas.

The first essay in *Breaking Ground* is archeological: it excavates almost forgotten American writers on modern art in the 1920s who practiced analysis of form. These early explorers, among them Henry McBride, Forbes Watson, and Thomas Craven, relied on the English critics Clive Bell and Roger Fry as their primary reference point. They explored formalism much as American painters in those years explored Cubism, embracing it, modifying it and doubting it. Craven and Watson later became advocates for Regionalism and American Art.

The second chapter discusses the writings of Sheldon Cheney, an eager proselytizer for modern art in the theater as well as visual art. I had the good fortune to interview him in 1979, the year before he died. His enthusiasm to help people to understand the creative process is very much in tune with the early twentieth century when accelerated change marked all aspects of life. Cheney's reference points are not only the formalism of Roger Fry and Clive Bell, but also Leo Tolstoy's *What is Art?* Tolstoy embedded art in moral principles and believed that good art was not beautiful or pleasant, but reflected the "conditions of human life."

In dramatic contrast to these writers, the third chapter addresses the dynamic Jane Heap who also worked in New York City in the 1920s. Heap personally knew and understood the artists of Dada, Surrealism, and Constructivism. While other writers wrote on familiar artists, like Picasso, she struck out into unfamiliar territory in *The Little Review* magazine and gallery. As a lesbian, she was acutely aware of the outsider status of both her thinking and that of the artists she championed. But perhaps even more formative was her childhood as the daughter of an employee of an insane asylum. She grew up feeling that the insane were far more interesting and intelligent than the sane.

Alfred Barr attended several of Jane Heap's exhibitions and echoed them in his choice of shows at the Museum of Modern Art. The fourth essay mainly focuses in detail on Alfred Barr's "Cubism and Abstract Art" exhibition at the Museum of Modern Art in 1936. The destruction of art in Hitler's Germany drove Barr to create that exhibition. Prior to visiting Germany in 1933 Barr inclined in his taste toward the eccentric, the surreal, and the expressionist. Following it, he created a seamless evolution based on formalism and abstraction that survives even to the present day in various ways. The 2019 iteration of the Museum of Modern Art strives to move beyond his deterministic model, but still clings to the anchor of his "greatest hits".

The next two essays address critics and artists of the 1930s who embraced the political concerns of the time. One focuses on Elizabeth McCausland who articulately espoused the rise of a new art that engaged social issues. She also experimented with evoking her intense sexual feelings toward Berenice Abbott in her radical prose. Artists Ben Shahn and Bernarda Bryson redefined the conventions and content of history painting as they worked for the Federal government. This essay closely examines their mural in what was known then as Jersey

Homesteads, now as Roosevelt, New Jersey. Again I was fortunate to be able to base this essay on extensive interviews with Bernarda Bryson in her home in Roosevelt in 1992. Their thinking as embodied in the mural cycle incorporates formalism as well as a radical rethinking of what constitutes American history.

The ongoing Pittsburgh Carnegie International just celebrated its 57th exhibition. But without the extraordinary work of the curator and critic Homer Saint-Gaudens from 1922 to 1950, it would probably not have survived. As he negotiated those complicated and turbulent years, Saint-Gaudens transformed the Carnegie International from a parochial event into an innovative cross section of European and American contemporary art. He also succeeded in engaging the American press and the public through various theatrical tricks and gambits. His theoretical perspectives were embodied in the exhibitions. His deep commitment to diversity and inclusion forecasts our perspectives today.

Finally, my study of Clement Greenberg's formative years in the late 1930s provides new insights that shed light on his outsized influence after World War II. It is hard to recall his pervasive influence today. Starting in the 1960s art criticism moved beyond formalism, through postmodern theory in the 1990s, and today embraces the complexities of the intersections of art and politics. Yet Greenberg's and Alfred Barr's obsession with formalist abstraction still resonates strongly in contemporary practice. We have forgotten how arbitrary, politically motivated and even mythical that idea was in its earliest formulation in the 1930s.

This collection of essays demonstrates that critics first embraced formalism in the 1920s under the impact of the English theorists Roger Fry and Clive Bell, then expanded their thinking during the Depression, the influence of Socialism and Communism, and the rise of Fascism. But those same political pressures also led to stripping an inclusive and radical vision back to a formal analysis of art and an elevation of abstraction.

# Clive Bell and Roger Fry Transform American Art Criticism in the 1920s *(1986)*

TODAY, FORMALISM IS INEXTRICABLY ASSOCIATED with the name and generation of Clement Greenberg. Scholars recognize that formalism, that method of art criticism that analyzes the abstract elements of form, color, line, space and composition, rather than story or content, has evolved from such late nineteenth century writers as Heinrich Wölfflin, through the early twentieth century English critics, Clive Bell and Roger Fry. Fry and Bell, in turn, are generally acknowledged as the primary source for Clement Greenberg's writings of the 1940s and later.

A fascinating, early chapter of formalism has been overlooked in this careful geneology. In the 1920s, a little studied generation of critics provide an important link between the first articulation of a developed formalist theory by Fry and Bell and the emergence of Greenberg's important writings. Writers such as Walter Pach, Forbes Watson, Guy Eglington and Henry McBride, all embraced the new theories of formalism and used them as fruitful, if controversial means for understanding and writing about the art of Paul Cézanne, Pablo Picasso, Henri Matisse, John Marin and Charles Sheeler, among many others. As these writers adopted the formalist method, they constantly analyzed its validity, recognized its shortcomings and discussed its strengths, in an extensive body of literature that has not heretofore been examined.

Before examining these writings, a brief summary of the theories of Bell and Fry themselves is helpful in clarifying their contributions to the introduction of formalism into America. While the two critics shared the idea of looking at a work of art in terms of form that led to an emotional response, they diverged significantly in their manner of presenting that idea. They will therefore be treated separately here.

## Clive Bell

While Roger Fry had articulated a rudimentary approach to formalism in *The Burlington Magazine* as early as 1908,[1] Clive Bell's popularization of those ideas in his book *Art,* written in 1913, first introduced formalist ideas to the general public. Bell's theory as presented in *Art* is general and all encompassing. Two key phrases stand out: "aesthetic emotion" and "significant form." Bell's definition of these terms is most frequently circular, that is, the presence of one means the presence of the other, but careful examination of *Art* does reveal the specific context in which he used the terms, if not an exact definition.

Bell was reacting to Victorian esthetics in developing the idea of "aesthetic emotion" and "significant form." He opposed art that was descriptive, informational, historical, literary or scientific. He believed that art should be detached from the "concerns of life." His model for good art was the painting of Paul Cézanne. In response to that work he felt "aesthetic emotion," and found an example of "significant form." The "aesthetic emotion" was distinct from common emotion: it made the viewer ecstatic and even giddy, but it was a feeling "lifted above the stream of life." Bell writes of Cézanne that he "carried me off my feet before ever I noticed that his strongest characteristic was an insistence on the supremacy of significant form." That form has no associations with life; it can be representative, but that is irrelevant; it must have "lines and colors combined in a particular way ... that arouses "aesthetic emotion." "Significant form" is an "ultimate reality," an "end in itself." Bell goes on to suggest in subsequent chapters of *Art* that "significant form" and "aesthetic emotion" exist in selected

---

1     Roger Fry, "The Last Phase of Impressionism," *The Burlington Magazine,* March 1908, 375-376.

examples of art throughout history. He sees art and religion as similar manifestations of "spiritual universals." On the other hand, although "significant form" is apparent in many stages of art, it disappears in the nineteenth century, until Cézanne, who is, according to Bell, "the Christopher Columbus of a new continent of form."[2]

Bell's book is a readable treatise on aesthetic theory. The energy and style with which he presents his terms led to a widespread and positive response. During the late teens and early twenties, Bell wrote frequently for American magazines such as *The New Republic*, *Vogue*, and *Vanity Fair*.[3] These articles primarily elaborated on his original principles in various ways. They never superceded the general public's identification of Bell with his first book, or the identification of that book as the primary treatise on modern aesthetics. The impact of *Art* was immediate. Shortly after its publication Elizabeth Luther Cary quoted passages in the *New York Times*."[4] By 1916 it was familiar to intellectuals.

One excited response to Bell's book appears in an autobiography by Madge Jenison, owner of the Sunwise Turn Bookshop, an intellectual center in the late teens and early 1920s. She writes: "I began to think about Clive Bell's essay on art. I had often thought of it that winter. Mr. Arthur Davies had brought it back from England in the fall and we had passed it around and talked it up to midnight."[5] As a result of that experience, Jenison decided to open her bookshop in 1916 to make *Art*, in particular, available to the general public.

Another example of Bell's influence that is clearly acknowledged appears in the writings of Sheldon Cheney. Cheney had begun his career as a theatre critic, but in the late teens he read Clive Bell's book and began utilizing the terminology of "significant form." It became the basis for his explanation of modern art in his influential *Primer of*

---

2     Clive Bell, *Art* (New York: G.P. Putnam's Sons, 1958), pp. 17-18,27,36 46,54,63,139.

3     Clive Bell, "The Rise and Decline of Cubism," *Vanity Fair*, February 1923, p.53: Clive Bell, -Modern Art and How To Look At It," *Vanity Fair*, April 1924, pp. 56, 58.

4     Elizabeth Luther Cary, *The New York Times*, January 26, 1913, sec. 7, p. 10.

5     Madge Jenison, *Sunwise Turn, A Human Comedy of Book Selling* (New York: E.P. Dutton, 1923), pp. 2-3.

*Modern Art* published in 1924. In the introduction to the *Primer* he states: "the clearest elementary treatise about [form] … is to be found in an admirable little book titled *Art* by Clive Bell. … Despite the dangers in such a catch phrase, it is so serviceable that I shall use it often."[6] The *Primer* remained in print for over forty years, with only minor editorial changes, and was read by generations of introductory classes in modern art. A clearer documentation of Bell's influence cannot be imagined.

A humorous glossary of art terms written in 1925 parodied Bell's terminology, particularly with respect to his accessibility and popularity. The "Complete Dictionary of Modern Art Terms for the Use of Aspiring Amateurs" commented on Bell near the end of the lengthy series of articles, although he is also mentioned at the beginning as one of the authorities consulted:

> Form—An ancient deity whose empire, however, only reached its widest sway in the year 1920, which saw the publication of Mr. Clive Bell's *Art*. True, He bore a brand new name, having been hailed by Mr. Bell by the title of Significant, but neither Mr. Bell, nor any of his followers were at all clear as to the meaning of this new distinction. Having prostrated themselves before the altar of an Unknown God, they merely hoped that the addition of a still more ineffable and, by the same token, indefinable, title, would render His throne for all time unassailable. Alas for their piety. They were born in an age of Unbelievers and Blasphemers, who subjected their God to so merciless a fire of criticism that after five years the greater part of His empire has been wrested from Him and His title even to what remains in question. [7]

This lengthy parody foreshadows the objections to formalism that began to surface around the middle of the 1920s. While in 1922 Bell was celebrated by *Vanity Fair* as a nomination for the "Hall of Fame"[8]

---

6     Sheldon Cheney, *A Primer of Modern Art* (New York: Boni and Liveright, 1924), pp. 39-40. See next essay in this collection.

7     Guy Eglington, "Art and Other Things," *International Studio*, August 1925, p. 377; other installments of the "Dictionary" appeared in Eglington's column *International Studio* throughout 1925.

8     "We nominate for the Hall of Fame," *Vanity Fair*, September 1922.

and described as a "bringer of enlightenment," by 1926 he was being attacked as too far removed from the real world.

One important article in *The Journal of the Barnes Foundation* provides the summary of the arguments over formalism. The article admits the importance of Bell in the opening paragraph by saying that he "expressed a conviction and a standard widely influential in contemporary art criticism," that of the importance of form over subject. Bell is also credited with "driving home to the popular consciousness the truth that a picture is not good because it resembles the original." The objection was to the idea that a picture was "independent of its relationship to any real thing." In other words, art that was not an illustration was acceptable, but art that was unrelated to life in any definable way was not acceptable.[9] This subtle distinction would be the basis for the heated attack on formalism and abstract art in general. In a 1928 *Nation* review of a later book by Bell, *Landmarks in Nineteenth Century Painting*, the author attacked his "inadequate notion of life which more than anything else has led Mr. Bell to alienate and esotericize art. It is clear enough that Mr. Bell does really consider modern industrial and social life to consist in humdrummery. The ideal artist is removed from the forces of our age because art has nothing to do with our crass concerns."[10] Bell's intellectuality was an issue in a review of another book by Bell, *Civilization, An Essay.* The critic was even more adamant than the *Nation* reviewer had been: "Mr. Bell's reverence and Platonic adoration of the mind and understanding of man entangled him in a chain of conceits and abstractions from which all observations of experience are excluded. ... Mr. Bell's civilized state mirrors only a conception of beauty, unreal and changeless."[11]

The reference to Bell's intellectuality relates to his formation as part of the Bloomsbury group, a brilliant group of thinkers that included Virginia Woolf, Maynard Keynes, Lytton Strachey, and Roger Fry.

---

9       Laurence Buermeyer, "Pattern and Plastic Form," *The Journal of the Barnes Foundation,* January 1926, reprinted in John Dewey, *et. al., Art and Education* (Merion: Barnes Foundation Press, 1929), pp. 99-102.

10      Henry Ladd, "Art: Since Clive Bell," *The Nation,* January 4, 1928, p. 28.

11      Leo Gershoy, "Review of Civilization, An Essay," *The Arts,* November 1928, p. 296.

Yet, this sophisticated metaphysical aspect of his thinking was generally lost, in the interest of his catchwords, "significant form" and "aesthetic emotion." Bell's oversimplification of complex ideas made him an easy target for superficial understanding.

## Roger Fry

While Bell was a successful popularizer, although with a solid intellectual foundation, Roger Fry was a systematic analyzer. Initially, his ideas were the springboard for Bell's book.[12] In 1909 Fry's "Essay on Aesthetics," carefully identified what he calls the emotional elements of design: rhythm, mass, space, light and shade, color, order and variety. Even as Fry was more systematic and specific, he shared with Bell an emphasis on the emotional response to art. But that emotional response was not identified by a cliché, rather it manifested itself throughout Fry's writings, in his very personal response to individual works of art. Fry builds and expands beyond his initial thesis in a rich series of essays and lectures that encompass his excited responses to a wide variety of art from many artistic traditions. Fry, trained as a painter, as well as a critic and intellectual, allows the formal analysis to become a method, as much as a theory.

Fry dwelt on "vision" more than Bell. Where Bell defined a particular feeling in response to the work of art, Fry defined a type of looking: "This is at once more intense and more detached from the passions of the instinctive life. Those who indulge in this vision are apprehending the relation of forms and colors."[13]

Fry then, like Bell, considers art and the art experience as a separate sphere from ordinary life. Yet, at the same time, in his discussion of particular work, he responds to art sensitively and specifically. He

---

12    Frances Spalding, *Roger Fry, Art and Life* (Berkeley: University of California Press, 1980, p. 164.

13    Roger Fry, *Vision and Design* (London: Chatto and Windus, 1925), p. 49. All further references are to this edition, unless otherwise indicated.

speaks of Mayan sculpture or the painting of Giotto equally eloquently using the language of form:

> Now with Giotto, beautiful as his line undoubtedly is, it is not the first quality ... that impresses us. ... It is in its significance for the expression of form with the utmost lucidity, the most logical interrelation of parts that his line is so impressive ... we feel at once the relation of the shoulders to one another, the relation of the torso to the pelvis.

Thus, Fry looks at art concretely. While Bell introduced the general ideas of formalism, Fry demonstrated how they could be used creatively and not poetically.

Fry was familiar to the major art critics, less familiar to the general public. For example, Arthur Dow, Professor of Art at Columbia University, cited Fry in his 1917 discussion of modernism. While he also mentions Bell, Dow's definitions of modernism read like an excerpt from Fry's "Essay in Aesthetics."[14]

The important philosopher-critic, Willard Huntington Wright, mentions the English critics as "the ablest and most discerning defenders of the modern spirit in England."[15] In Wright's 1916 essay, "The Aesthetic Struggle in America," he attacked American criticism, suggesting Fry and Bell as standards."[16] In his own book on art, *Modern Painting*, Wright differs from Fry and Bell by giving more emphasis to color and depth, as well as to the philosophy of Frederich Nietzsche. But he also adopted the language of formalism from the English critics. Wright was widely read by American critics, and reinforced the attention given to formalism in the 1920s.

Another reflection of the influence of Roger Fry in particular appears in reviews of his book *Vision and Design. The Arts*, a widely read

---

14    Arthur Dow, "Modernism in Art," *American Magazine of Art*, January 1917, p. 116.

15    Willard Huntington Wright, *Modern Painting Its Tendency and Meaning* (New York: John Lane, 1915), p. 341.

16    Willard Huntington Wright, "The Aesthetic Struggle in America," *The Forum*, February 1916, p. 208.

and influential art magazine, carried two reviews of the book because the editor, Hamilton Easter Field, was a friend of Fry's. He saw Fry as a fellow Quaker and embraced the book as an example of tolerance. The first review, by Alan Burroughs, quoted extensively from the text and contrasted Fry's broadmindedness with Bell's narrowness. The second review, by Field himself, developed the issue of Fry's separation of "actual life and imaginative life." He took exception to Fry's attempt to separate them, although he otherwise celebrated the critic. The reviews are significant, not only for their careful appraisal of Fry's ideas, but also for their lengthy quotations, which ensured direct transmission of Fry's ideas.[17]

An even more detailed discussion of Fry's ideas was carried by *The Dial,* a magazine directed to the intellectual at large, rather than the art world specifically. Thomas Craven, a critic better known today for his regionalist criticism in the 1930s, stated that "*Vision and Design* is one of the few books written on art in the last decade that are worth reading."[18] He went on to state Fry's premise that "the meaning of art lies in its forms," but criticized him for failure to distinguish between meaning and representation. In subsequent issues of *The Dial,* Craven adopted Fry's principles of form in a lengthy examination called "The Progress of Painting," his own version of the history of art.[19]

The discussion of Fry's views continued in *The Dial* in 1924. Laurence Buermeyer, an associate of the Barnes Foundation, objected to Fry's failure to distinguish between the aesthetic imagination and mere daydreaming. He also found Fry's separation of the emotions and the senses erroneous. He went on to attack Craven's articles as well.[20] Craven rebutted with a third article that claimed he had identified the

---

17    Alan Burroughs, "Review of *Vision and Design,*" *The Arts,* May 1921, pp. 57-58. "Hamilton Easter Field, "Review of *Vision and Design,*" *The Arts,* May 1921, pp. 57-58.

18    Thomas Craven, "Mr. Roger Fry and The Artistic Vision," *The Dial,* July 1921, pp. 101-106.

19    Thomas Craven, 'The Progress of Painting," *The Dial,* April 1923, pp. 357-367 and pp. 581-593.

20    Laurence Buermeyer, "Some Popular Fallacies in Aesthetics," *The Dial,* February 1924, p. 116.

weakness in the English critic's ideas, particularly concerning the "indi-visibility of form and content."[21]

By 1928, a review in *The Arts* stated more directly the central reservation about Fry's aesthetics and summed up the position of critics who were gradually rejecting formalism. The author, Virgil Barker, praised Fry for his brilliant writing and sensitive eye, but spoke of the "limitations of pure art." He saw Fry's purist aesthetic theories developing in a culture where "art itself has been reduced to a side issue out of touch with the main current of life. [22]

Even as a growing sentiment resisted the separation of art from life in the reviews of Fry's books, the methods of formalism were being increasingly adopted. One evidence of this approach appears in the theoretical treatises by artists published throughout the 1920s. Much like the watered down influence of Cézanne and Cubism on American painting, these treatises watered down formalism and combined it with individual artists' prejudices. Thomas Hart Benton's series of articles called "The Mechanics of Form Organization in Painting," is one example of this use of formalism. Benton combined ideas of Fry, Bell, Wright and other sources into a theory that formed the basis for his teaching at the Art Students League.[23]

## Formalism and the Art Critics

A specific analysis of the writings of selected critics demonstrates how they used formal analysis. In very few cases did a critic of the 1920s adopt it as the only perspective. The nature of the art under review determined the appropriate use of the formal terminology. Naturally, it

---


21     Thomas Craven, "Psychology and Common Sense," *The Dial*, March 1924, p. 240.

22     Virgil Barker, "Aesthetics and Scholarship," *The Arts*, January 1926, p. 64.

23     Thomas Hart Benton," The Mechanics of Form Organization in Painting," *The Arts*, November 1926, pp. 285-289; December 1926, pp. 340-342; March 1927, pp. 145-148. For another discussion of Benton's aesthetics see my Masters thesis "Thomas Hart Benton as Aesthetic Theoretician" (Brown University, 1972).

appeared most frequently in discussion of artists whose pictorial aims were more abstract.

## Forbes Watson

Forbes Watson, a prominent critic of the 1920s, combined his duties as editor of *The Arts* with a regular column in the *New York World*. Watson had graduated from Harvard University and received a degree from Columbia Law School, but decided to pursue a career in art criticism instead. By the time of the Armory Show in 1913, he was already an established, if not particularly avant-garde, commentator on the art scene. In his newspaper column, written for a general audience, he utilized formal analysis to demonstrate that modern art was not illustration. Watson specifically praised Fry as "one of the best writers on art alive."[24]

For *The Arts,* by contrast, he wrote long monographic articles, a novelty for art critics in those years. They were on a range of artists from the Renoiresque William Glackens to the more up-to-date Charles Sheeler. His criticism of Sheeler most clearly demonstrates his use of a formal vocabulary combined with his own concern with the indigenous design tradition:

> What he evidently looks at and strives, successfully I believe, to put down, is its (the barn's) structural character—the rela-tion of its planes, the inherent quality of its materials, the meaning of its forms. How do the planes move one against the other? ... In his exquisite arrangement of space, in his complete destruction of the superfluous, Sheeler reaches the cool, refreshing heights of the best periods of American design and, most important of all, his work is imbued with the necessary element of life, that native tang and fragrance, that sense of inherent quality without which art-cannot rise above logic.[25]

---

24    Forbes Watson, clipping from *The World,* February 1, 1925, n.p. on microfilm 1349, Archives of American Art, Smithsonian Institution, Washington, D.C..

25    Forbes Watson, "Charles Sheeler," *The Arts,* May 1923, pp. 341, 344.

In the art of Sheeler, Watson found a combination of form consciousness and meaning that he felt necessary for the highest quality in art.

While in *The Arts* Watson increasingly bemoaned the theoretical aspects of modern art and formalism, in his newspaper column for a more general audience, he emphasized the absence of literalism and photographic qualities, using more formal language. About Picasso's work in 1923 he wrote: "The parts are welded together in a whole, the quality of the form and the quality of the color belong together."[26] Careful reading of Watson's criticism reveals that he rarely analyzed individual works of art, but most often used the art as a support for a political position with respect to his ideas on modernism or nativism. As the decade progressed he increasingly supported the latter view and supported the artists like Grant Wood and Thomas Hart Benton who emphasized subject matter reflecting American themes.

## Henry McBride

Henry McBride was easily the best known critic of the 1920s. He began his career as a painter in New York City, created an art school for the Educational Alliance in the late years of the nineteenth century, then became director of the Trenton Industrial Art School. From 1900 to 1912 he travelled in the United States and Europe, reading extensively in American literature. His career as an art critic began with *The New York Sun* in 1912; the Sunday art page of that newspaper remained his main affiliation until 1920, when he also joined *The Dial.*[27]

McBride met Roger Fry as early as 1910, for he describes Fry showing him Matisse's bronze relief sculpture, at that time in London.[28] As a result of his early awareness of modern art and literature (he was also a close friend of Gertrude Stein), McBride's perspective was more sophisticated than that of many other critics. He could analyze work

---

26     Forbes Watson, "Pablo Picasso Knocks Loudly at the Doors," *The World,* November 25, 1923.

27     Henry McBride Papers, microfilms NMcB 7, frames 350-648 (miscellaneous letters and journals).

28     Henry McBride, *Matisse* (New York: Knopf, 1930, pp. 14-15.

with magnificent sensitivity if he chose, although more frequently he enjoyed the gossip of the art world or more general issues.

In a 1924 review of the work of Abraham Walkowitz he admitted his bias toward formal components more than subjects. In speaking of Walkowitz's subjects he writes that it was "one of the rare instances in which I find myself as a critic thinking of the matter that an artist presents rather than the manner."[29]

On the other hand, his style of analysis was Whitmanesque, or perhaps influenced by the aesthete Walter Pater. Like them, he felt the energy of the work as much as the form. About Charles Demuth he said evocatively: "The Demuth color is like light that has glanced through jewels on its way to the paper."[30] On John Marin, McBride wrote: "The opposing currents of modern life beat in upon Marin's spirit relentlessly. He feels each jerky jazzlike force that comes along and, to the death, must translate into rhythms." McBride believed that Nadelman had "a sure enough knowledge of form, but doesn't hesitate to sacrifice a muscle or two for the sake of the greater rhythms."[31]

Although McBride knew formalist aesthetics, his analysis was impulsive and intuitive rather than systematic. He believed that people should learn about art by looking at it rather than by reading about it, and he was at heart an elitist. In a letter to Gertrude Stein, in which he remarked on a review of Stein's writing, he wrote: "It is fine—but I almost regret she did it, and I hated to see her help the mob so much."[32] He also had a low opinion of American modern art, although he frequently editorialized about his desire to see a strong modern tradition develop in America. Again to Gertrude Stein, he commented: "I dare say that our modernists are all replicas of Paris originals, just as our impressionists were."[33] Thus, McBride's use of formalism was certainly

---

29    Henry McBride, "Walkowitz and the Parks," *International Studio,* November 1924, p. 156.

30    Henry McBride, "Modern Art," *The Dial,* June 1926, p. 527.

31    Henry McBride, "Modern Art," *The Dial,* April 1927, p.353.

32    Henry McBride, letter to Gertrude Stein, December 12, 1913. McBride Papers, Yale University, New Haven.

33    Henry McBride, letter to Gertrude Stein, January 5, 1920. McBride Papers, Yale University, New Haven.

part of a much larger position, based on his real understanding of modern art and modern aesthetics, but disdainful of derivative modernism.

## Walter Pach

Walter Pach's criticism was also a peculiar blend of formalism and other theories. Pach was trained as a painter and lived for many years in Paris. Although he was more directly involved with French aesthetic theory than with English formalism, he acknowledged a debt to Roger Fry in an article of 1922.[34] As one of the most informed commentators on the Armory Show of 1913, Pach had written on modern art frequently since that year. In a 1913 magazine article he commented, for example, that Post-Impressionism was "the embodiment of living ideas in forms which respond to the sense of beauty in men… [It is] the conveying of the particular emotion which has seemed important to the producer.… [It is] an aesthetic equivalent of thought!"[35] While Pach gave the "particular emotion" a more intellectual quality than did Fry or Bell, he shared with them a concern for separating responses to art from other types of experiences.

Pach was usually vague when he wrote about an artist's work, preferring to use sweeping generalities that implied an on-going development or evolution, rather than examining a piece in detail. For example, he identified Picasso's "investigation of pictorial structures."[36] When he looked at a painting by Matisse he interpreted it as an intellectual act: "[The] purity of design, the calm beauty of color…are guarantees that the image has passed through the alembic of his mind." His wedding of an intellectual version of formalism with evolutionary determinism is clear in his comment on Diego Rivera: "The lines and colors of his frescoes are brought to a unity even severer, more organic than that which he could attain in the previous stage of his evolution."[37]

---

34    Walter Pach. "An Artist's Criticism," *The Freeman,* October 25, 1922, p. 165.

35    Walter Pach, "The Point of View of the Moderns," *International Studio,* April 1914.

36    Walter Pach *The Masters of Modern Art* (New York: B.W. Huebsch 1924), p. 94.

37    Ibid., pp. 98, 99.

By the mid 1920s Pach's combination of formalism and, evolutionary determinism was considered obsolete as a method of analysis of modern art by the more up-to-date commentators. The clearest statement on Pach's critical position as a promulgator of formal aesthetics was made by his colleague, Guy Eglington, in a review by Pach's 1924 book *The Masters of Modern Art*. He writes:

> [One] is grateful to Pach for reminding us that there are still a few people in the world capable of thinking clearly on art and presenting their conclusions logically and with concision. ... [This book] gives such a definite expression to accepted-modern esthetic theory, that one is tempted to wonder whether that theory has not seen its best days. ...

> It has long been growing evident that the greatness of these men is dependent on other things besides their mastery over light. ... Likewise ... the concept of *form* [emphasis Eglington] too is a useful illusion that has had its day. ... Pach's book carries the theory almost to a point where further development is almost impossible.[38]

## Guy Eglington

Guy Eglington, author of the review, was one of the most outspoken critics of the period. He is unknown today because his career was cut short by accidental drowning at the age of thirty-two in June 1928.[39] An Englishman who had studied in Germany, Eglington came to the United States as editor of *The International Studio,* a post he held from November 1920 to March 1922. He later became co-editor of *The Art News.* While his signed articles in the latter publication are few, he wrote anonymous reviews that *The Art News* carried during the middle

---

38     Guy Eglington, "Art and Other Things," *International Studio,* January 1925, p. 341. Another review that criticized Pach was by Robert Allerton Parker in *The Arts,* January 1925, pp. 51-52.

39     "Eglington Drowned," *The Art Digest,* July 1928, p. 4. The article mentions that Eglington had been in a German detention camp during World War I where "he had nothing to do but read and think, and ponder upon the meaning of things."

years of the 1920s. Eglington's relationship to formalism is sophisti-cated. He used it as a means to analyze art, but never let it become a limitation in his interpretation of the object.

Eglington's real contribution to the art criticism of the 1920s was in his skeptical attitude to the overuse of the language of criticism: he is the author of the "Complete Dictionary of Modern Art Terms" already quoted above. Utilizing specific analysis of a painting was an unusual approach for him. In 1925 he writes in an article on Seurat's *Baignade*:

> (The *Baignade*) is the outcome of two preoccupations which he was later to subordinate, the preoccupation with light, … which grew out of his crayon drawings, and a preoccupation with mass, which he had been developing simultaneously in the drawings and in his early essays in paint. If he relies here as later on the horizontal, it is by instinct and not in response to any compositional theory, and the too logical corollary of the horizontal, the perpendicular, is conspicuously missing... he is not concerned with subtle distortions in the direction of compositional angles, but is content to let figures and trees keep their own shapes. …[40]

Eglington's analysis is underlaid by a subtle determinist or evolu-tionary strain that he shared with Walter Pach; he looked at an early work in relationship to what he knew would come next.[41] On the other hand, the freshness and accuracy of the analysis puts him in a separate class from the other critics concerned here. Unfortunately, he chose to use his sensitivity to mock the use of art critical terms rather than fully develop his own approach to art criticism.

---

40    Guy Eglington, "The Theory of Seurat," *International Studio*, July 1925, p. 290.

41    The clearest statement of Eglington's interest in evolution as a method of criticism is in his "The American Painter," *The American Mercury*, February 1924, pp. 218-220.

## Thomas Craven

The heavy debt that Thomas Craven owed to Roger Fry has been established earlier in this article by analysis of his reviews of Fry's *Vision and Design*. Craven taught English to support himself as a poet in the teens. He became affiliated with *The Dial* in 1920. Since McBride was the art critic for that publication, his writings for it were mainly book reviews. Occasionally he wrote longer articles such as his "Progress of Painting," a rudimentary history of art.[42]

Craven's coverage of specific artists appeared in *Shadowland*, a theatre and movie publication. In a series of essays written between 1921 and 1923, Craven looked at the art of Thomas Hart Benton, John Marin, Edwin Dickinson, Charles Demuth, Joseph Stella and Charles Sheeler, His articles usually opened with a theoretical discussion. In the Benton piece, for example, he treated the connection between modern and classic art in their dependence on the principles of form. Craven, like Pach and Watson, rarely treated specific works, but generalized about compositions and colors. For Craven, Benton's compositions were "still an exceedingly conscious process with him and his struggles to make a form obey a certain curve or fill a given amount of space are evinced in the finished work,"[43] In an article an Marin, he primarily commented on Marin's own art theories, but finally declared about the recent painting that "his design is larger, more direct and strengthened in general effect by heavier masses and sharper more assured drawing."[44]

Craven reveals his formalist approach most clearly in his analysis of Charles Sheeler's painting and photography:

> Compare his oil study of skyscrapers with his camera study
> of the same. In the painting I find a certain definite quality,
> a linear precision and a remarkable tonal range which sug-
> gest the photograph, but the beauty of the painting lies in its
> design, in the imaginative reconstruction of the basic planes

---

42    Craven, "Progress," see footnote 19.

43    Thomas Craven, "Thomas Hart Benton," *Shadowland*, September 1921, p. 66.

44    Thomas Craven, "John Marin," *Shadowland*, October 1921, p. 77.

to produce a new form stronger than the literal object of the negative.[45]

In the late twenties Craven took up the cause of Thomas Hart Benton, abandoning intellectual subtlety for a celebration of American subject matter and a denigration of modern theory. Craven dismisses the carefully argued subtleties of his reviews of Fry's *Vision and Design* over the relationship of art and life, and adopts instead a harsh rhetoric in support of American art. Yet, even at the height of his success as promoter of Regionalism, Craven maintained a clear respect for Bell and Fry. In a bibliographic note for his survey of art called *Men of Art*, published in 1931, he concludes:

> Fry *Vision and Design, Transformations*. Miscellaneous essays by one of the best living critics. Fry is an ardent champion of modernist art which he defends with the highest intelligence. Bell *Art, Since Cézanne*, art for art's sake applied to the Modernists.[46]

## John Dewey

Perhaps the most surprising analysis from the waning days of the first wave of formalism came from John Dewey, the inspiration of critics like Forbes Watson and Thomas Craven, who sought an alternative to the formal approach to art. In a 1931 lecture Dewey acknowledged the importance of Fry with lengthy quotations from the English critic about aesthetic vision. Dewey comments that Fry gives an

> excellent account of the sort of thing that takes place in artistic perception and construction. It makes clear two things: Representation is not, if the vision has been artistic of 'objects as such'. ... It is not the kind of representation that a camera would report. ... [47]

45    Thomas Craven, "Charles Sheeler," *Shadowland*, March 1923, p. 71.

46    Thomas Craven, *Men of Art* (New York: Simon and Schuster, 1940) p. 516.

47    John Dewey, *Art as Experience* (New York: GP Putnum's 1958) p. 87.

However, in a crucial passage Dewey goes on to say that "one thing may be added. ... The painter did not approach the scene with an empty mind, but with a background of experiences."[48] Thus, Dewey's philosophy of the importance of experience in art is basically an elaboration and response to Fry's formalist esthetics. Such a closely reasoned study of Fry by the man who most effectively offered an alternative to formalism suggests the profound importance of that aesthetic theory in yet another context.

## Conclusion

The formalist criticism of the 1920s is, then, a crucial chapter in the history of American art criticism. While individual contributions are not heroic, the collective writings of American art critics of the 1920s form an important episode, particularly with respect to the assimilation of the theory of formalism articulated by Clive Bell and Roger Fry. That theory constituted a well-defined focal point for the understanding of modern art. British formalist theory was a rallying point that led American critics to assess their ideas and to formulate their positions. The American awareness of formalism can be documented so thoroughly that, even with the controversies that followed it and the alterations that were made to it, the debt that the American critics owed to their English colleagues cannot be obscured.

Even the episode of Regionalism in the 1930s, that style and criticism that celebrated subject matter, can be seen as much as a reaction against formalist methods as a celebration of American scenes. Thomas Craven's writings are but one clear example of a critic who began with a belief in formalism, but subsequently embraced Regionalism. Other critics like Forbes Watson went through a similar philosophical shift.

In the mid to late 1920s, while the critics treated in this article were still discussing the validity of the ideas of Clive Bell and Roger Fry, the next generation of critics, such as Alfred H.Barr, Jr., Clement Greenberg, and Harold Rosenberg had their first contacts with the

---

48     Dewey, *Art as Experience,* p. 87.

art community.[49] Their earliest exposure to contemporary art criticism would probably have included reading magazines such as *The Arts, The Dial,* and *Vanity Fair,*[50] where articles on and by Clive Bell and Roger Fry were often prominently featured. Certainly, these later American writers were also subject to other influences. Yet, writings such as Barr's catalogs for the Museum of Modern Art in the 1930s,[51] and the art criticism of Greenberg and Rosenberg of the 1940s and 1950s,[52] can be regarded as a sophisticated development that builds on the complex, sometimes awkwardly self-conscious, occasionally incredibly informed, American formalist art criticism of the 1920s.

---

49　Clement Greenberg attended the Art Student's League in the mid 1920s. Harold Rosenberg published poetry in the "little" magazines toward the end of the decade.

50　Alfred Barr declared "I read such American magazines as the *Arts.*" William S. Lieberman (ed), "Introduction, *Art of the Twenties* (New York: Museum of Modern Art, 1980), p. 7.

51　Alfred Barr's catalogs for the Museum of Modern Art in the 1930s reflect a sophisticated evolution within his critical awareness. (See article in this collection).

52　The best known work by Clement Greenberg is *Art and Culture* (Boston: Beacon Press, 1961). Harold Rosenberg has written numerous books of art criticism including *The Anxious Object* (New York: Collier, 1966.)

# Sheldon Cheney: Crusader for Modernism (1985)

*"When you say that you were one of the wilder men, what did you do in terms of being wild?"*

*SHELDON CHENEY: Well, I wrote about modern art; that was wild enough. (Interview, November 1979)*

IN THE EARLY TWENTIETH CENTURY, modern art was promoted with crusading fervor by the initiated few who understood the principles of abstraction. Katherine Dreier, founder and director of the Société Anonyme, the leading organization in support of modern art in the 1920s, was a committed writer on the subject. Henry McBride, Forbes Watson, Alfred Stieglitz, and Paul Rosenfeld supported modern art in various books and articles.[1] Sheldon Cheney (1886-1980) was one of this group of writers who dedicated their lives to explaining the principles of art since Cézanne to the uninitiated public. He alone has not been examined by historians.[2]

1    Katherine Dreier, *Western Art and the New Era* (New York: Brentano's, 1923); Daniel Catton Rich, *The Flow of Art: Essays and Criticism of Henry McBride* (New York: Atheneum, 1975); Herbert Seligmann, *Alfred Stieglitz Talking: Notes on Some of his Conversations, 1924-1931* (New York: Yale University Press, 1966).

2    Robert L. Herbert, Eleanor S. Apter, and Elise K. Kenney, *The Société Anonyme and the Dreier Bequest at Yale University* (New Haven: Yale University Press, 1984). See also Ruth Bohan, *The Société Anonyme's Brooklyn Exhibition* (Ann Arbor: UMI Research Press, 1982); William Homer, *Alfred Stieglitz and the American Avant-Garde* (Boston: New York Graphic Society, 1977); Paul Rosenfeld, *Port of New York*, with an introductory essay by Sherman Paul (Urbana and London: University of Illinois Press, 1966); Sandra S. Philips, "The Art Criticism of Walter Pach," *The Art Bulletin*, (March 1983): 106-121; Susan Noyes Platt, *Modernism in the 1920s* (Ann Arbor: UMI Research Press, 1985).

Yet of all the writing on modern art in the 1920s, only Cheney's remained continuously in print until the middle of the 1960s. They form a tangible link between the first generation of analysis of modern art and later developments in modernist criticism. As recently as the early post-World War II era, they were used as important references. Clement Greenberg has stated that Sheldon Cheney's writings were an important introduction to modern art in his early career.[3] Also significant are the generations of college students for whom Cheney's books provided the first, and sometimes the only, explanation of modern art. Beyond that, Cheney's books have always had a wide appeal to the general public.

Cheney's popular reputation, however, helped lead to his neglect. His translation of complex ideas into language understandable to the general public has caused historians to overlook his real achievement as a synthesizer of avant-garde theory. The interdisciplinary character of his writings may be another factor. Cheney wrote pioneering books on avant-garde theatre and architecture as well as on avant-garde visual art. He became a writer on visual art only after making a considerable contribution to the literature on modern theatre in the late teens.

As an undergraduate at the University of California, Berkeley, in the early years of the twentieth century, Cheney studied the principles of architecture and performed in the innovative outdoor Greek theatre.[4] The study of architecture gave Cheney the background to understand the significance of avant-garde modern architecture later in his career. Cheney's work with the theatre group soon led to an interest in the avant-garde principles of Gordon Craig, the prophet of modern stage design. It also impressed on Cheney the impact of presenting culture to a mass audience, certainly the purpose of his own writing throughout his career.

Cheney's concern for the relationship of art to the average person was initially encouraged by a study of the writings of Leo Tolstoy. He was profoundly affected by Tolstoy's essay "What is to Be Done?"

---

3    Clement Greenberg Interview with Susan Noyes Platt, San Francisco, July 1, 1984.

4    Sheldon Cheney interview with Susan Platt, Berkeley, November 18, 19, 1979, Archives of American; Sheldon Cheney to Susan Noyes Platt, June 15, 1980.

an analysis of the causes of poverty in Moscow slums.[5] Tolstoy's book *What is Art?* suggests that art as practiced (in the nineteenth century) was meaningless to the general public because it failed to communicate a feeling based on experience.[6] Tolstoy suggested that art needed to be purged of the meaningless idea of beauty, in order to create a more direct expression of life. This same concept permeates Cheney's writing throughout his career. Cheney, however, never embraced the masses in the same way as Tolstoy. He was equally influenced by an important theorist of early modern art, Willard Huntington Wright, who adopted a more Nietszchean approach suggesting that art was the creation of the exceptional individual.[7] Cheney's goal was to uplift the masses by educating them to modern art. Tolstoy's goal, by contrast, was to bring himself in touch with the revitalizing simplicity of the masses. Thus, although Tolstoy inspired Cheney at a crucial early period of his development, he provided only a point of departure for Cheney's commitment to modern art as a source of spiritual renewal. He felt that society needed renewal by purging what he perceived as the deadening influence of the status quo. In an interview just before his death, Cheney recalled the conservatism that he sought to counter, both at the University of California and in New York City.[8] The desire to be a source of revitalization for the individual and for society permeates all of his writings.

Cheney first approached the avant-garde in 1913 by writing a study of the new movements in the theatre, with a focus on the pioneering role of Gordon Craig. Craig advocated the elimination of traditional

---

5     Sheldon Cheney, "The Value of Tolstoy's 'What is to be Done?' to the Present Rebuilding of the Social Structure," University of California Prize Essays, 1912, pp. 55-122. Around this time Cheney also created a pageant in the Oakland Auditorium, which he called "Redemption, A Masque of Racial Betterment." Tolstoy was an ongoing inspiration for Cheney as evidenced by his 1920 play based on Tolstoy's *The Light that Shines in the Darkness* preserved in the Cheney Archives at the Bancroft Library, University of California, Berkeley. Sheldon Cheney, "The Open-Air Theatre," *The Craftsman* (August 1916): 435-437, 519. The subtitle of the article was "Seeing Our Plays Out-of-Doors: What this May Do to Create a Healthful Civic Sense."

6     Leo Tolstoy, *What is Art?* (New York: Thomas Crowell, 1899), p. 43.

7     Willard Huntington Wright, *Modern Painting, Its Tendency and Meaning* (New York: John Lane, 1916).

8     Interview with Platt, November 18, 19, 1979.

scenery and an emphasis on the formal components of light, color, space, and rhythmic movement. These principles laid the foundations for both expressionist and constructivist stage design in the teens and twenties.[9]

Cheney's understanding of the principles of abstract art in the theatre supported his later study of expressionism in the visual arts. As editor of *Theatre Arts Monthly* in the teens, Cheney introduced the radical new stage designs of the expressionist theatre to America. He moved the magazine to New York in 1917, and by 1919 he was writing of interconnections among the various avant-garde art forms in an exhibition of painting and sculpture representing modern dance. In the catalogue to the exhibition, Cheney states that "the essential thing in life is the creative, the inspirational—the spontaneous expression that goes beyond creeds, conventions and outward semblances." He contrasts this type of creative expression to the "sentimental and amusing," which he considered superficial and insignificant.[10]

A small pamphlet of 1921 documents his early thinking on the interrelationships of avant-garde theatre and visual arts. He compares the rejection of representation in stage design to the movement toward abstraction in modern art:

> The general trend of modern art is unmistakably toward abstract or non-representative means. In the theatre there are these parallels: the use of the mask in acting, or better still the actor's consciousness of his body and face as an emotional mask; the use of words not only literally but tonally, musically; the use of line and color, in the background for emotional reinforcement, without purpose to imitate actuality or suggest reality; and a frankly theatrical approach, abandonment of any effort at illusion ... I wish not to overlook the close connection between progress on stage and progress in the painter's studio.

---

9    Sheldon Cheney, *The New Movement in the Theatre* (New York: Kennerley, 1914), esp. pp. 302-303. Sheldon Cheney, *The Open Air Theatre* (New York: Kennerley, 1918) and *The Art Theatre* (New York: Knopf, 1917).

10   Sheldon Cheney, "The Dance and Modern Art," *Exhibition of Paintings and Sculpture Representing the Dance in Modern Art* (Tarrytown: Elizabeth Duncan School and the Bourgeois Gallery, 1918), p. 15.

What is generally called 'modern art'? In its negative aspect it
is a revolt against the representative basis in painting, against
descriptive painting, illustrative painting. ...

In its constructive aspect it is creation as contrasted with
imitation, expression as contrasted with representation. It is
concerned with ... the rhythm or essential reality or structural truth of nature and then with the artist's emotion and
his individual emotional way of conveying what he has felt
or divined.[11]

In the same essay Cheney introduces the phrases "significant
form" and "aesthetic emotion," terms taken from the lexicon of the
popular formalist theories of Clive Bell.[12] Cheney's awareness of Bell's
work resulted from his contact with the Société Anonyme's Katherine
Dreier. Dreier, too, sought to educate the uninitiated into the mysteries
of modern art as a virtually religious cause. At the Société Anonyme,
which Cheney joined at its inception in 1920, Dreier created exhibitions
of recent art, accompanied by brochures and publications. Cheney, as
part of the library committee of the organization, had access not only
to the public exhibitions, but also to the most sophisticated library on
modern art in New York in the early 1920s.

The importance of the Société Anonyme for Cheney emerged
clearly in a November 1979 interview; as he talked, he revealed the
stratified character of the modern art environment in New York and his
status as something of an outsider in that world.

*CHENEY: Well, there was an organization of modernists, they
formed in New York, the Société Anonyme ... and I don't know
how I got into it, but anyway, ... we used to meet for lunch
occasionally, and ... we were not welcome at the museums, and
so on ... in those days to be invited to lunch was something. See,
I came up through that business having no money back of me. I
got into it because I wrote a few articles for magazines.*

---

11      Sheldon Cheney, *Modern Art and the Theatre. Being Notes on Certain
        Approaches to a New Art of the Stage with Special Reference to Parallel
        Developments in Painting, Sculpture and the other Arts* (Scarborough-
        on-Hudson: The Sleepy Hollow Press, 1921), pp. 4, 9.

12      Clive Bell, *Art* (London: Chatto and Windus, 1913; New York: G.P.
        Putnam and Sons, 1968).

*SUSAN PLATT: Did you know Marcel Duchamp?*

*CHENEY: He was rather above us, of course; he was French in origin, anyway ... he knew the scene a great deal better than we did. ...*

*SP: Did Katherine Dreier suggest that you write a book about modern art, or was that your own idea, that you write a primer so that people could understand?*

*CHENEY: I started out and wanted to be a writer and those other people weren't necessarily writers....*

*SP: Did you know Henry McBride? He was involved with that group.*

*CHENEY: I knew him, but he was a little earlier, I think, wasn't he? He was already established and I was a beginner... He was, I think, quite liberal, but he was not a crazy modern like me.*

*SP: Christian Brinton?*

*CHENEY: He was more conservative ... He did the reviews, for one of the more conservative magazines. For these people I was a wild man.*

*SP: What about Frank Crowninshield who was the editor of Vanity Fair?*

*CHENEY: That was up above us. I knew Crowninshield, but still I wasn't one of his people in any sense.*

*SP: So, it was kind of a social thing, when you say he was up above you? They were a little private world of the elite?*

*CHENEY: Yes, and they had connections with the big magazines and a person like me had to be content to sell to the little magazines.[13]*

---

13      Interview with Platt, November 18, 19, 1979; edited by the author.

So Cheney first published articles on modern art in "little" magazines, although in his case they were often commercial. His first published essay on art, for the movie magazine *Shadowland*, focuses on the principle of expressionism, or the importance of emotion in art of all types, as well as on the principle of aesthetic form. The title, "Expressionism: Art's Latest Revolution, How It Threatens Our Theatres as Well as Our Exhibition Halls," lent a note of drama.[14] The term "expressionism" referred to "all currents flowing against the centuries old realistic tradition."[15]

Alfred Stieglitz, the pioneer supporter of modernism in America, wrote to Cheney as a result of the article:

> *Shadowland*, October was sent to me a day or two ago ... In poking through it I ran across your paper on "Expressionism." I read it aloud to Miss O'Keeffe. We both enjoyed it greatly and felt it was the best thing we had read on kindred subjects since Willard Huntington Wright's articles in *The Forum* five or six years ago. We enjoyed the genuinely free spirit and the fine toleration. ... I do hope we'll run into each other in the near future for we certainly have common interests.[16]

Cheney and Stieglitz continued their correspondence, and Stieglitz became an important source of inspiration for Cheney.[17]

Cheney's most radical article, "Why Dada?," appeared in one of the most conservative journals of the twenties, *The Century*, with the subtitle "An Inquiry into the Connection Between War's Ruins, Peacetime Insanity and the Latest Sensation in Art." Cheney relished the opportunity to spread distress among the bourgeois audience of the magazine by describing the extravagant anarchism of the Dada artist. He surveyed recent literary and theatrical events as well as those at the

---

14    Sheldon Cheney, "Expressionism: Art's Latest Revolution," *Shadowland* (October 1921): 59-61.

15    Ibid., p. 59.

16    Alfred Stieglitz to Sheldon Cheney September 14, 1921, Sheldon Cheney Papers, Archives of American Art.

17    Sheldon Cheney, "Pioneer of Modern Art," *Wings* (December 1934): 10-12, 26.

Société Anonyme with the overall purpose of spreading revolutionary impulses:

> Art is no longer an expression of life; it has become a theocracy and a priesthood, cultivated like a religion. ... The man who dares to seek out new forms of beauty and express them nakedly is made an example and outcast ... We need a Dada to destroy our whole mechanized system which has blindly clamped the acquisitive supply-and-demand principles of business over the realms of art and spiritual life. ... This is Dada's virtue, that it goes beyond all other iconoclasts. Destroying images is not enough. It is necessary to go on and destroy iconoclasm.[18]

Shortly after the completion of "Why Dada?" Cheney persuaded the publisher Horace Liveright to give him a five-hundred-dollar advance to write an introduction to modern art.

Cheney spent the winter and spring of 1922 in Europe. A diary from the trip records visits to cities in England, Germany, France, and Northern Italy. During his travels, he evaluated art in terms of emotional expressionism and formal sophistication,[19] and although the main purpose of the trip was to conduct research on avant-garde visual art, Cheney's wide-ranging interests led him to inspect museum installations, attend performances by Sarah Bernhardt and the followers of Loie Fuller, visit the school of dance run by Isadora Duncan's sister, Elizabeth, and observe modern architecture. While stranded in Berlin for six weeks, he studied German Expressionism both in the visual arts and in the theatre. One comment from his diary on visiting the British Museum suffices to establish his perspective throughout the trip and the perspective of the book that resulted from it. It illustrates Cheney's impatience with realism and his search for meaningful expression in an art based on the principles of form and expression:

> It is becoming clearer where the fallacy of later art originates—the clever mind, reproducing and decorating ... the

---

18    Sheldon Cheney, "Why Dada?" *The Century Magazine* (May 1922); 29.

19    The unpublished European diary. 1922, in the collection of John Cheney, Washington, D.C. [at time of writing].

surface clearly molded, correct portraiture, detail decorative (sometimes formalized nicely which gives another sort of art of pleasure) ... but form and aesthetic expression are gone.[20]

Cheney completed *A Primer of Modern Art* by October 1923. It was published in early 1924, virtually simultaneously with Katherine Dreier's survey, *Western Art and the New Era,* and Walter Pach's *Masters of Modern Art.* In contrast to the serious, pedantic style of these two books, Cheney's *Primer* sets a casual yet aggressive tone on the first page in discussing a self-portrait of Oscar Kokoschka:

> This is an example of Modern Art. It is a good example. It has all the earmarks. It is not in the least photographic. Almost any student of drawing could copy the outlines and shading. It is not prettily finished—indeed it is very rough.... Let me right out with it. Not to be able to appreciate Kokoschka's paintings just because they seem rough and unphotographic argues plain ignorance.[21]

The blunt style paired with comprehensive discussions of modern art and theory proved an appealing formula to the general public. Cheney also used modesty and dedication:

> Now please don't think that I am setting up as less ignorant than you on most questions. God forbid that I should so forget my place. But in this one little matter of art appreciation I have worked myself out of something that I look back to as a sort of prison. I should like to help clear the way for you, take down a bar or two, help you to blow some of the dust off your mind.[22]

Following its didactic and aggressive opening, the *Primer* presented the theory and history of modern art with the same informal

---

20    Excerpt from European diary, 1922, unpaginated.

21    Sheldon Cheney, *A Primer of Modern* Art (New York: Boni and Liveright, 1924); Katherine Dreier, *Western Art and the New Era, An Introduction to Modern Art* (New York: Brentano's, 1923); Walter Pach, *Masters of Modern Art* (New York: B. W. Huebsch, 1924); see also Eli Faure, *Modern Art.* trans. Walter Pach (New York: Harper Bros., 1924).

22    Cheney, *Primer,* p. 3

but persuasive tone. Dada was included with Futurism in the chapter titled "Schools, Fads and Sensations," with much of the material taken from his "Why Dada?" article.[23] In addition to its personal style, the *Primer* was remarkable for its use of one hundred seventy-five illustrations juxtaposed to appropriate passages. Reproductions in art books in the early 1920s were typically skimpy, hard to see, or clustered together in a special section. In addition, Cheney's interdisciplinary approach included theatre and architecture as well as painting and sculpture. The *Primer* included one of the earliest English-language discussions of the architecture of Frank Lloyd Wright and the Bauhaus.

Most important, though, was Cheney's combination of French and German art and theory. Although Katherine Dreier's book focused on Kandinsky and Pach's book on the new French aesthetics, only Cheney elucidated the full range of modern art by bringing together his knowledge of Gordon Craig's writings, German Expressionist theory, and formalist aesthetics.

The first edition sold out immediately, and by 1929 the book had gone through five editions. The sales of the book increased even in the midst of the Depression. Critical praise spread from coast to coast, from New York art critic to small-town journalist.[24] Cheney had succeeded in reaching the mass audience he sought to enlighten. Alfred Stieglitz captured the spirit of the crusade for modern art in his letter to Cheney:

> I am having a great time with the book *A Primer of Modern Art*. It is certainly most timely and most entertaining. ... I am only glad that someone has dared what you have dared ... Thanks for your delightful inscription. Yes, I'll fight to the finish for all that is Living and that includes the *Primer*.[25]

Stieglitz's enthusiastic support for Cheney's book suggests that despite its popularizing approach and purpose, ordinarily an anathema

---

23    Ibid., p. 5.

24    For the response of a New York critic, see Henry McBride, "Modern Art," *The Dial* (November 1924): 444, and for a popular journalist's discussion, see "What Do You Know About Modern Art," *Columbia South Carolina Record* (June 22, 1924).

25    Alfred Stieglitz to Sheldon Cheney, February 24, 1924, Sheldon Cheney Papers, Archives of American Art.

to Stieglitz, Cheney was able to explain difficult concepts in simple terms with complete accuracy.

In the early 1930s, Cheney wrote a second introduction to modern art. While the *Primer* was a survey of the new movements in the visual arts with an emphasis on the chronological sequences of events, *Expressionism in Art* followed a more conceptual approach based on the theories of Hans Hofmann. Cheney gained access to Hofmann's concepts through his friendship with Glenn Wessels in Berkeley, who translated Hofmann's recently completed manuscript from German in 1931. With Hofmann's permission, Cheney included significant segments of Hofmann's theory of "picture building" in the 1934 book.[26] Cheney continued to use the term "expressionism" to identify modern art in general, but he now linked that term to the ideas of the foremost theoretician of expressionist art in America.

By the mid-1930s, as a result of the efforts of the Museum of Modern Art and its scholarly catalogues. As well as the proliferation of other books on modern art, the pioneering and exploratory excitement of the early writings by Cheney and others had passed. Cheney's *The Story of Modern Art*, published in 1941, already reflected the new, more objective historical approach to modern art.[27] Rather than a revolutionary treatise, this is a college textbook. Yet even in this ponderous format, Cheney enlivens the details, writes engagingly, and presents complex material in understandable language.

While Cheney is best known for his books on modern visual art, he continued throughout his career to write on other aspects of the avant-garde. In 1928, following the death of Isadora Duncan, Cheney edited her writings into a book he titled *The Art of the Dance*.[28] In the same year, he published a survey of stage decoration that included the most recent developments in constructivist and expressionist designs

---

26    Sheldon Cheney, *Expressionism in Art* (New York: Liveright, 1934). See especially chapters vi-x and the introduction, p. ix. The manuscript for Hofmann's essay "Creation in Form and Color: A Textbook of Instruction in Art," is preserved at the Archives of American Art, microfilm roll 1355.

27    Sheldon Cheney, *The Story of Modern Art* (New York: The Viking Press, 1941).

28    Isadora Duncan, *The Art of the Dance*, ed. Sheldon Cheney (New York: Theatre Arts, 1928).

from the 1920s as well as an examination of Gordon Craig's important role in the development of stage design.[29] In 1930, a book on the history of the theatre included an overview of drama, acting, and stagecraft.[30]

Another contribution to the historiography of modern art is Cheney's 1930 study of modern architecture, *The New World Architecture*. In this book he examined Frank Lloyd Wright's work and developments in the 1920s in Europe, including buildings by Dutch, French, and German architects. Cheney's book preceded the Museum of Modern Art exhibition defining the International Style by two years, and provided, from the perspective on early modern architecture today, a more comprehensive explanation of its rise during the 1920s.[31]

During the early 1930s, Cheney was active in promoting modern art through lectures and informal groups. He founded the School for Open Mindedness in Berkeley as a protest against the lack of concern for modern art at the University of California at Berkeley.[32] Frank Lloyd Wright invited Cheney to participate in his Taliesin community in 1932, but Cheney declined.[33] From the mid-1930s to the mid-1970s, Cheney lived in rural Pennsylvania, although he continued to make national lecture tours throughout the country to speak on modern art. After publishing *Expressionism in Art* in 1934, Cheney collaborated with his wife to produce *Art and the Machine* (1936), a discussion of the industrial design of the mid-1930s.[34] This book marks the last of Cheney's explorations of the different aspects of the avant-garde.

---

29     Sheldon Cheney, *Stage Decoration* (New York: John Day, 1928).

30     Sheldon Cheney, *The Theatre, Three Thousand Years of Drama, Acting and Stage Craft* (New York: Longman, Green and Co., 1930).

31     Sheldon Cheney, *The New World Architecture* (London, New York: Longmans, Green and Co., 1930). The book also included earlier architecture and a discussion of the importance of the machine's impact on architecture. It omitted discussion of Russian developments, the importance of which were still only little known. The Museum of Modern Art exhibition by Henry Russell Hitchcock and Philip Johnson, *The International Style* (New York: Museum of Modern Art, 1932), dominated our understanding of modern architecture for decades.

32     John Cheney to Susan Noyes Platt, November 3, 1985.

33     Frank Lloyd Wright to Sheldon Cheney, February 24, 1932.

34     Sheldon Cheney with Martha Candler Cheney, *Art and the Machine* (New York: Whittlesey House, 1936).

In 1945 Cheney published an historical account of the lives of several mystics, including Lao-Tse and William Blake. Writing during World War II, he commented on the existence of mystics as "a reminder that in whatever depths of … moral confusion mankind may have sunk, there have been always spiritual guides, adventurers in holiness and calm. …"[35] The statement also suggests the basis for Cheney's interest in mystical modern artists such as Kandinsky.

During the later years of his career, Cheney continued to write on visual art, most notably in a history of sculpture published in 1968.[36]

Sheldon Cheney made a significant contribution to the understanding of modern art in America both in his in-formal, confessional work of the 1920s and early 1930s and in the more art historical works of his later career. His development as a writer echoes the shift in the way people saw modern art—from eccentric and inaccessible avant-garde experiment to accepted art history—also reflected in the evolution of art writing from subjective interpretation to more objective recounting of fact. Cheney was important not only for what he wrote but also for how he wrote it, for his continuing receptiveness to modern art, and for his success in explaining the difficult principles of modernism to a wider audience than perhaps anyone else in the twentieth century. Even in the year before his death in 1980, he spoke of modern art with a sense of excitement.[37] For those of us who, as teachers, still seek new ways to convey the unique vision of twentieth century art, his achievement is impressive.

## NOTE:

This article is dedicated to the memory of my father, Rutherford Platt, who wrote on nature in the same spirit that Sheldon Cheney wrote on modem art.

I would like to express my particular appreciation to John Cheney for his assistance in various aspects of the research, particularly in arranging the interview with his father.

---

35     Sheldon Cheney, *Men Who Have Walked with God* (New York: A. A. Knopf, 1985), p. 384.

36     Sheldon Cheney, *Sculpture of the World, A History* (New York: Viking Press, 1968).

37     Interview with Platt, November 18, 19, 1979.

# Mysticism in the Machine Age: Jane Heap and *The Little Review (1989)*

*We need fights, discussion—hot and impolite, jeering and insulting, to knit the thing together, to find and bring out a definite creative harshness in this pulp of art in America.*

-Jane Heap in The Little Review

WITH THE CURRENT ABUNDANCE OF LAVISHLY illustrated periodicals on every conceivable topic, we can only imagine eagerly awaiting issue of one small, poorly illustrated, cheaply printed magazine. Yet, during the early years of American modernism, many experimental writers and artists regarded *The Little Review* with exactly that attitude. It played a crucial role in disseminating modernist writing, theory, and art to the avant-garde intellectual community. The magazine was founded in 1914 by Margaret Anderson (1886-1973). In 1917 Anderson moved her periodical from its original home in Chicago to New York, where it continued to appear until 1927. A single farewell issue materialized in 1929. During the 1920s, Jane Heap (1883-1964) emerged as the dominant editor.

Whereas Anderson wrote several autobiographies and is familiar in the context of *The Little Review*, Heap's career has barely been acknowledged. Except in the last years of the magazine, she herself strove to be almost invisible; even when she signed her name, she generally did so in lower-case initials, until the Spring 1925 issue when she finally used her full name in the masthead of the magazine. She has been lost to history even further because scholarship has focused on the publication's middle years when Ezra Pound was an editor, whereas Heap's most significant activity came later. In these last years of *The*

*Little Review*, she was also involved with the avant-garde visual arts. In later life, mystical practice shrouded her personality.[1]

This article focuses on Jane Heap as a central figure in the history of *The Little Review*. It reconstructs her background, insofar as it can currently be outlined, and integrates her activities with the larger avant-garde and feminist environment of the 1920s. It also demonstrates how Heap created a unique wedding of mysticism to the just-emerging theory and art of the Machine Age. Her enigmatic and difficult endeavor provides a new perspective on a complex period in the history of modernism.

*The Little Review* went through three distinct phases. It first emerged in Chicago during that city's short-lived renaissance of culture known as the Liberation. An atmosphere of change and experimentation inspired Margaret Anderson, an idealistic young book reviewer recently arrived from Indiana, to found a magazine with only the slightest financial backing. She announced *The Little Review* in the summer of 1913, not long after the Art Institute of Chicago showed the Armory exhibition of postimpressionist painting. Starting in March 1914, the monthly magazine presented young Chicago writers along with energetic articles on the political and philosophical issues of the day, such as feminism, anarchism, and Nietzscheanism. In this first phase, it featured contributions of such later famous writers as Sherwood Anderson and Edgar Lee Masters.[2]

In 1917 The *Little Review* moved to New York. There it was dominated by Ezra Pound as foreign editor in London and was financially sponsored by Pound's friend, the New York lawyer John

---

1    Unless otherwise designated, the archival sources for this article are *The Little Review* Archives at the University of Wisconsin-Milwaukee. That archive contains many letters to Jane Heap; however, they are sometimes difficult to locate because they are catalogued under the writer's name. For this reason, as well as the focus by scholars on Ezra Pound, the extent of the material on Jane Heap has long been underestimated.

2    See my article "*The Little Review* and the Early Avant-Garde in Chicago," Sue Ann Prince, ed, *The Old Guard and the Avant-Garde, Modernism in Chicago 1910- 1940* (University of Chicago Press, 1990), pp. 139-154; See also my *Modernism in the 1920s: Interpretations of Modern Art in New York from Expressionism to Constructivism* (Ann Arbor: UMI Research Press, 1985).

Quinn. During this second, famous chapter of the magazine's history, it published excerpts from James Joyce's masterpiece-in-progress *Ulysses*, as well as writing by T. S. Eliot, Wyndham Lewis, and Pound himself. Explicitly sexual references in *Ulysses* sparked clashes with the United States Post Office and the legal system: the magazine was accused by the Society for the Suppression of Vice of publishing obscenity, and the editors were brought to trial and found guilty in the spring of 1921.[3] Reincarnated shortly after, an engagement with the international avant-garde in the visual arts gave *The Little Review* a new distinction. This chapter of great importance to the history of the early twentieth-century avant-garde in America has been glossed over by scholars of the period.

Heap connected the avant-garde visual artists and *The Little Review*. While Anderson remained on the title page and Pound provided the initial contacts, Heap was the driving force behind the increased commitment of the magazine to stage design, architecture, painting, and sculpture.

Particularly after 1924, when Pound moved to Italy and Anderson settled in Europe, Heap worked almost alone to produce the magazine as a quarterly. From 1924 to 1927 she also ran an eponymous art gallery.

As editor of *The Little Review*, Heap proceeded along two distinct lines. First, she was a key liaison between the European avant-garde, particularly those artists concerned with the Machine Age, and

---

3      For an important study of the roles of Margaret Anderson and Ezra Pound at the magazine, see Jackson Bryer, "A Trial-Track for Racers: Margaret Anderson and the 'Little Review'" ( Ph.D. diss., University of Wisconsin-Madison, 1965). Although the bulk of his study is devoted to the Pound phase, Bryer provides a reconstruction of the early years. Part of the title of Bryer's dissertation is taken from Jane Heap's editorial in the last issue of *The Little Review* ("Lost: A Renaissance," *The Little Review* 12, no. 2. [May 1929]: 5-6). See also Jackson Bryer, "Joyce, 'Ulysses' and 'The Little Review,'" *South Atlantic Quarterly* 66 (1967): 148-64. Other works that illuminate this early era are Frederich J. Hoffman, *The Little Magazine, A History and a Bibliography* (Princeton, N.J.: Princeton University Press, 1946), 52-66; Abby Ann Arthur Johnson, "The Personal Magazine: Margaret C. Anderson and *The Little Review*, 1914-1929," *South Atlantic Quarterly* 75 (1976): 351-63; and Thomas Scott, *Pound/The Little Review: The Letters of Ezra Pound to Margaret Anderson* (New York: New Directions Press,1986).

the small but influential American audience that avidly followed the magazine. Second, she linked the Machine Age to the mystical teachings of Georgei Ivanovitch Gurdjieff, an Armenian mystic. Gurdjieff surfaced in New York, via Moscow, Constantinople, London, and Paris, just at the time that Heap took full responsibility for *The Little Review* in 1923-24. Heap's dual commitment to art and mysticism is crucial to understanding her unique and sometimes problematic activities.

By befriending artists directly, Heap made *The Little Review* a conduit for European modernism. She published work by Francis Picabia, Theo van Doesburg, Laszlo Moholy-Nagy, and Tristan Tzara and collaborated with Frederick Kiesler, Brancusi, Jacques Lipchitz, Naum Gabo Anton Pevsner, Ossip Zadkine, and Fernand Léger sent their work and writing to her. Through such direct contacts, Heap received material from an even broader range of the avant-garde, among them El Lissitzky in Russia, Kurt Schwitters in Germany, Josef Peeters in Belgium, and Szymon and Helen Syrkus in Poland. Heap's interests also encompassed avant-garde music through her friendship with George Antheil and her knowledge of the work of Igor Stravinsky, Edgard Varese, and the emerging group known as the Six that included Darius Milhaud.

During and after World War I, many of the artists who contributed to *The Little Review* were obsessed with the relationship of art and the machine. As mechanization increasingly entered daily life, the efficiency, simplicity, and functionalism of the machine influenced esthetics. Machine-made materials such as plastics were popular. Many artists also experimented in their art with machines as images, as objects, and as processes.

Their preoccupation with the machine led foreign artists to endow America with nearly mythical stature. Except for the handful of artists who visited New York, however, their main knowledge of American machines came from American films. Thus, artists were highly receptive to Heap as an American editor who could both inform them on American art and machines and publicize their work in New York.

The resulting activities would have been inconceivable only a few years later, for both financial and political reasons. In some cases, the photographs, literature, and even art sent to Heap became the only documents published on or by those artists in the United States for many decades.[4] The direct transmission to *The Little Review* also reflected the informal character of the art world, when artists were still accessible as individuals; galleries, dealers, and museums played a minor role. Indeed, some of Heap's difficulties could have been ameliorated had a more sophisticated support system been available to her and the artists.

In the second aspect of her activities, Heap combined admiration for the machine in art with pursuit of mysticism as a means of enhancing life. In early 1924 she came in contact with the teachings of G.I. Gurdjieff and his disciple Alfred Richard Orage, formerly an influential London editor. They profoundly affected Heap with a message of the necessity for spiritual renewal. The basic issue of Gurdjieff's teaching was that for the unenlightened, life functioned mechanistically, based on laws and natural processes. Understanding those mechanisms led to a more developed level of self-awareness and spirituality. The means of coming to this understanding was mystical, not rational, although Gurdjieff employed practical exercises that ranged from ritual dances to manual labor.[5]

Beginning in 1924 Heap indirectly promoted these ideas through her activities at *The Little Review*. She connected the new art and Gurdjieffian principles through the idea of the machine: just as the machine was transforming art, likewise understanding the mechanical principles at work in our own lives would transform us spiritually. For three years Heap worked with this unusual and difficult alliance of ideas, but by 1927 a sense of frustration with the art world, as well as an increased allegiance to Gurdjieff, led her to abandon the international artistic avant-garde.

Only for a few years in the mid-1920s were Heap's artistic and spiritual concerns mutually reinforcing. Her activities in the arena of modern art, intersecting with her pursuit of mysticism, led to an

---

4     For a compilation of monographs on major women writers of this era see Shari Benstock, *Women of the Left Bank, Paris 1900-1940,* (Austin, University of Texas Press, 1986).

5     James Webb, *The Harmonious Circle: The Lives and Work of G.I Gurdjieff, P.D. Ouspensky and their Followers* (New York G. Putnam's Sons, 1980).See also Linda, D. Henderson, *The Fourth Dimension and Non-Euclidean Geometry in Modern Art* (Princeton University Press, 1982, reissued 2017, MIT Press).

extraordinary effort to bring the art of the Machine Age to New York. That particular conjunction is the climax of her career at *The Little Review*, her unique contribution to the understanding of modernism in America, and the central concern of this article.

## Early Career

Heap's early career does not forecast her dramatic activities of the 1920s. As a result of her decision, after making a full commitment to Gurdjieff, to be as anonymous as possible, her first thirty years are difficult to document. A few facts emerge, however. Heap was the daughter of an English father and a Norwegian mother, the granddaughter of a Lapp whose relatives lived near the Arctic Circle.[6] She grew up in Topeka, Kansas, where her father was a supervisor at an insane asylum. Coming to Chicago at the turn of the century, she attended art school, apparently inspired to creativity by the example of Sarah Bernhardt.[7] Initially enrolling in a Saturday morning art education class, she eventually graduated from the Art Institute in 1905 after having achieved some distinction in the academic mode taught there. She is once again documented as attending the Art Institute as an evening student in 1909 and 1911.[8] Sometime after 1912, she participated in Maurice and Ellen Browne's avant-garde theater group known as the Little Theater, then went to Europe to study art in Germany.[9]

When Margaret Anderson met Jane Heap, she immediately became infatuated with her. As many of the writers and artists who had given the magazine its first support dispersed, Anderson was feeling a need for fresh inspiration. She was overwhelmed by Heap's brilliant conversation, as well as her imposing personal demeanor. The two women became lovers, a radical act of overt lesbianism for that time.

6     Webb, *Harmonious Circle*, 277-78.

7     J(ane)h(eap], "Mary Garden," *The Little Review* 3, no. 9 (March 1917): 5-6. Subsequent references to articles by Jane Heap signed with her initials will be designated "jh."

8     Mary McIsaac, Archivist, School of the Art Institute of Chicago, to author, 22 June 1987.

9     Dale Kramer, *Chicago Renaissance, The Literary Life in the Midwest 1900-1930* (New York: Appleton-Century, 1966), 315-16 .

After an intense spring and summer, Anderson convinced Heap to write for the magazine.[10] Their close personal and professional relationship sustained the magazine for six years, and the two women remained friends throughout their lives.

Even within the orbit of *The Little Review* in the late teens and twenties, Heap's style was unique. One writer referred to her as having a "personal magnetism that was almost visible!"[11] The best-known photograph of Heap, taken by Berenice Abbott in Paris in the early 1920S, shows her dressed in tuxedo jacket and bow tie. She apparently wore this with a long black skirt, a popular garb of lesbians of that era.[12] As one writer commented, she "had the most stimulating and penetrating mind of any American woman I have ever met and like all people with strong positive vibrations, her negative ones were equally strong. She could be quite ruthless, regardless of near friend or old foe, when she wanted something. She had a strong masculine side."[13] One friend of Anderson's described Heap in terms that may characterize her as she was seen by other women:

> That Jane exists in the way she does fills people with strength and new realizations in those parts of their beings which sometimes shrivel emotionally. She is always staunchly herself, and her humor, always flickering, delights one. Though she is overwhelmed with work, and fatigue, and illness, she endures it all with the utmost fortitude.
>
> When one is under great strain, for which no words can be found, she always finds the right way to prove that she has understood through all one's incoherence. She becomes a kind of benign wizard, warm and with a mysterious kindness and affection. She is like a "home" in herself full of a

---

10    Margaret Anderson, *My Thirty Years' War* (New York: Covici, Friede, 1930), 107-8.

11    Webb, *Harmonious Circle*, 432.

12    Benstock, *Women of the Left Bank*, 177-84 treats the complex issues of dress among lesbians in this era.

13    Webb, *Harmonious Circle*, 279. Comment is by C. H. Nott.

loving security which banishes tensions, so that one becomes momentarily, a new being.[14]

Heap and Anderson were part of an informal network of brilliant, predominantly lesbian, women who congregated in Paris and London in the teens and twenties. Many of these women, including Gertrude Stein, Djuna Barnes, Hilda Doolittle, and Mary Butts, also contributed to and were celebrated by *The Little Review*. Although they produced an extraordinary outpouring of literature and art in the 1920s, their careers are, for the most part, only now being documented, analyzed, and interpreted. Despite their appeal to feminist scholars today, most did not make feminism a major issue in their careers. Anderson and Heap, for example, were more engaged with running a magazine and publishing high-quality writing and art than with creating a publication by and for women. They chose lesbian lifestyles, but also interacted with the entire avant-garde community.

With her artistic background, Heap immediately transformed the appearance of *The Little Review* in 1916. Instead of drab brown covers, the magazine now carried a brilliant pink or deep blue jacket. More art appeared, although initially it was rather tame. Heap's first contribution to the magazine was a series of cartoons showing Anderson and herself enjoying a playful summer in California. These cartoons followed sixteen blank pages, Anderson's "want ad" for more exciting material to put in the magazine.

---

14    Margaret Anderson, *The Strange Necessity* (New York: Horizon Press, 1970), 23-24. Comment is by Elspeth Champcommunal. Few letters between Jane Heap and the women of the Left Bank have survived, so Heap's exact relationships with these women are difficult to establish. Margaret Anderson's is the only documented intimate relationship, but Heap also certainly had a strong rapport with Gertrude Stein and they had a lengthy correspondence (Gertrude Stein Papers, Beinecke Rare Book and Manuscript Library, Yale University). Djuna Barnes had a crush on her in the teens and early 1920s. Benstock, *Women of the Left Bank*, 232, 239; Andrew Field, *Djuna, The Formidable Miss Barnes* (Austin: University of Texas Press, 1983), 102. A more recent article is by Linda Lappin "Jane Heap and Her Circle" *Prairie Schooner* Vol. 78, No. 4 (Winter 2004): pp. 5-25 focusing on Heap's personal relationships.

Heap's writing first appeared in *The Little Review* in late 1916, primarily in brief comments signed with her initials in lower case. Her first major article celebrated Mary Garden, the eccentric dancer whose performance in 1910 had been halted by the police. The article, accompanied by the first tipped-in illustration to be used in the magazine, made a strong statement concerning the role of the artist in society: "Many long for a share in that which the artists are making in the silence of their soul. But who is there except the artist who is willing to feel in this/thing the imminence of something beyond life and personality?" The same article provided an unusual autobiographical summary that puts her uncompromising and strongly felt opinions into perspective:

> When I was a child I lived in a great asylum for the insane. It was a world outside of the world, where realities had to be imagined and where, even through those excursions in illusions and hallucinations, there ran a strange loneliness.... There was no one to ask about anything. There was no way to make a connection to 'life'. ... Very early, I had given up on everyone except the Insane. The others knew nothing about anything or knew only uninteresting facts. From the Insane I could get everything.[15]

She likened the insane to creative artists in their "adventures in illusions and hallucinations." The perspective she reveals here led to her skepticism and impatience with traditional thinking and attitudes.

Another major statement from the spring of 1917 focused on James Joyce's first book, *A Portrait of the Artist as a Young Man*:

> His story is told the way a person in a sick room sharply remembers all the over-felt impressions and experiences of a time of fever; until the story itself catches the fever and becomes a thing of more definite, closer-known, keener-felt consciousness—and of a restless oblivion of self-conscious-ness.[16]

These striking perceptions, couched in a subtly shaped metaphor, demonstrate Heap's importance to the intellectual caliber of *The Little Review* and foretell her later ability to establish rapport with sophisticated

---

15      jh, "Mary Garden": 5-6.

16      jh, "James Joyce," *The Little Review* 3, no. 10 (April 1917): 8-9.

European artists. By contrast, Anderson appears naively enthusiastic when she writes of the same book as "the most beautiful piece of writing ... to be seen on the horizon."[17] Heap brought to Anderson's initial enthusiasm for the idea of renewal in the arts an astute, critical mind that never hesitated to inveigh against the mediocrity of much American culture.

Most of Heap's writings in the early teens responded to readers' letters that objected to the magazine's modern work:

> What do you mean by Beauty?—the idea that education puts upon the minds of people, meaning lovely, pleasing to the senses and the emotions? That isn't Art; it is not necessarily a feature but may be an instrument' of Art. What of real Beauty, which surpasses the spirit of joy or tragedy? ... The artist does not falsify or interpret life; he creates with joy!— even if the joy in the creating is the surplus of his agony.[18]

Not yet seen in Heap's early writing is the celebration of the machine and avant-garde visual art that would become so important for *The Little Review* in the 1920s. Indeed, scattered references suggest a negative attitude to the machine.[19]

During the magazine's middle phase, from 1917 to 1921, it was dominated by Ezra Pound, his contributions from London, and the hectic pressures of publishing chapters from *Ulysses*. Heap continued to write initialed comments in response to letters until her outrage over the suppression of Joyce's novel motivated her to move to the front of the magazine:

> The heavy farce and sad futility of trying a creative work in a court of law appalls me. Was there ever a judge qualified to judge even the simplest psychic outburst? How then a work of Art? Has any man not a nincompoop ever been heard by a jury of his peers?[20]

---

17    Margaret Anderson, "James Joyce," *The Little Review* 3, no.10 (April 1917): 9.

18    jh, "Growing Pains," *The Little Review* 3, no. 8 (January 1917): 25.

19    jh, "Push-Face," *The Little Review* 4, no. 1 (June 1917): 4-5.

20    jh, "Art and the Law," *The Little Review* 7, no. 3 (September-December 1920): 5. Heap's wrath even led her to sign the article at the beginning and to use a larger typeface for her initials.

The crisis of the trial and the related stress of losing her youthful illusions in the cause of truth and beauty soon led Anderson to a nervous breakdown. In its wake she initiated an emotional relationship with Georgette Le Blanc, singer and former wife of Maurice Maeterlinck, and moved to Bernardsville, New Jersey.[21] As a result of these circumstances, and the breakdown of the editors' personal relationship, Anderson proposed terminating *The Little Review*. Heap was adamantly opposed.[22]

Meanwhile, through Pound, the avant-garde in Paris began to embrace the magazine. Pound sent a Dada Manifesto from a "Contra Marinetti" demonstration in Paris. Appropriately, it appeared in the same issue as Anderson's article on the trial.[23] Pound also asked Francis Picabia to be the foreign editor: "But I have a present for you in the form of Picabia, who doesn't contribute to reviews, but was interested in my statement that you wd. [sic] go the whole hog. ... I believe he will give some live stuff, at any rate he and Cocteau are intelligent, which a damn'd large number of Parisians aren't. I don't know when you are going to 'resume'; but it ought t [sic] be with a swish when it does occur."[24] Pound sent Jean Cocteau's poem "The Cape of Good Hope," newly translated by Jean Hugo, and photographs of Brancusi's sculpture taken by the artist himself: "N.B. that Brancusi (photos, posted today) has just refused '*L'amour de l'Art*; *L'Esprit Nouveau* and *Lumur* of Prague, all of which noted art reviews want to pub. photos of his stuff So that you are free to consider this lot as both a scoop and an honour."[25]

---

21    Margaret Anderson, *My Thirty Years' War*, 218-26, 231. Anderson's memoirs are often vague and inaccurate in their details, but they clearly reflect her spirit during these years. Her disillusionment is also reflected in "Ulysses' in Court," *The Little Review* 7, 10, no 4 (January-March 1921): 22-25.

22    Anderson, *My Thirty Years' War*, 230-32. See also jh, "Gardening with Brains," *The Little Review* 9, no. 3 (Autumn 1922): 33; and Margaret Anderson, "Dialogue," *The Little Review* 9, no. 2 (Winter 1922): 24-25 for indications of stress between the editors.

23    Ezra Pound to Margaret Anderson, c. 17 January 1921 [dates inscribed on letters by another hand are designated with "C."); "Dada souléve tout," *The Little Review* 7, no. 4 (January-March 1921): 62-63.

24    Ezra Pound to Margaret Anderson, c. 20 April 1921.

25    Ezra Pound to Margaret Anderson, c.7 April-May1921.

The photographs of Brancusi's sculpture and the Cocteau poem created a stunning image for the Autumn 1921 issue, which proclaimed: "As PROTEST against the suppression of the *Little Review* containing various installments of the 'ULYSSES' of JAMES JOYCE, the following artists and writers of international reputation collaborating in the autumn number of the Little Review: BRANCUSI, JEAN COCTEAU, JEAN HUGO, GUY CHARLES CROS, PAUL MORAND, FRANCIS PICABIA, EZRA POUND."[26] Both the Brancusi sculpture, in its simplicity and finished surfaces, and the poem by Cocteau, a homage to his friend the aviator Roland Garros, directly reflected the fascination with the machine, machine technology, and machine-related esthetics then raging in Paris. Cocteau's poem played with images from American movies and machines in such passages as "very smooth Underwood typewriter/detective/in the saddle/and (a good shot with the pistol) the telephone girl of Los Angeles/ revives/ the old gallop/the Indians on their poneys."[27]

These contributions brought *The Little Review* up to date with regard to both the visual arts and the next generation of the Parisian literary avant-garde. The issue had a magnificence, both visually and conceptually, that did create a "swish" and a fitting response to "the dung of ignoble animals," as Pound referred to the New York legal system.[28] Hamilton Easter Field, editor and critic of *The Arts*, leading art magazine of that time, commented: "The Brancusi reproductions (twenty-four in number) are well worth the price of the issue and you get Ezra Pound, Picabia, Jean Cocteau, and Kenneth Burke thrown in. You also get a cover page which ought to make those responsible for the cover of *The Arts* blush for shame."[29]

As the magazine moved beyond the *Ulysses* trauma, it increasingly featured visual art. The entire Spring 1922 issue was produced by new foreign editor Francis Picabia. It featured numerous reproductions of his mechanomorphic art as well as several essays, including one in cel-

---

26    *The Little Review* 7, no, 1 (Autumn 1921): 2.

27    Jean Cocteau, "The Cape of Good Hope," *The Little Review* 7, no.1 (Autumn 1925): 76-77.

28    Ezra Pound to Margaret Anderson, c. 22 April 1921.

29    Hamilton Easter Field, "Comments," *The Arts* 6 (December 1921): 186.

ebration and support of *The Little Review*: "'Little Review' is certainly the only magazine which at the present moment desires to give the public the work of men whose new quests are the aim in art—whether in painting, music, sculpture or literature."[30] Picabia went on to reflect the Parisian avant-garde's impatience with traditional art and ideas. He used different arguments than Heap but pointed to the same issues:

> There is sometimes more art in knowing how to drink a cocktail than in knowing how to mix blue or vermilion with white, more art in designing the practical side of an automobile than in imitating the buttocks of an Italian model of the Place Pigalle, more art in constructing a motor than in copying a poilu with this twenty kilos of imbecility on his back, more art in making a watering pot than in making the portrait of an apple.[31]

In the late fall of 1922, with Heap now taking the main responsibility, *The Little Review* began to engage the New York art scene as well as the Parisian, with an issue featuring the art of American Futurist Joseph Stella, along with the first installment from Guillaume Apollinaire's *Aesthetic Meditations* in translation and numerous reproductions of cubist painting and sculpture. The appearance of Stella and Apollinaire reflects contact with New York's Société Anonyme, an organization created in 1920 by Katherine Dreier in collaboration with Man Ray and Marcel Duchamp. Its activities encompassed a broad spectrum of the avant-garde, mixing American, French, and German art.[32] Yet, despite the fact that both Dreier and Heap were supporters of the European avant-garde in America, interaction between Dreier and *The Little Review* was erratic.

Heap, in one of her first independent moves following the *Ulysses* trial, and apparently in response to a suggestion from Pound,[33] contacted

---

30    Francis Picabia, "Anti-cog," *The Little Review* 8, no. 2 (Spring 1922): 42.

31    Picabia, Ibid.

32    Stella Number, *The Little Review* 9, no. 3 (Autumn 1922). The Société Anonyme sponsored the translation of the Apollinaire book. The Stella issue of *The Little Review* coincided with a Société Anonyme exhibition of his work which was publicized in the magazine.

33    Ezra Pound to Margaret Anderson, c. 1 April-2 May 1921.

Dreier and invited her to advertise in *The Little Review*.[34] While this letter
is the only direct communication between them that survives from this
time, the interaction apparently led to the Apollinaire/Stella issue of the
following fall. Since Dreier did not have a regular publication of her
own, *The Little Review* could well have appealed to her. In the winter
of 1922 *The Little Review* continued the collaboration by publishing
photographs of the machine-influenced sculpture of John Storrs, who
was having an exhibition at the Société Anonyme.[35] However, by 1924,
following a year abroad, Dreier was distancing herself from Heap, saying she did not have time for Heap's projects.[36] Dreier withdrew because
she was uncomfortable with Heap's manner of operation in her promotion of modernism.

Heap's experience with *The Little Review* up to the early 1920s had
always been in tandem with Anderson and with the support of Pound.
As she began to make her own way in the New York art world, she lacked
organization and support. Though Dreier and Heap shared interests
and promoted many of the same artists, their personal and intellectual
styles were diametrically opposed. Dreier, a native New Yorker from an
intellectual German family, was at ease in New York. Moreover, she was
a recognized abstract painter, with a firsthand knowledge of Kandinsky
and his theories. She was an experienced and orderly administrator of
her organization, concerned about educating the public and systematic
in her activities. Heap, on the other hand, took pride in making "no
compromise with the public taste."[37] Despite her established reputation
with writers, Heap was new to the New York visual art scene. She had
given up painting to become a critic, and had no experience with art
administration. When she began working with art, rather than just literature, her haphazard organization incurred the wrath of many artists.
She particularly appalled the systematic and conscientious Dreier.

---

34    Jane Heap to Katherine Dreier, undated, Société Anonyme Archives,
      Beinecke Rare Book and Manuscript Library, Yale University.

35    Ezra Pound to Margaret Anderson, Anderson, 28 December 1922;
      John Storrs to Margaret Anderson, 27 December 1922. He sent
      his photographs, chosen by Pound, as a request for publicity in
      conjunction with his exhibition at the Société Anonyme.

36    Katherine Dreier to Jane Heap, 9 January 1924, Société Anonyme
      Archives, Beinecke Rare Book and Manuscript Library, Yale University.

37    This slogan by Ezra Pound appeared on the cover of *The Little Review*
      for several years.

Thus, when Heap sought Dreier's support in a new community called "Inter Arts, A Guest House for Work and Play," she was rejected. The brochure that Heap sent to Dreier proclaimed a "Society" with "Painters, poets, scientists, engineers, musicians, actresses, opera-stars and enthusiasts." Each sponsor was asked for $5000. The project never developed, except in the guise of the Little Review Gallery, but its definition already suggested the direction that Heap would take as she made her own place in the avant-garde scene. Around this same time in the Winter 1922 issue, she declared:

> The American [sic] artist is in a bad way. He has never established his social function in the minds of the public. In Europe groups of artists have revolted against the existing state of consciousness; they have ceased to act as the medium and have become masters of the spiritual situation.
>
> Many artists in this country … whine about the terror of the 'mechanistic age.' What belief in the power and function of art, to be terrorized by the power of plumbing systems and engines. …
>
> The artist … must establish [his] social function … He must affiliate with the creative arts in the other arts, and with the constructive me of his epoch; engineers and scientists etc. Until this is established a great spiritual waste is going on through the dispersed unrecognized or unattained energy of the true artist. *The Little Review* has long been working on a plan to promote this idea, and to bring the artist into personal contact with the consumer and the appreciator.[38]

This polemical statement, like the Inter Arts guest house project, promotes Heap's new connection of the artist and the engineer, the theme that would be so important to her subsequent activities for *The Little Review*. The writing of Picabia, Cocteau and other contributors to the magazine who frequently referred to machines as superior to traditional art, along with the appearance of mechanical elements in satirical art of the World War I period, must have reinforced Heap's long-standing and deep seated disgust with any form of tradition.

---

38      jh, "Independents, etc.," *The Little Review* 9, no. 2 (Winter 1922): 22. In 1922, the Winter issue followed Spring and Fall, as a result of post office regulations.

Along with this outspoken editorial, the reproduction of Vladimir Tatlin's radical and extraordinary "Monument to the Third International" in the same Winter 1922 issue further signaled Heap's independence from Pound, Anderson, and even Dreier, in terms of her awareness of avant-garde concerns. Tatlin's "Monument" joined engineering and art in a building that was to have been the heart of both the new Soviet government and the communication system for a new society. *The Little Review* may have acquired the photograph through its friends in the literary sphere, for a diagram of the "Monument" appeared around the same time in another American periodical, *Broom*.[39] It was also in the winter of 1922 that Tatlin and the Russian constructivists first emerged in Western Europe. Heap's Tatlin reproduction therefore marks her awareness of the mid-twenties cutting edge.

From spring until late fall of 1923 Heap, along with both Anderson and Le Blanc, visited Paris for the first time. The trip was a major turning point in Heap's life for two reasons. First, Anderson decided to stay in Europe as piano accompanist for Le Blanc's concerts and therefore turned the primary editing of the magazine over to Heap. While Anderson did return to New York often during the 1920s, and even was involved with Heap's endeavors at *The Little Review*, particularly with respect to Gurdjieff, her attention was on Le Blanc and Europe.[40] Second, the trip to Paris was important because Heap directly engaged the European avant-garde scene. She and Anderson met their former European editor, Ezra Pound, and through him the artists he admired: Léger, Brancusi, Cocteau, and Picabia. Yet, Heap and Anderson also quickly became acquainted with a broader spectrum of people than they could meet through Pound (whose status in the clannish Parisian

---

39    *Broom* 3, no. 3 (October 1922). 234. This issue of *Broom* also published Enrico Prampolini, "The Aesthetic of the Machine and Mechanical Introspection in Art," 235-37, an essay that would appear in *The Little Review* to, no. 2 (Autumn-Winter 1924-25): 49-51 and again in the catalogue for the "Machine Age Exposition" *Machine Age Exposition* (New York: The Little Review, 1927). Another possible source for the Tatlin photograph is Louis Lozowick, who was already writing occasionally for both The *Little Review* and *Broom* by 1922. *Broom* 5, no. 1 (August 1923) declared "The Age of the Machine" as an age of "spiritual change" in an advertisement in the back of the magazine.

40    Anderson, *My Thirty Years' War*, 265.

art scene was problematic).[41] Through Brancusi and Gertrude Stein, as well as others, they met most of the Parisian avant-garde artists and writers, including the just emerging surrealists and, of particular importance to the later history of the magazine, the major promoter of Dada, Tristan Tzara.[42]

Starting in the fall of 1923, Tzara provided Heap with manuscripts, photographs, and contacts that included van Doesburg and de Stijl.[43] Publicist that he was, Tzara saw an opportunity for bringing himself and his artists before an American audience, a possibility he was apparently thinking about as the Dada movement in Paris was going through its last rites. Even before Tzara began contributing, however, Heap celebrated machine principles with her pioneer publication of Fernand Léger's important essay "The Esthetics of the Machine" in the first issues of *The Little Review* after her return from Paris.[44] That essay proclaimed the new Machine Age esthetics that celebrated engineering principles as more vital than traditional painting. Heap's publication of Léger's statement, a major and much quoted essay of the early Machine Age, demonstrates Heap's astute engagement with the latest ideas on the revitalization of art through the machine.

Just after the publication of the Léger articles, in the winter of 1923-24, Heap became involved in Gurdjieff's mystical teachings. His ideas provided the backbone for her increasingly self-assured work in the mid 1920s. Heap's first documented contact with Gurdjieff's teach-

---

41      Tristan Tzara to Jane Heap, undated, saying that Satie and Brancusi did not like Léger and Pound, but they promised to send something if Pound's and Léger 's influence was at an end. "If you can certify that, Satie will give you an article made just for you."

42      Anderson, *My Thirty Years' War*, 252-64. See for example Tristan Tzara to Jane Heap, 23 November 1923, with a long list of works enclosed.

43      See for example Tristan Tzara to Jane Heap, 23 November 1923, with a long list of works enclosed.

44      Fernand Léger, "The Esthetics of the Machine," *The Little Review* 9, no. 3 (Spring 1923): 45-49; 9, no. 4 (Autumn-Winter 1923-24): 55-58. Although the first issue is dated Spring 1923, internal evidence indicates that it, was published after the trip. The essay was dedicated to Ezra Pound. It is not known whether Heap received it directly from Léger or from Pound while she was in Paris, but this is the first recorded publication of the essay based on Léger's lecture to the Collége de France in the spring of 1923.

ings came through the intermediary of Alfred Richard Orage in late December 1923. Orage had played a central role first in the Theosophical Society in England, then as pioneering editor of *The New Age* magazine from 1907 until 1922. As one writer has put it, "The New Age and its circle became the most articulate section of Progressive idealism in Britain."[45] Orage's publication, like *The Little Review* on a less powerful level, pioneered in areas ranging from politics to esthetics.[46] While Orage had always been interested in spiritual and occult ideas, contact with the ideas of Gurdjieff in London during February 1922 led him to abandon *The New Age* and become a follower.[47] When he decided to bring the Gurdjieff teachings to America, he turned to *The Little Review* editors as supporters.

On Orage's arrival in the United States, "he went straight from the boat to the office of *The Little Review* on east Eleventh Street near Fifth Avenue, where Anderson and Heap awaited him."[48] For Orage, "his hopes as well as his drive was for a new, as yet unimagined, development of skills the machine age would make possible."[49] As a well-known editor of an avant-garde publication, Orage appealed to New York intellectuals and created receptivity to Gurdjieff when the teacher himself arrived in February 1924. Gurdjieff's teachings synthesized the

---

45    Webb, *Harmonious Circle*, 208.

46    Of a slightly older generation than Pound, Orage supported the younger writer but critiqued his work and that of Joyce as they appeared in *The Little Review*. Wallace Martin, ed., *Orage as Critic* (London and Boston: Routledge and Kegan Paul, 1974), 151-156. Orage also contributed "Henry James and the Ghostly," *The Little Review* 5, no. 4 (June 1918): 41-43. Tom Gibbons outlines Orage's early activities in *Rooms in the Darwin Hotel* (Nedlands: University of Western Australia, 1973), chapter 4.

47    Orage had already been inspired by P. D. Ouspensky's teachings in London from August 1921. Both the personal and intellectual connections between Gurdjieff and Ouspensky are complex. See Webb, *Harmonious Circle*, 218-26 for a discussion of this intermediate stage in Orage's spiritual quest.

48    Louise Welch, *Orage with Gurdjieff in America* (Boston: Routledge and Kegan Paul, 1982), 1; since Welch specifically mentions Anderson as also present, this is one instance of her continued involvement with Heap's activities at *The Little Review*. No correspondence with Orage on this meeting survives in *The Little Review* Archive.

49    Welch, *Orage with Gurdjieff in America*, 9.

physical sciences, Christianity, and Eastern mysticism. What attracted Heap initially was the notion that the mechanical aspect of life might be understood as a source of transformation.

Gurdjieff saw the human body as mechanical[50] and human beings as therefore limited. However, he also believed that by acknowledging the mechanical, transformation to a higher level of consciousness would be possible. Since he emphasized the mechanistic aspect of life, he also emphasized the mechanistic aspect of art:

Q. Is mathematics the basis of all art?

A. All Eastern ancient art.

Q. Then could anyone who knew the formula build a perfect form like a cathedral, producing the same emotion?

A. Yes, and get the same reactions too.

Q. Man has an octave inside him; but what about higher possibilities? A. This is the aim of all religions to find how to do. It cannot be done unconsciously, but is taught by a system. ...

Q. With mathematical law could everyone be developed to a higher degree? A. The body when born is the result of many things and is just an empty possibility. Man is born without a soul, but it is possible to make one. ... I must be a slave of either science or religion. In either case man is a slave of this objective law. It is impossible to free oneself from it. Only he is free who stands in the middle.[51]

Gurdjieff supported the idea of understanding and utilizing the mathematical and scientific laws of the universe as a means of creating

---

50    G. I. Gurdjieff, *Views from the Real World* (New York: E. P. Dutton, 1973), 119; Gurdjieff's teaching also included sacred dances with mechanical movements such as stop motions. Welch, *Orage with Gurdjieff in America*, 5. Webb, *Harmonious Circle*, 540-41, analyzes the complex sources of Gurdjieff's teachings, ranging from Buddhism and Sufism to Gnosticism, Neoplatonism, and Rosicrucianism, and points out the parallels in Gurdjieff's thought to Theosophy He also makes a comparison with respect to the mechanical references in Gurdjieff to behaviorism, p. 436.

51    Gurdjieff, *Views from the Real World*, 185, 190, 191, 199.

both art and, more profoundly, a soul. His emphasis on science and its laws appealed to Heap. In supporting the machine as a new creative force, she sought to "stand in the middle" between science and religion, or in her case, science and art, and thus to create the possibility of transformation. Through these teachings she saw the machine as "a mysterious and necessary part of our evolution."[52] Extolling the machine dovetailed with Léger's theory of the importance of the clean, impersonal esthetics of the machine and the exciting role of the engineer in modern society. For Léger, however, as for the Russian constructivists, Machine Age art was divorced from mysticism.[53] Thus, Heap created her own unique wedding of the machine and mysticism.

In the spring of 1924 Heap provided meeting space for study groups led by Gorham Munson, an important literary figure and follower of Gurdjieff.[54] That summer Heap visited Gurdjieff's Institute for the Harmonious Development of Man in a chateau near Fontainebleau, and in the summer of 1925 she returned to study there.[55] The following fall, Munson proposed that an entire issue of *The Little Review* be written by Orage:

52    jh, "Machine Age Exposition," *Machine Age Exposition* (New York: The Little Review, 1927), 36.

53    Gurdjieff's mysticism had its roots, in part, in the spiritualism of the upper classes of Russia and Armenia; rejection of that type of mysticism was an important dimension of the new art of the constructivists after the Russian Revolution.

54    Welch, *Orage with Gurdjieff in America,* 41. Munson was editor of *Secession,* another little magazine; it lasted only from 1922 until 1924. Hoffman, *The Little Magazine,* 93-101. Dickran Tashjian outlines the battle of spirituality and the Machine Age in another context that also included Munson. *Skyscraper Primitives* (Middletown: Wesleyan University Press, 1975), 116-142. Waldo Frank deplored the dehumanizing effects of technology while dada-influenced figures such as Matthew Josephson celebrated technology in the pages of Broom, See also Gorham Munson, *The Wakening Twenties,* (Baton Rough and London: Louisiana State University Press, 1985) chapter 15.

55    On Heap's and Anderson's visit to Fontainebleau *see Margaret Anderson, The Fiery Fountains* (New York: Horizon Press, 1951), 109-28. Another useful source is Margaret Anderson, *The Unknowable Gurdjieff* (London: Routledge and Kegan Paul, 1962). Anderson sometimes disagrees with other sources on chronological details. The book is dedicated to Jane Heap and gives her credit for many of the formulations. In the mid-1920s, perhaps partially motivated by the impulses of Gurdjieff's teachings, Heap adopted Margaret Anderson's two nephews, Fritz and Tom Peters, after their parents' divorce, Webb, *Harmonious Circle,* 290.

Here in better shape than I put it last night, is the germ of an idea for a special number of *The Little Review* devoted to Programs, or the problem of engineering a renaissance. Such a number, to my mind should contain

a.   Trotsky's concept of proletarian art

b.   The humanistic classical program of such men as Irving Babbitt

d.   The religious-romantic program of Middleton Murry, D. H. Lawrence

c.   The neo-classical program of such men as T. S. Eliot

e.   The mystical-naturalistic program of Waldo Frank....

f.   The program of Surreallisme [sic].

g.   The program of Orage.[56]

By the time Munson wrote, Heap had already turned in a different and more difficult direction than Munson suggested in order to "engineer a renaissance." Instead of emphasizing the literary figures who were directly involved with Gurdjieff, she expanded her art coverage. In the spring 1924 issue of *The Little Review*, immediately after her first contacts with Gurdjieff, Heap increased exposure of machine-related art by including illustrations of Russian constructivist work by Lissitzky, Gabo, and Pevsner,[57] along with Edgard Varèse's score for *Amériques*, his homage to New York, which incorporated sirens and other mechanical sounds. In addition, she launched her view of the machine as a religious expression, thereby directly promoting her Gurdjieffian ideas:

Today there are artists who are creating forms and beings which are the conscious expression of the unvarying and universal laws. These forms do not copy the organizations of Nature, but have a life of their own and extend Nature. Something very interesting could be written about the Machine

---

56   Gorham Munson to Jane Heap, 19 November 1925.

57   jh, "Comments," *The Little Review* 10, no. 1 (Spring 1924) 57.

as a religious expression as great if not greater than the great cathedrals.... I have thought of doing it.[58]

At this early stage of her spiritual study, Heap slightly manipulated Gurdjieff's ideas to her own purpose: she made the machine the counterpart of the cathedral as a manifestation of a religious consciousness, whereas Gurdjieff stressed the underlying principles of the machine as a process of transformation.

In the next issue, which she assembled in the autumn of 1924, Heap included machine-inspired art works in an issue dedicated to Juan Gris. A statement and score by Léger for his avant-garde film "Ballet Mecanique," an article by George Antheil on his machine-influenced music, and Enrico Prampolini's powerful statement on the "Esthetic of the Machine and Mechanical Introspection in Art," together created a dynamic impact both visually and verbally.[59]

For the spring 1925 issue Heap went even further: she announced plans for a major "Machine Age Exposition" that would feature the engineer:

> There is a great new race of men in America: The Engineer. He has created a new mechanical world, he is segregated from men in other activities. ... It is inevitable and important to the civilization of today that he make a union with the artist. ... A great many people cry out the Machine as the incubus that is threatening our "spiritual" life.
>
> The aims of this race have bred an incomplete man. ... His outer life is too full, his inner life empty. His religion is either dead or seems a hopeless misfit for life today. The world is

---

58    jh, "Comments," *The Little Review* 10, no. 2 (Autumn-Winter 1924-25): 22.

59    Fernand Léger, "Film by Fernand Léger and Dudley Murphy, "Musical Synchronism by George Antheil," *The Little Review* 10, no. 2 (Autumn-Winter 1924-25): 42-44; George Antheil, "Abstractions and Time in Music," 13-15. The Tristan Tzara contribution to this issue was a poem by G. Ribemont-Dessaignes, "Le Singe et le Singe," 42.

restless with a need to express its emotions. The desire for beauty has become a necessity.[60]

Under the impetus of Gurdjieff, Heap had developed within one year from an acerbic commentator into an active and public figure with a positive agenda for revitalizing art and life by uniting the dynamic, new engineer of the machine and the world's need for nontraditional religion. In this issue Heap published Theo van Doesburg's major statements "The Evolution of Modern Architecture in Holland" and "Literature of the Advance Guard in Holland," essays that Tzara had sent her the year before.[61]

The articles introduced principles of de Stijl architecture to America and were the magazine's first major plunge into modern architecture, a logical step given Heap's new perspective. De Stijl, as articulated by van Doesburg, emphasized the functional principles of the new architecture in terms of form, ideas that corresponded to the Machine Age principles that Heap promoted.

Around this time Heap launched The Little Review Gallery and exhibition program. Active from 1925 to 1927, the Little Review Gallery remains the least documented dimension of Heap's activities. Heap founded the gallery at 66 Fifth Avenue as an adjunct to the magazine and a gathering place for intellectuals. Financial backing was even more sporadic than for her magazine, and she apparently had no assistance. Consequently, the exhibitions and the logistics associated with them were often a nightmare for the artists involved. Although she promised exhibitions to many artists, most of the shows were miscellaneous groups of works by European modernists. For that reason, and because they were barely publicized even in the pages of *The Little Review,*

60      jh, "Machine Age Exposition," *The Little Review* 11, no. 1 (Spring 1925): 22. The final version of this article in the exhibition catalogue adds at the end of the first paragraph: "This affiliation of Artist and Engineer will benefit each in his own domain, it will end the immense waste in each domain and will become a new creative force." However, all of the second paragraph quoted here was omitted. "Machine Age Exposition," *Machine Age Exposition* (New York: The Little Review, 1927): 36.

61      Theo van Doesburg, "Evolution of Modern Architecture in Holland," *The Little Review* 11, no. 1 (Spring 1925): 47-51; Theo van Doesburg, "The Literature of the Advance Guard in Holland," 56-59. Tristan Tzara to Jane Heap, 27 April 1925.

the exhibitions were not reviewed in the art press. Despite its slightly recorded history, by early 1926 Hart Crane, in a letter to Heap, called the gallery "a rendezvous of talent, a galaxy of wit,"[62] a comment that suggests the gallery was more important as a place of discussion, probably Gurdjieffian discussion, than as a center for art.

In general, Heap's preserved correspondence about the gallery begins around 1925 in a cordial, friendly tone, and ends two years later in anger, frustration, and even open hostility. The endeavor started with the new-found inspiration of Heap's excitement with the Machine Age, ended as she increasingly disengaged from the art world and devoted herself to Gurdjieff.

Initially, European artists were flattered by her offer of an exhibition in New York. They thirsted for contact with and information about America. They even returned the invitation by asking Heap to write on American modern art for European publications. For example, Szymon Syrkus, Polish architect and editor of the periodical *Pressens*, wrote, "American modernism could not find a better representative than yourself, Madame, and we hope you are willing to send us, as soon as possible, not only the material on America that you had the kindness to promise, but also an article by you, treating modern art in America."[63] Moholy-Nagy asked her to contribute an entire book on "The New World" for the Bauhaus series.[64]

Léger, Moholy-Nagy, Anton Pevsner, Naum Gabo, Jacques Lipchitz, van Doesburg, Schwitters, and others all sent recent work to New

---

62    Hart Crane to Jane Heap, 19 January 1926.

63    Szymon Syrkus to Jane Heap, 15 July 1927 (translation from French by the author).

64    Laszlo Moholy-Nagy to Jane Heap, 12 September 1925. This book was advertised in a Bauhaus brochure as "Jane Heap (America) The New World." For an earlier version of this brochure see Hans M. Wingler, *The Bauhaus, Weimar, Dessau, Berlin, Chicago* (Cambridge and London: MIT Press, 1969), 131.

Heap also planned a book on modern art with Harcourt, Brace and Co. (Ray Everitt to Jane Heap, 27 December 1927).

York.[65] That Heap sometimes displayed machinery along with the art is documented in her comment that "in conjunction with these chemical paintings by Man Ray, we are exposing temperature regulators, chemical apparatuses, self-aligning ball-bearings and other 'ready-made' objects."[66] Kurt Schwitters, Hannah Hoch, Jean Arp, Pevsner, and Gabo all had significant shows accompanied by comments, of which the following brief statement is representative: "Kurt Schwitters lives in Hanover. He lives in a house papered with newspaper and tramway tickets. He is young and has the wit and mockery and poetry of a Dadaist writer, painter, sculptor and the editor of *Merz*. *The Little Review* has just closed an exposition of his pasted paper pictures." Other artists appearing in group exhibitions and illustrated in *The Little Review* included Ossip Zadkine, Lett Haines, Cedric Morris, Nicolai Granovsky, Pavel Tchelitchew, and a few American artists: John Storrs, Charles Demuth, and Henry McFee.[67]

The correspondence with Moholy-Nagy records the largest fiasco of Heap's career. In December 1926 Moholy-Nagy sent her virtually his entire production up to that time. He accompanied his work with lengthy statements and letters, in which he explained to Heap in detail his mechanical technique and philosophy, most of which was as yet unpublished. This large shipment was sent on the basis of two meetings, one in Paris in 1925, when plans were laid for a Bauhaus exhibition

---

65    Theo van Doesburg to Jane Heap, 20 April 1925. Léger said that he was "very touched that she has thought of him for this exhibition" (Fernand Léger to Jane Heap, 1924). Lipchitz's exhibition was to have been accompanied by articles by Jean Cocteau and Gertrude Stein (Jacques Lipchitz to Jane Heap, 4 January 1925). The articles were not published, although the latter article appeared later in Gertrude Stein, *Portraits and Prayers* (New York: Random House, 1934). Ossip Zadkine to Jane Heap, to April 1925. Laszlo Moholy-Nagy to Jane Heap, 12 September 1926.

66    jh, "Comments," *The Little Review* 9, no. 4 (Autumn-Winter 1923-24): 39.

67    *The Little Review* 10, no. 1 (Spring 1924): 58. One checklist for a group exhibition survives; one advertisement appears in *The Little Review* 11, no. 2 (Winter 1926): 123. Other references are occasional passing remarks in *The Little Review*. On Gabo and Pevsner, Henry McBride, "... Art of Two Constructionists," *New York Sun*, 1 May 1926, 9. Most of these artists first became known to Heap through Tzara (Tristan Tzara to Jane Heap, 27 April 1925; 28 May 1925)

in New York, and the second in 1926 at Dessau, when Heap visited Moholy-Nagy and his wife, apparently stimulating a profound respect and rapport.

In September Moholy-Nagy explained to Heap that a Bauhaus exhibition could not take place because other Bauhaus artists were concerned about not getting their work back from America (a well-founded concern, as it turned out), so he sent his own work for a one-person exhibition. By August 1927 he was horrified to discover that this work was still tied up at the harbor in New York. This astonishing situation apparently resulted from Heap's lack of funds, her illness (she suffered from diabetes), her increasing distraction with other activities (including Gurdjieff and the "Machine Age Exposition"), and her problems with customs over the importation of the works as art. Moholy-Nagy frantically corresponded with Heap throughout the fall to take care of the situation and finally acknowledged the return of his art in January 1928. His work never appeared in the Little Review Gallery.[68]

Although the Moholy-Nagy story was by far the most disastrous, other artists who sent their work for exhibition at Heap's gallery suffered similar anxieties. One of Gabo's constructions was broken in shipment. Zadkine, whose works were detained in a crate with those of Lipchitz, angrily wrote, "I warn you everybody is furious against you, and if you do not take any energetic steps to get our work out of this situation you will be [illegible] in the opinion of the Paris artists—a matter which is very serious."[69] Since this letter was received at the same time as the Moholy-Nagy letters, and those of several other artists, when Heap had already returned to France to study with Gurdjieff, she had to work long distance from Paris to extricate the work from customs in New York. Apparently, all the art works were finally returned to the artists,

---

68    The correspondence from Moholy-Nagy begins 22 August 1925 and continues through 27 June 1929. The crucial letter documenting the neglect of the pictures in the New York harbor and referring to Heap's comments that she was having trouble with customs is dated 5 August 1927. Moholy-Nagy also sent a five-page manuscript which appears to be a preliminary introduction to issues developed further in Moholy-Nagy's later publications. I am grateful to Horst Lueck for his assistance in translating the Moholy-Nagy/Heap correspondence.

69    Ossip Zadkine to Jane Heap, 8 August 1927.

although their varied reactions to the problems and delays is in itself a study in personalities.[70] Even Moholy-Nagy later forgave Heap and sent her some photograms and an essay for the final issue of *The Little Review* in 1929.[71]

In the midst of organizing small exhibitions at her gallery, Heap also played an important, although controversial, part in "The International Theatre Exposition/New York 1926." Created by the de Stijl-affiliated designer Frederick Kiesler, "The International Theatre Exhibition" was the decade's largest and most comprehensive exhibition of stage design based on mechanical principles. Heap stated in *The Little Review* that Tzara had suggested, while she was attending the 1925 "Exposition Internationale des Arts Decoratifs et Industrielles Modernes" in Paris, that she invite Kiesler to organize an exhibition in New York. Kiesler's display at the Paris exposition included a stunning futuristic urban design called "City in Space," a plan for a city suspended above the ground on steel girders.[72] Heap must have responded deeply to this utopian Machine Age vision, for it corresponded exactly to her hopes for a union of the engineer and the artist. Although she obtained support from other backers, such as the Theater Guild, to bring Kiesler and his exhibition to New York,[73] it was Heap (apparently along with

70      Léger was furious (Fernand Léger to Jane Heap, 18 April 1926). Moholy-Nagy was anxious (Laszlo Moholy-Nagy to Jane Heap, 24 and z6 August, 12 and 27 September 1927). Lipchitz was polite (Jacques Lipchitz to Jane Heap, 21 June 1927). Morris was sorry for the trouble to her (Cedric Morris to Jane Heap, undated).

71      Moholy-Nagy promised Heap some of his work. When he acknowledged that his work had finally come back, he wrote, "Please write me where I can send the pictures I have promised to you" (Laszlo Moholy-Nagy to Jane Heap, 28 February 1928). Moholy-Nagy's article is a response to a questionnaire. "In Answer to Your Interview," *The Little Review* 12, no. 2 (May 1929):54-56.

72      R. L. Held, *Endless Innovations, Frederick Kiesler's Theory and Scenic Design* (Ann Arbor: UMI Research Press, 1982), 39.

73      Although the Kiesler literature and reviews give little space to Heap's role, Held, *Endless Innovations*, 40, does state that Heap "was impressed and wrote the Theater Guild to help support the magazine's efforts to bring the exhibition to New York with Kiesler as its director." Newspaper references to the exhibition's sponsorship consistently give her the credit, with one exception, which states that Maurice Lagner of the Theater Guild made the arrangements. *Chicago Tribune*, 5 January 1926, unsigned, untitled clipping, Frederick

Margaret Anderson) who greeted him in New York when he arrived with the many crates for the exhibition.[74]

The grandiose Kiesler and the idealistic, inexperienced Heap were a poor combination. Kiesler created an exhibition much larger than Heap's gallery could accommodate. To make matters worse, the backing for Kiesler fell through, leading to much embarrassment for *The Little Review*.[75] Yet, finally a coalition of support was gathered, and the exhibition opened in Steinway Exposition Hall on 27 February 1926 with 1,541 exhibitions of stage design from fifteen countries including Czechoslovakia, Yugoslavia, Romania, Hungary, Sweden, Poland, and the U.S.S.R., as well as France, Holland, Germany, Belgium, and the United States.[76] Kiesler used radical installation methods that placed the exhibits on trestles in circles and spirals. Extensive press coverage orchestrated by the theater and art critic Sheldon Cheney made Machine Age stage design and constructivism familiar concepts in America.[77]

Heap herself publicized the exhibition by publishing a revised version of the exhibition catalogue as an issue of *The Little Review*. She retained Kiesler's radical format, including typography that presented

---

Kiesler Archives, Archives of American Art, microfilm roll 147. The Theater Guild, the Provincetown Playhouse, Greenwich Village Theater, and Neighborhood Playhouse were listed as sponsors in the catalogue.

74    "Design's Bad Boy," *Architectural Forum* 86, no. 2 (February 1947): 88-99, 138, 140, especially 88. Kiesler's ego was wounded by *The Little Review's* failure to produce a major reception for him. His ideas were neglected in America partly because of the power of the International Style in the 1940s and 1950s. See "Kiesler's Pursuit of an Idea," *Progressive Architecture* 52, no. 7 (July 1961): 104-23.

75    "Design's Bad Boy," 88.

76    Kiesler's own exhibits attracted attention with the idea of the "endless theater" which was an "immense indoor theater shaped like a bowl with concentric rings for horse races, motor races, a grandstand for music, a grid for sports and twisting in and out, up and down, among these promenades, automobiles, roads, etc." (unsigned clipping, American Art News, 6 March 1926, Kiesler Archives, Archives of American Art, microfilm roll 147). The reviewer concluded that it sounded "like the tenth circle of Dante's inferno." From our contemporary perspective, it sounds similar to an amusement park or a prototype for Disneyland.

77    The Kiesler Archives (Archives of American Art) preserve much of the publicity for his exposition, indicating that he managed to achieve a good deal of attention. Most of the criticism was positive.

text in different directions and sizes, and reprinted provocative articles by Hans Richter, Léger, Prampolini, and Kiesler. Other material on constructivist principles in the U.S.S.R. and Poland informed New Yorkers, practically for the first time, about the Eastern European avant-garde. Heap added to these original essays an article by her partner in Gurdjieffian pursuits, Alfred Richard Orage, who connected theater design to Gurdjieffian ideas.[78]

Kiesler's use of technology to reshape the stage combined the mechanical and the human. He called for "the vitality of life itself, a vitality which has the force and the tempo of the age.[79] Likewise Heap declared:

> We will endeavor to show that there exists a parallel develop-
> ment and a balancing element in contemporary art. The men
> who hold first rank in the plastic arts today are the men who
> are organizing and transforming the realities of our age into
> dynamic beauty. They recognize [the machine] as one of the
> realities.[80]

Kiesler and Heap had a compatible sense of mission in their desire for change. By developing the mechanized stage and radically reshaping

---

78     A. R. Orage, "The Theatrical Theatre," *The Little Review* 11, no 2 (Winter 1926): 33-36. Exposition (New York: *The Little Review*, 1927), 5-6.

79     Frederick Kiesler, "Debacle of the Modern Theatre," *The Little Review* 1r, no. 2 (Winter 1926): 67.

80     jh, "Machine Age Exposition," *Machine Age Exposition*, 36. In bringing Kiesler to New York, Heap had also helped him to realize his own hopes: according to some Paris newspapers, he had been planning to go to New York in order to obtain the engineering expertise he needed for his projects. "Mr. Kiesler must next go to America to confer with experts on the means of constructing a city in space ..." (unidentified clipping, Kiesler Archives, microfilm roll 147). Another article stated that "Kiesler expects to visit the United States in connection with his work on a huge model of his city built in space. He will confer with American experts on traffic problems" ("Artist Plans City in Air ...," Kiesler Archives, microfilm roll 147). Heap apparently also lost a good deal of money as a result of the endeavor (J. O'H. Cosgrove to Jane Heap, undated). Cosgrove, also a Gurdjieffian, encouraged Heap to proceed with her plans for her own exhibition, despite her financial setbacks.

space, Kiesler completely altered the traditional theatrical experience. He provided Heap with a tangible example for the use of machines as a means of transformation of spiritual as well as material life.

Partially inspired by Kiesler's elaborate scale of operation, Heap finally realized her own "Machine Age Exposition" in the spring of 1927. Held in a large warehouse space, adjacent to where Kiesler's exhibition had been, it presented Heap's version of a radical installation with "the unpainted white plaster finish of the walls, columns, beams, girders, and floor slabs of an unpartitioned office floor of a common type of building erected for commercial renting. An amusing touch was the use of ordinary tin pails inverted as reflectors in place of lighting fixtures."[81]

Combining models, photographs, and art, and sometimes called an architectural exhibition in press releases, Heap's show was officially titled "Machine Age Exposition" only near the end of the preparations. As one review detailed, it comprised "radio sets, valves, gears, propellers, metal cupboards, ventilators, aeroplanes, diving apparatus, rifles and machine guns, slicing machines, harvesting implements, scales, gas manufacture, piano frames, motor car designs and electric light bulbs" as examples of manufacturing. Photographs of "broadcasting stations, grain elevators, power plants, airports, garages, warehouses and factories" accompanied the machines. The exposition also featured engineering techniques such as "day lighting, ventilation, and transportation."[82] The exhibition borrowed a double-ended coffee mill from International Business Machines, a model of an electric farm from International Harvester, and machine guns from the United States Army.

In juxtaposition with the manufactured objects, Heap included painting and sculpture that suggested a Machine Age esthetic in their imagery, materials, or handling. Much of the visual art was drawn from artists who had shown in her gallery, including Demuth, Man Ray, Alexander Archipenko, Storrs, Gabo, Pevsner, van Doesburg, Zadkine, Lipchitz, and Arp. The painting and sculpture from Europe, which constituted most of the art, was probably still on hand because of Heap's

------

81    Herbert Lippman, "The Machine Age Exposition," *The Arts* 12, no. 6
        (June 1927): 324.

82    Ibid., 324

disorder in returning work; many of the sculptures were the subject of the controversy over return shipments outlined above.

Architecture was the most historically significant and innovative aspect of the "Machine Age Exposition." In line with Heap's goal, she juxtaposed photographs of raw sulfur storage plants in Germany, a church in Poland, and the new Bauhaus architecture. She also introduced a broad spectrum of modern architecture to New York. In some cases, as with Le Corbusier and the Bauhaus, this was almost the first American documentation of work that would soon become internationally renowned. Fritz Hoeger's Chile House in Hamburg is still used as an example of an early high rise in Europe, while the garden built from the model for a terraced garden by Gabriel Guevrekian now appears as an example of landscape architecture in the *Encyclopedia of World Art*.[83] From America, the exposition featured Hugh Ferriss's model for a glass skyscraper and a model of three stages of development in the Radiator Building by Raymond Hood. Other Americans included Arthur Loomis Harmon (architect of the Shelton Hotel), William Lescaze, and Eliel Saarinen.

Heap also included less-known European modern architects such as the Germans Hans and Wassili Luckhardt; the Poles Bohdan Lachert, Josef Szanajka, and Barbara and Stanislaw Brukalski; and the Belgians Louis van der Swaelmen, Jean Eggericx, and Victor Bourgeois. For these important architects of the 1920s, the 1927 exhibition of their work in New York can now be seen as a poignant event at the end of that hopeful and heroic era of early modernism. These artists were not numbered among the architects of the influential International Style as defined by the Museum of Modern Art in 1932, and they were unable to work later in the 1930s and 1940s because of the Nazis and World War II.

As the publicity poster emphasized, the mixture of architecture, technology, and fine art was collected under the impetus of the "inter-relation-inter-influence of architecture, engineering, industrial arts, and

---

83    The Chile House is reproduced in Vittorio Magnago Lampugnani, ed., *The Thames and Hudson Encyclopedia of 20th Century Architecture* (London: Thames and Hudson, 1983), 94; a photograph of the completed garden by Guevrekian appears in the *Encyclopedia of World Art* (New York and London: McGraw Hill, 1958), 7: plate 450.

modern art." The effort to include such diverse expressions made the exhibition unique. Moreover, the timing was sensational: the "Machine Age Exposition" appeared in New York as transatlantic airplane flights were constantly in the news. Halfway through the exhibition, on 22 May 1927, Charles Lindbergh successfully completed his flight over the Atlantic Ocean, an event seen as the ultimate wedding of humanity and technology, and an appropriate accompaniment to the goals of the exhibition.[84]

In the press release, Heap explained her attitude toward the show: "The modern architect is giving a new aspect to the world. ... The automotive, mechanical, electrical, chemical, and civil engineers have replaced the Seven Wonders of the World with their Wonders. In the machine we have a new plastic-mystery which is influencing and energizing all the Arts."[85] The reference to mystery suggested the larger philosophical underpinning for the exhibition. Heap celebrated a positive development in the evolution of the human mind, which had in the past been aided in its development by contact with art. By bringing together the engineer and the artist, she encouraged the artist to "transform the realities of our age into a dynamic beauty." She believed that the exhibition demonstrated the wedding of beauty and utility, achieving what she termed, in a catalogue essay phrase borrowed from the Italian Futurist Prampolini, a "plastic-mechanical analogy."[86]

The catalogue for the "Machine Age Exposition" brought together various aspects of mid-1920s theory and provided something of a retrospective of Heap's concerns between 1925 and 1927. It demonstrated her support for current thinking on the machine and modern architecture and her unique understanding of the art theory as it combined with her mysticism. First, and forming an important record, are the

---

84     "Lindbergh Does It! To Paris in 33 1/2 hours. Flies Miles Through Snow and Sleet; Cheering French Carry Him off Field. ... Ate Only One and a Half of His Five Sandwiches," *New York Times,* 22 May 1927, 1. Such a headline underlines the interaction of the human and the technical. Almost the entire first section of the paper was devoted to Lindbergh, who actually was only one of many fliers engaged in the transatlantic flying endeavors of that time. His solo success stole the headlines, however.

85     Regrettably, the New York papers virtually entirely ignored the exhibition, perhaps because of their preoccupation with Lindbergh.

86     jh, "Machine Age Exposition," *Machine Age Exposition,* 36.

catalogue essays that defined modern architectural thinking before the formularization of modernism. Andre Lurçat, a leader of a group characterized as "young French architects" that included Le Corbusier and Mallet-Stevens, spoke of the importance of "unity of appearance and simplicity of expression" in buildings that also "avoid the dangers of the machine-attitude." Syrkus from Poland spoke of the destruction of volume and "new technical possibilities and new experiences."[87] Significantly, the first essay in the catalogue, "Architecture of this Age" by Ferriss, an American Gurdjieffian, spoke of leaving "the pleasant security of forms ... matured by others," because "another stream is already beginning to flow."[88] The idea of the watershed experience of spiritual renewal is just below the surface in Ferriss's metaphors.

Heap republished Prampolini's "The Aesthetic of the Machine and Mechanical Introspection in Art," which had already appeared in *The Little Review*:

> Is not the machine today the most exuberant of the mystery of human creation? Is it not the new mythical deity which weaves the legends and histories of the contemporary drama? ... We today ... see now the outlines of the new aesthetic of the Machine appearing on the horizon like a fly wheel all fiery from Eternal Motion.[89]

For futurists such as Prampolini, the esthetic of the machine had the religious dimensions of a new deity. Of all the European artists who celebrated the machine, the Futurists came closest to Heap's own perspective by incorporating a mystical dimension in their writings.

---

87      Andre Lurcat, "French Architecture," *Machine Age Exposition* (New York: The Little Review, 1927), 22-23; S(zymon) Syrkus, "Architecture Opens Up Volume." 30.

88      Hugh Ferriss, " Architecture of This Age," Machine Age Exposition, (New York *The Little Review* 1927) 5-6.

89      Enrico Prampolini, "The Aesthetic of the Machine and Mechanical Introspection in Art," *Machine Age Exposition* (New York: The Little Review, 1927), 9-10. Henry Adams had long since been among the first to suggest a negative response to the idea of the machine as a new divinity. Henry Adams, "The Dynamo and the Virgin," *The Education of Henry Adams An Autobiography* (Chicago and New York: Houghton Mifflin, 1918) 379-390.

In addition to discussions of contemporary architecture and Futurism, Heap included Louis Lozowick's "The Americanization of Art," an essay that spoke of the trend toward order and standardization in industry that was affecting the "whole of mankind."[90] Significantly missing from the catalogue were essays by Léger and the Bauhaus artists, although illustrations of Bauhaus architecture appeared. Léger's essay of 1923, "The Esthetic of the Machine," which had provided a beginning point for Heap's celebration of the engineer, along with Moholy-Nagy's ideas on the mechanical production of painting, as he had sent them to her in 1925, would have been important additions to her summary of Machine Age ideas in 1927.

But Heap did not intend for her endeavor to be a systematic overview of Machine Age theory. For her, the issue was above all spiritual, inextricably linked to her understanding of the teachings of Gurdjieff. More than synthesizing the ideas of Constructivism, Futurism, de Stijl, *l'Esprit Nouveau* (as she knew it from Léger), and the Bauhaus artists, she placed all their art and theory in the context of a spiritual enlightenment. Heap believed, as she interpreted Gurdjieff, that "great cathedrals were built with a conscious purpose—to elevate for a moment the vibrations of people. This was a conscious attempt to leaven the masses."[91] The modern counterpart of the cathedral was the machine. The evolution of civilization depended, thus, on understanding the mathematical (mechanical) laws that constitute the underpinning for all of life. By studying the workings of these laws, individuals could discern that

> ideas are a pattern of thinking—a great machine. At the base of things there is not just a mystery. The nature of things lies together in harmony. The real world is the evolution of an idea. Man's obligation is to co-operate with the laws which

---

90    Louis Lozowick, "The Americanization of Art," *Machine Age Exposition* (New York: *The Little Review*, 1927), 18-19. Louis Lozowick, *Modern Russian Art* (New York: Société Anonyme, 1925) demonstrated that Lozowick had a more accurate grasp of Russian ideas than most writers. See also Louis Lozowick, "A Note on Modern Russian Art," *Broom* 4, 110. 3 (February 1934): 202.

91    Anderson, *Unknowable Gurdjieff* ,51. Anderson states that her formulations are based on Heap's teachings of Gurdjieff's principles.

operate the universe. The realization of the workings of certain laws is the kingdom of heaven.[92]

Thus, the machine was both a manifestation of the structure of the universe and the next step in its spiritual evolution. By understanding the workings of the machine, the artist could utilize that structure to create a meaningful art for the new spiritual age. In the catalogue for the "Machine Age Exposition," Heap's commitment to spiritual evolution appeared not only in her own essay but also particularly in those of other Gurdjieffians: Hugh Ferriss, the visionary architect cited previously, and Mark Turbyfill, a Chicago poet. Heap commented that the "extension of the human mind as evidenced in this invention of Machines, must be a mysterious and necessary part of our evolution."[93] Turbyfill spoke of the "Poetry of Forces." He celebrated the scientist as providing "symbols for our work." The work was to "turn perception in a direction where it no longer views the evolution of ages, but where it beholds the instantaneous manifestation of forces."[94]

The "Machine Age Exposition" apparently satisfied Heap's desire to bring together the artist and the engineer. In the summer of 1927, by returning to Fontainebleau, she shifted her focus from promotion of Machine Age art to her spiritual studies. The next and last issue of *The Little Review* appeared two years later, in May 1929. Its content was based on a questionnaire that reflected a Gurdjieffian orientation, although no one not engaged with mystical practices would have recognized that from the questions. [95] Responses to the questionnaire came from writers and artists who spanned the history of *The Little Review* from its earliest years in Chicago. Most of them were already of major stature by 1929. Their willingness to write personal statements for the magazine reflected the important place of *The Little Review* in their careers and personal affections. Gertrude Stein summed that up in her own way in a tribute to Heap:

---

92      Ibid., 23.

93      jh, "Machine Age Exposition," Machine Age Exposition, 36.

94      Hugh Ferriss, "Architecture of This Age," *Machine Age Exposition* (New York: *The Little Review*, 1927), 5-6; Mark Turbyfill, "The Poetry of Forces," 38.

95      Webb, *Harmonious Circle*, 351.

Jane was her name and Jane her station and Jane her nation and Jane her situation. Thank you for thinking of how do you do how do you like your two percent. Thank you for thinking how do you do thank you Jane thank you too thank you for thinking thank you for thank you.[96]

Heap's own statement of disillusionment, "Lost: A Renaissance," declared, undoubtedly based on her new spiritual perceptions of the unenlightened state of humanity: "I do not believe that the conditions of our life can produce men who can give us master-pieces. ... If there is confusion of life there will be confusion of art."[97]

In order to try to clarify some of the "confusion of life," Heap spent the rest of her life as one of Gurdjieff s leading disciples and teachers, mostly organizing study groups from among select women intellectuals of the Left Bank.[98]

Heap's activities in the mid-1920s had a significant legacy. One visitor to the "Machine Age Exposition" was Alfred H. Barr, then a young art history professor at Wellesley College. He also followed other activities of *The Little Review,* for he recommended that his students visit the Little Review Gallery as a place to find "always something interesting."[99] When Barr became the first director of the Museum of Modern Art only two years later, the imprint of the exhibitions of *The Little Review* appeared in several of his projects for the museum. During the first five years of the Museum of Modern Art, it showed modern architecture in 1932,[100] a display of theater art in 1934, and a "Machine Art" exhibition the same year. In the catalogue for the latter, Barr made a specific reference to Heap's 1927 exhibition with a description that suggested he was impressed by it, although he saw it as an example of "the romantic attitude toward the machine."[101]

96    Gertrude Stein, "J. H. Jane Heap Fairly Well/An Appreciation of Jane," *The Little Review* 12, no. 2 (May 1929):10.

97    jh, "Lost: A Renaissance," 5.

98    Webb, *Harmonious Circle,* 431, 476.

99    Rona Roob, " Alfred H. Barr, Jr.: A Chronicle of the Years 1902-1929," *New Criterion,* special issue (Summer 1987): 13.

100   Henry-Russell Hitchcock and Philip Johnson, *The International Style* (New York: Museum of Modern Art, 1932).

101   A[lfred]. H[amilton]. Bfart-l., Jr., " Foreword," *Machine Art* (New York: Museum of Modern Art, 1934), unpaginated.

However, the Museum of Modern Art pared down Heap's visionary, wide-ranging effort. It promoted instead an austere, modern form that derived primarily from the Bauhaus. This formalist, puritanical, and ascetic canon stripped modernism of all references to social, religious, or political ideals. The Museum of Modern Art's "Machine Art" exhibition, for example, presented only pristine objects that avoided any sense of complexity or multiplicity of styles. As one scholar has described them, they were "clean machines."[102]

Heap presented a more accurate vision of a society transformed by the machine and the mechanized. In the mid-1920s *The Little Review* as well as its gallery expositions reminded New York that "it was twenty years behind the times instead of twenty years ahead."[103] These important shows accompanied by the documentation in *The Little Review* form the only record of Heap's significant contribution to dissemination of information on the European avant-garde of the 1920s in America.

Never again did Heap make public statements, wide-ranging contacts with the European avant-garde, or daring plans for international exhibitions. The only record of the last thirty-seven years of her life is Margaret Anderson's book on Gurdjieff based on Heap's teachings. Heap's heroic effort of the 1920s had been motivated by a spiritual mission, which would ultimately become the end, rather than the means; but for a few short years it inspired her to provide New York with an extraordinary exposure to the most recent ideas and art of the Machine Age. Her spiritual mission, arising out of the trauma of the obscenity trial of *Ulysses*, provided a bridge for her personally and for New York in general from provincialism to a more sophisticated grasp of the avant-garde. It would be another decade before America would seize the cultural initiative, but without Heap's efforts, it might have been even longer.

Heap belonged to that generation of intellectuals of the late nineteenth and early twentieth centuries who sought to break art out of

---

102    Sydney Lawrence, "Clean Machines at the Modern," *Art in America*, 72, no. 2 (February 1984): 127-68. An even greater contrast to Heap's exhibition was seen in a recent exhibition that presented the Machine Age with an Art Deco interpretation. Richard Wilson, *et al.*, *The Machine Age in America 1918-1941* (New York: Abrams, 1986).

103    McBride, "... Art of Two Constructionists," 9.

its esthetic isolation. Groups such as the Futurists and Constructivists sought to bring art in touch with the world.[104] In that pursuit they created an art that was interdisciplinary, international, political, and even spiritual. That was the art Heap presented in the pages of *The Little Review* and in her exhibitions. Tragically, these avant-garde hopes were not enough to counter the Machine Age's destructive potential when it got the upper hand in the mid-1930s. Had the wedding that Heap sought of the engineer, the artist, and the mystic experience been more permanently realized, history might have taken a more enlightened path.

---

104    Peter Burger, *Theory of the Avant Garde* (Minneapolis: University of Minnesota Press, 1984).

# Modernism, Formalism, and Politics: "The Cubism and Abstract Art" Exhibition of 1936 at The Museum of Modern Art *(1988)*

THE "CUBISM AND ABSTRACT ART" EXHIBITION, held at The Museum of Modern Art in New York City during the spring of 1936 and subsequently in six other cities, marks a watershed in the historiography of early-twentieth-century modernism. Earlier, the critical analysis of modern art had been complex, individual and often contradictory. Interpretations in America by such writers as Katherine Dreier, Alfred Stieglitz, and Walter Pach, for example, depended on a combination of personal prejudices and sporadic interaction with European and American publications and artists. These early critics developed categories, styles, and motives anew for each publication.[1]

"Cubism and Abstract Art" together with the widespread dissemination of its influential catalogue, established Cubism as the central issue of early modernism, abstraction as the goal. It made Cubism and

---

1     See, for example: Katherine Dreier, *"An International Exhibition of Modern Art Assembled by the Societe, Anonyme,* exh. cat., Brooklyn, The Brooklyn Museum, 1926. This exhibition was the most comprehensive effort to show modern art up to that time, and included Eastern as well as Western European art. The book was organized around six categories invented by Dreier. For a complete study of this exhibition, see: Ruth Bohan, *The Societe Anonyme's Brooklyn Exhibition: Katherine Dreier and Modernism in America,* Ann Arbor, 1982, Walter Pach, *Masters of Modern Art,* New York, 1924, included chapters on "After Impressionism," "Cubism," and "Today."

what it characterized as its descendants into a completed history. At the same time, in a significant contradiction, it removed Cubism from its own historical, social, and political context. These ideas dominated understanding of the early-twentieth-century developments in modernism for decades. It affected later histories of early modern art written by European as well as American critics. The effectiveness of the exhibition and its catalogue from the perspective of our jaded, satiated late-twentieth-century art world is startling. Yet, when the contents of the exhibition, the basis for the interpretations it proposed, and its development within the context of the political events of the 1930s are subjected to scrutiny, the reasons for its impact emerge clearly.

As visitors entered the exhibition, they were immediately confronted with Picasso's *Dancer* (1907) juxtaposed to an African figure. In another room, Boccioni's bronze *Unique Forms of Continuity* in *Space* was paired with a plaster cast of the *Winged Victory of Samothrace*.[2] These juxtapositions of modern art and its purported sources were intended to educate viewers to the revolutionary development of modern art as well as to its historical roots in the familiar art of the classical era.

Alfred Barr, the curator of "Cubism and Abstract Art," presented an apparently absolutely systematic version of the development of Cubism. This grand scheme was epitomized in an evolutionary chart that traced the ancestry and descendants of Cubism. The chart was posted throughout the exhibition and used on the dust jacket of the catalogue. Divided into five-year periods, the chart presented a genealogy of modern artistic styles. At the top it demonstrated that Redon, Van Gogh, Gauguin, Cézanne, Seurat, and Rousseau generated Fauvism and Cubism, whose non-European and non art sources were set off in red boxes. About midway through the chart, Cubism was shown as the progenitor of Futurism, Purism, Orphism, Neoplasticism, Suprematism, and Constructivism, with Fauvism, less centrally, as the direct ancestor of Abstract Expressionism and Surrealism. Finally, these styles evolved into just two directions: "geometrical abstract art" and "nongeometrical abstract art."

---

2    Henry McBride, "Exhibition of Abstract Art at the Museum of Modern Art," reprinted in *The Flow of Art, Essays and Criticisms of Henry McBride*. ed. Daniel Catton Rich, New York, 1975, pp. 333-36; the review originally appeared in *The New York Sun*. March 7, 1936.

The thesis and structure of the chart was reflected in the order and sequence of the installation. Here for the first time Cubism was displayed as an historically completed style with demonstrable derivation from earlier sources and inevitable progeny in the later styles of abstraction. On the first floor, immediately after the entryway with the *Dancer* and the African figure, Barr grouped his designated precursors in a source room. Next came a step-by-step development of early Cubism, with Cubist works paired with appropriate works of African sculpture and Cézanne. Later Cubism was represented with works such as Picasso's *Table, Guitar and Bottle* (1919) along with Futurist examples, early Delaunay, and Léger's *Luncheon* (1921). This section culminated with Picasso's *Studio* (1927-28) and *The Painter and His Model*(1928) which were given entire walls to themselves.

Barr divided Cubism distinctly and unequivocally into two phases: "Analytic" and "Synthetic." These were terms that had appeared frequently in literature on Cubism almost since its inception, but with varying connotations.[3] Here, for the first time, those terms were used with capital letters to define clear-cut stylistic stages in the history of Cubism. Other sections of the exhibition included the Orphism of Delaunay, the development of Neoplasticism in the work of Mondrian, Suprematism (Malevich's *Red Square and Black Square* (1914-15) was hung upside down and reproduced that way in the catalogue), and the Constructivism of Tatlin and Popova, represented by photographic reproductions. Finally, "Abstract Expressionism," the term Barr used for the works of Kandinsky, appeared near the end of the exhibition, as did "Abstract Dadaism" and "Abstract Surrealism."

In addition to the traditional mediums of painting and sculpture, the exhibition featured abstract film, photography, and the application of

---

3     Lynn Gamwell, *Cubist Criticism*, Ann Arbor, 1980, pp. 33-35, 95-100, carefully outlines the various usages of these terms in the early literature. By the mid 1930s they were widely known. See, for example: Maud Dale, *Picasso*, New York, 1930, p.1, in which Picasso's work is divided into analytic and synthetic phases; and James Johnson Sweeney, *Plastic Redirections in Twentieth-Century Art*, Chicago, 1934, p. 28, where the terms are used as adjectives and with lower-case letters to apply to Cubism in its development. Sweeney, in 1935, arranged an exhibition at the Museum of Modern Art. Thus, he was part of the circle in which Barr worked and his book would have been easily accessible to Barr.

the modern vocabulary to architecture, chair design, and small household objects such as plates and cups. In all, nearly 400 objects were exhibited. Barr enhanced the dignity of the work by his spare installation. Such touches as the exhibition of Malevich's *White on White* between two windows on which the white window shades had been lowered exactly halfway made a point about the painting and underscored its inherent elegance.

In the exhibition catalogue, Barr systematically laid out a history of Cubism. The emphasis throughout the essay, as in the chart, was on the development of the styles of modern art, rather than on details of the individual artists' careers. Barr repeated the juxtapositions of the installation in the catalogue, filling in works that did not appear in the exhibition, such as the *Demoiselles d'Avignon*, for which the *Dancer* was probably the stand-in. Each style was given a chronology, a summary, and pictorial documentation. The book concluded with a list of the works, carefully catalogued as to size and source, and a bibliography compiled by Beaumont Newhall, who also took the installation photographs.

The theoretical principles and models used to explain the development of modern art in "Cubism and Abstract Art" were in some ways the distillation of many years of thought for Barr. In other ways, the essay was a significant departure from his earlier writings, a departure generated by the political pressures of the mid 1930s. Examination of his earlier essays reveals the moment at which politics began to affect Barr's concerns as an art historian.

As Director of The Museum of Modern Art from its founding in 1929, Barr formulated preliminary versions of Cubism and Abstract Art in the early 1930s. Even before he became Director, he had frequently combined teaching with modern-art exhibitions. But in the mid thirties a sudden and brilliant amalgamation of his earlier experiences as curator and teacher found expression in the startling clarity of the 1936 exhibition. Seeking to educate the public in the art of their own century, he used the established methodologies of traditional art history to validate it.

Barr received a Bachelor of Arts degree from Princeton in 1922 and a Masters degree in 1923. His attitude to an instructional survey of modernism was the product of his training in the methodologies of art history as they were practiced in the early 1920s, when the focus was formalist. The historians who influenced Barr's approach to the 1936 exhibition—Charles Rufus Morey and Frank Jewett Mather[4]—were among the founders of the disciplines of art history and connoisseurship in America.

Morey, in particular, influenced Barr throughout his career. Two aspects of Morey's approach had particular importance for Barr. First, he impressed on Barr the idea that all the expressions of art had validity no matter what medium was used, a perspective that was at variance with traditional notions of the superiority of painting and sculpture. Morey's courses included the so-called minor arts as well as painting, sculpture, and architecture. Barr's catalogues would later include film design as well as painting and sculpture. Second, Morey, who was a classical archaeologist before he turned to medieval art, held the classical tradition in high esteem. Yet, influenced by Alois Riegl, the theorist of late Roman art, Morey also subscribed to the principle of a biological model for the history of art—growth, flowering, and decay.[5] Morey characterized art as an abstract flow of form, which existed independently of the individual artists. He strongly influenced Barr to conceive of art history as a detached event with its own internal development rather than as a phenomenon subject to social, political, and personal pressures.

In Frank Jewett Mather Barr encountered a professor of art history engaged with contemporary criticism, as well as with earlier art. Mather's background was in literature rather than art history. His historical studies echoed the chatty, informal approach to art criticism as it was often practiced in the teens. Yet his less scholarly approach was as instrumental to Barr's development as was Morey's more analytical approach, although Mather was less obviously an intellectual role model.[6]

---

4   For an account of Barr's early experiences with these professors, see: Rona Roth, "Alfred H. Barr, Jr., A Chronicle of the Years 1902-1929," *The New Criterion*, special issue (Summer 1987), pp. 2-4.

5   Charles Rufus Morey, *Medieval Art*, New York, 1942, p. 21.

6   Barr's lifelong devotion to both Morey and Mather was reflected in the dedication of his monograph on Matisse to them as well as to Paul Sachs (Alfred H. Barr, *Henri Matisse*, New York, 1951).

Barr began doctoral study at Harvard University in 1924. Among the professors who most influenced his later work was Paul J. Sachs. Connoisseurship, the direct examination and evaluation of the work of art without regard for its authorship, was the particular emphasis of Sachs's courses. Sach's close friend and even mentor was Bernard Berenson,[7] whose role as the formulator of the methodology of connoisseurship is crucial to an understanding of Barr's later writing.

In an early work, *The Study and Criticism of Italian Art* (1901), Berenson explained his methodology:

> The history of art should be studied much more abstractly than it has ever been studied and freed as much as possible from entangling irrelevancies of personal anecdote and parasitic growths of petty documentation. ... [T]he world's art can be, nay should be, studied as independently of all documents as is the world's fauna or the world's flora. The effort to classify the one should proceed along the line of the others. ... Such a classification would yield material not only ample enough for the universal history of art, but precise enough, if qualitative analysis also be applied, for the perfect determination of purely artistic personalities.[8]

Berenson built on the scientific approach of the pioneer of connoisseurship, Giovanni Morelli, but added to that writer's quantitative approach "the element of quality."[9] It was in this scientific, rational, yet subjective determination of quality that Sachs trained his students at Harvard. In a seminar presentation for Sachs's course on the history of engraving and drawing, in the spring of 1925, Barr attempted for the first time, as far as is known, to adapt the methodology of connoisseurship to modern art:

---

7     Paul Sachs, unpublished autobiography, "Tales of an Epoch," Archives of the Fogg Art Museum, Harvard University, Cambridge, Mass., p. 276. See also: Ernest Samuels, Bernard Berenson: The Making of a Connoisseur, Cambridge, Mass., 1979, p. 171; and *The Berenson Archive: An Inventory of Correspondence*, Nicky Mariano, compiler, Cambridge, Mass., 1965, p. 86

8     Bernard Berenson, *The Study and Criticism of Italian Art*, reprint ed., London, 1903, pp. vi, vii.

9     Ibid., p. viii.

> If all artists painted or drew Madonnas as they once did, how conveniently we could compare them—but they don't. So I will show you a series of portraits. ... I will be emphasizing neither personalities nor chronologies, nor nationalities. I will merely propose a series of comparisons from which you must draw your own conclusions.[10]

Barr then presented an overview of modern engraving and drawing by connecting the works on the basis of such style elements as line. He thus created an anonymous stylistic history of modernism based on qualitative differences he perceived in the works themselves.

At the same time, Barr created, in an exhibition that accompanied the lecture, sequences and juxtapositions of images to suggest stylistic developments; lengthy wall labels explained how the works related to earlier, contemporaneous, and later works. They also provided a rudimentary explanation of Cubism and its background:

> [Picasso] began with Steinlen... played with negro sculpture; with Braque created Cubism; and deserted that for a return to nature and to Ingres. ... Cubism was the invention of Picasso and Braque but it was inspired by Cézanne who pointed out that natural forms if simplified to geometrical essentials become cubes and cylinders. This was the first stage of Cubism. Having reduced the form to cubes and cylinders and spheres, it is not a difficult step to juggle them somewhat to combine in one picture the front and back of the same figure, to substitute the concave for the convex and to do all of these things according to the aesthetic sensibility of the artist.[11]

Barr arranged the prints in the exhibition in what he called "an almost mathematical progression from Impressionism to Cubism." Analyzing individual Cubist works in the tradition of the connoisseur, he emphasized their formal elements, treating the line, plane, and shape of the works very much in the way he had been trained to analyze

---

10     The Museum of Modern Art Archives: Alfred Hamilton Barr, Jr., Papers, unlabeled lecture notes for seminar report (dated on internal evidence to Spring 1925.).

11     Ibid.

Renaissance painting. He indicated that Cubism had been abandoned for a return to Ingres, but an Ingres "simplified and continuous in contour, based ... on profound knowledge."[12]

Even in this rudimentary student exercise Barr revealed his dual allegiance to the current critical dialogue on Cubism and to the methodologies of connoisseurship and art-historical analysis. In that spring of 1925, as Barr was presenting his report and exhibition, the prevailing attitude in American criticism was that Cubism was finished. The development of the so-called neoclassical style by Picasso was seen as an indication that, as one critic put it, the "game is about up." The critics of art celebrated what they saw as a return to sanity and realism.[13]

On the other hand, some writing on recent modern art was available in New York by 1925: three surveys of modern art had appeared in 1924, as well as an English translation of Apollinaire's *Aesthetic Meditations*.[14] Thus Barr, as a young art historian focusing on the scholarly approach in which he had been trained, had literary sources on which to draw. And although he was aware that Cubism was considered already a completed event, unlike the more reactionary critics, he could appraise and analyze the tradition itself with his scholarly tools.

Following graduate school, Barr arranged an exhibition in conjunction with teaching a course in modern art at Wellesley in 1927. His first exhibition with a printed catalogue and extensive explanations, it bears a close relationship to his activities at The Museum of Modern Art in the early 1930s. The title of the exhibition, "Progressive

---

12    Ibid.

13    "Arch Cubists Recant?" *American Art News,* 19(June 12, 1920) p.1. For more information on American criticism of Cubism in the early 1920s, see: first article in this book.

14    Guillaume Apollinaire, "Aesthetic Meditations," *The Little Review,* 8 (Spring, 1922), pp. 7-19; "Aesthetic Meditations II," *The Little Review,* 9 (Autumn 1922), pp. 41-59; "Aesthetics Meditations II (continued)," *The Little Review,* 9 (Winter 1922), pp. 49-60. The three surveys are: Sheldon Cheney, *A Primer of Modern Art,* New York: 1924; Katherine Dreier, *Western Art and the New Era.* New York, 1923; Pach (cited n. 1). Earlier surveys include Arthur Jerome Eddy, *Cubists and Postimpressionism* Chicago, 1914; Willard, Huntington Wright, *Modern Painting: Its Tendency and Meaning,* New York, 1915; and Jan Gordon, *Modern French Painters,* New York, 1923. Of all these books, Wright's seems to have been the most direct source for some of Barr's comments.

Modern Painting from Daumier and Corot to Post Cubism," reflected the principle of situating Cubism in relation to earlier developments of the mid nineteenth century. This historical approach continued in later exhibitions; even the emphasis on Corot and Daumier as ancestors of modernism was again propounded in early individual exhibitions for each of these artists at The Museum of Modern Art—a lineage for modernism very different from today's proposal of Manet and Courbet as progenitors. Also to reappear later is the categorizing of groups and tendencies, and the filling in of blanks left by crucial works that do not appear in the exhibition by means of accompanying remarks.

Cubism, although only skimpily represented—by Juan Gris, Jean Metzinger, Fernand Léger, and Marie Laurencin—was acknowledged as a central event with Futurism and Expressionism in what Barr referred to as Period II. The wall label for Juan Gris treated the nature of Cubism by formal analysis of the painting. Although the work was a collage, the term "Synthetic Cubism" did not appear in the discussion. Most important in light of later developments, Cubism was viewed as a prewar movement that was followed by "Period III," which was compartmentalized into "The Neo-Realists," "the Neo-classicists," "The Constructivists," and "The Super-realists."[15]

In his modern art course, too, Barr allotted much more space to the range of approaches in modern art than to the role of Cubism. The course studied all the directions outlined in the sections of the exhibition as well as "industrial architecture ... appliances [and] graphic arts. ... primitive and barbaric art, the psychology of expressionism, the discipline in Cubism and constructivism and the importance of the machine."[16]

---

15    Wall labels, Archives (cited n. 10). Part I was Cézanne, Renoir, Degas, Van Gogh, Gauguin, Les Fauves, and Die Brucke. Barr corresponded with Katherine Dreier, Director of the Société Anonyme, an authority on modern-art exhibitions. He even tried to get part of Dreier's modern-art collection for display at Wellesley College, a project that fell through owing to cost and logistical problems. Alfred H. Barr, Jr, to Katherine Dreier, February 7, February 27, and March I, 1927, and Katherine Dreier to Alfred H. Barr, Jr., February 19, March 4, 1927, Archives of the Société Anonyme, Beinecke Rare Book and Manuscript Library, Yale University.

16    "Wellesley and Modernism," Boston Transcript, April 27, 1927, n.p. This article also mentions that color reproductions were used for study; color reproductions of art were becoming available for the first time in the late 1920s.

In 1927-28 Barr went to Europe, supported by a small grant from Paul Sachs, in order to research his dissertation. On that trip Barr met a number of contemporary artists through letters of introduction given to him by the German art dealer J.B. Neumann. Neumann, who had immigrated to New York in 1923, had been Barr's close friend and supporter from his earliest years of teaching. Through Neumann's letters, Barr met most of the major figures of German contemporary art, such as the Bauhaus group, the Neue Sachlichkeit, and the dealers and critics that supported them.[17] But he went beyond even Neumann's contacts by visiting Russia in the spring of 1927. There he met Diego Rivera as well as members of the Russian avant-garde. His introduction to the extremely politicized artists in Russia had a permanent effect on his awareness of the interaction of art and politics. Thus Barr became an amalgam of the detached connoisseur-theoretician and an engaged art critic aware of the impact of Marxism and politics in general on the arts. During that sojourn in Russia, he not only met with revolutionary artists, but also undertook a pioneering study of the anonymous Byzantine icons of Russia.[18]

After his return from Russia, Barr resumed teaching at Wellesley. In a five-part lecture series in the spring of 1929, Barr presented his more fully developed analysis of modern art. The comprehensive Part I included:

---

17      Neumann's friendship with Barr is recorded in the letters from Barr to Neumann preserved in the I. B. Neumann Papers, Archives of American Art, Washington D.C., and was central to Barr's early years. That relationship is reflected in his collaboration with Barr in the exhibition of German art at The Museum of Modern Art in 1931, for which he was curator and Barr the writer of the catalogue. A. H. B[arr]., Jr, *German Painting and Sculpture,* exh. cat., New York, The Museum of Modern Art, 1931.

18      See: "Russian Diary" (reprinted from October [Winter 19781), in *Defining Modern Art: Selected Writings of Alfred H. Barr, Jr.,* ed. Irving Sandler and Amy Newman, New York, 1986, pp. 103-37. Barr wrote several articles as a result of this Russian trip: "The Researches of Eisenstein," *Drawing and Design,* 4, pp.155-56; "The 'LEF and Soviet Art," *Transition* 13/14 (Fall 1928), pp. 267-70; "Sergei Michailovitch Eisenstein," *The Arts,* 14 (December 1928), pp. 316-21; "Notes on Russian Architecture," *The Arts,* 15 (February 1929), pp. 103, 144, 146; "Otto Dix," *The Arts,* 17 (January 1931), pp. 234-51. In addition to these articles on modern art, Barr wrote "Russian Icons," *The Arts,* 17 (February 1931), pp. 296-313, 355-62.

Modern Painting: The Ideal of a "Pure" Art. The important tendencies in painting of twenty years ago: the neo-renaissance in Derain; the decorative in Matisse; the cubistic in Picasso. The formalist attitude toward Medieval, Renaissance, and Baroque painting. The immediate antecedents of cubism: Dégas, Gauguin and the "angle shot"; Seurat and the theory of pure design; Cézanne's natural geometry; abstraction in primitive art. The development of cubism in Paris. Kandinsky and abstract expressionism in Germany. The final purification of painting: Mondrian in Holland; the suprematists in Russia. Andre Lhote and the new academic. The influence of abstract painting upon architecture, the theatre, the films, photography, decorative arts, typographical layout, commercial art. Conclusion: the "demon of the absolute."[19]

Following this section were four more parts: "The Disintegration Since Cubism"; "Modern American Painting"; "The Bauhaus"; "The Lyef Group in Moscow." Cubism was thus buried in the early stages of the lecture series, followed by many subsequent developments. Part I would become the prototype for the "Cubism and Abstract Art." exhibition.

Lillie P. Bliss, Abby Aldrich Rockefeller, and Mary Sullivan founded The Museum of Modern Art in the spring of 1929; Paul Sachs recommended Alfred Barr as its first Director. Between 1929 and 1936, Barr arranged more than twenty exhibitions. Several had specific references to Cubism, and some can be seen as preliminary versions of the 1936 exhibition.

The first exhibition to outline the history of early-twentieth-century art was the 1930 "Painting in Paris from American Collections." As in the Wellesley exhibition of 1927, the disparities between what Barr perceived as the central issues and artists and the actual artists who were available in American collections were compensated for in the introductory essay. As both connoisseur and historian he suggested that even as he created order in modern art with the exhibition, the final

---

19     Archives (cited n. 10). The lecture series is reprinted in Sandler and Newman (cited n. 18), pp. 67, 68.

document was the work of art itself. At the same time he demonstrated his greater awareness of recent art in his introductory statement:

> Ten years ago it might have been possible to generalize about modern art. In fact, even at present there are some who are courageous—or blind—enough to declare that modern art has one dominant characteristic such as the belief in pure self-expression, or an exclusive interest in form, or a contempt for natural appearances but the truth is that ... contemporary art ... is merely so extraordinarily complex that it defies generalization. ... Any attempt to classify modern artists must lead to treacherous simplification. But it may not be too misleading to suggest a chronology and some description of terms, trusting that the paintings themselves will contradict inevitable error.[20]

His systemization included Fauves, Cubists, and Surrealists. Cubism was traced from its beginnings in mere simplification through ten years when it

> passed through three or four distinct phases each more complicated in appearance and in explanation. But by 1917 a distinct clarification occurs. ... The influence of cubism has been immense, but its nearly complete elimination of naturalistic imitation has brought about equally extreme reactions. ... It is noteworthy that almost without exception the original members of both the fauve and cubist groups have in their recent work given far more recognition to the values of objective representation.[21]

---

20    Alfred H. Barr Jr., "Foreword," *Painting in Paris from American Collections*, exh. cat., New York, The Museum of Modern Art, 1930, p. 11. See also Eunice Lipton, *Picasso Criticism, 1901-1939 The Making of an Artist Hero*, New York, 1975, pp. 335-36.

21    Barr (cited n. 20), pp. 13, 14. The idea of several stages for the development of Cubism was common in the early literature on the style. See, for example: Gordon (cited n. 14), p. 137, which outlines eight stages.

Barr's attitude towards contemporary art and his thoughts about the direction in which it was moving were most clearly stated in his next words: "[The] puritanical exclusion of all sentimental and 'human' values by the cubists of 1908 ... has induced in the last generation a reaction which has produced painting of extraordinary originality ... surrealism."[22] In 1930, thus, Barr held the opinion that Surrealism was the most interesting dimension of contemporary art. He devoted more than a page to its concerns and artists.

In the spring of 1932 Barr organized "A Brief Survey of Modern Painting", which was divided into several parts that echoed the subdivisions of the 1927 Wellesley exhibition, but expanded them. The historical part included: "Painting Fifty Years Ago: French and American" and "Cézanne and the Post Impressionists." Twentieth-century painting was divided into subcategories: Section III, which included "Expressionism," "Psychological and Decorative," "The 'Wild Animals,'" "The 'School of Paris'"; and Section IV, which included "Picasso and Cubism, Futurism, Abstract Design, Super-realism." Cubism was still presented here as a gradual "removal from realism ... until there were few traces of any recognizable objects in their pictures. [T]heir chief interest is in the design, in aesthetic qualities of line, color, texture."[23]

The catalogue in a significant contrast to the earlier statements also claimed that

> the principles of Cubism and Abstract Design [Kandinsky, Mondrian, and Rodchenko] spread all over the world and influenced many of the artists in this exhibition, for example, the Germans, Marc and Klee, the Americans, Marin, Demuth and Dickinson, the Italians, Chirico and Severini.

---

22     Ibid., p. 14. The same essay appeared in a catalogue for an exhibition shown in Detroit in the spring of 1931: A. H. B., Jr., "Introduction," *Exhibition of Modern French Painting*, exh. cat., Detroit, The Detroit Institute of Arts, 1931. The exhibition apparently included the same group of works.

23     A[lfred] H. Barr, Jr., *A Brief Survey of Modern Painting*, exh. cat., New York, The Museum of Modern Art [1932], n.p. This exhibition consisted of color reproductions rather than original works, thereby allowing Barr more flexibility in the selection of works

Cubism and Abstract Design have also had an immense influence upon 'modernistic' furniture, textiles, architecture, painting and advertising.[24]

Even more significant was Barr's statement that the Surrealists or, as he called them, the "Super-realists," "came as a violent reaction to the Cubists' exclusive interest in the problem of aesthetic design and color. The Super-realists asserted the value of the astonishing, the fantastic, the mysterious, the uncanny, the paradoxical, the incredible."[25] Barr concluded the exhibition with recent painting in which many different directions were developing at the same time but in which a "gradual, but widespread return to the realistic representation of nature has been in progress since the War."[26] Barr's statement expanded on the earlier essays: it gave "Cubism and Abstract Design" more emphasis, but it gave equal coverage to "Super-realism" and a multifaceted realism.

In the summer of 1933, while Barr was on leave in Germany, the trustees of the Museum arranged an exhibition, "Modern European Art," which Barr summarized in the *Museum Bulletin* the following October.[27] A subtle shift had now occurred in Barr's discussion of the historical survey of modern art, perhaps as a reaction to Hitler's rise to power and the beginning of the oppression or the avant-garde in Germany. Barr now praised the "Abstract paintings" including the Cubists, Kandinsky, and Mondrian as "the most striking." He spoke of Klee and Chirico, also included in the show, as pioneers against "pure design," and as part of the "Romantic Reaction." Finally, he spoke of the "Super-realists ... who insist fanatically upon the exclusive validity of the imagination." Barr here introduced a negative judgment in the discussion of Surrealism.[28] This exhibition once again relied on American collections,

---

24    Ibid.

25    Ibid.

26    Ibid.

27    No documents survive on Barr's specific role in the choice of works for the exhibition, but given his detailed correspondence with Frank Goodyear on other aspects of the museum activities during his leave, he probably had some influence. See: Alfred H. Barr, Jr., to Frank Goodyear, March 23, 1934, Archives (cited n. 10).

28    Alfred Hamilton Barr Jr., "Summer Show," *The Bulletin of The Museum of Modern Art,* 1 (October 1933), p. 2.

but Barr promised future shows of " 'Cubism and Abstract Painting' illustrating prototypes and analogies, sources, development, decadence, influence and recent revival" and " 'Post War Romanticism' illustrating Dadaism, Superrealism and other movements concerned with the mysterious, fantastic or sentimental together with their ancestry and analogs."[29]

Thus by the fall of 1933 Barr was granting Cubism central importance in relation to a major group of artists. One year later the Museum celebrated its fifth anniversary with the exhibition "Modern Works of Art" (November 1934—January 1935). It was accompanied by a much longer essay by Barr, and included works of sculpture and examples of American, as well as European, art. All works exhibited, like those in previous exhibitions, came from private collections in New York. Barr now analyzed the development of Cubism much more thoroughly:

> Under the influence of Cézanne and primitive negro sculpture they [Braque and Picasso] had begun about 1907 to reduce landscapes or figures to block-like forms with surfaces of flat planes. Two years later they had broken up these block-like forms, shifting their planes about, mingling the planes of foreground objects with the background. ... Gradually in this process of disintegration and re-integration, cubist pictures grew more and more abstract, that is abstracted from ordinary resemblances to nature. ... As a natural consequence of the elimination of subject they began to vary the surface of the painting by pasting on bits of newspaper.[30]

This was the first instance in Barr's treatment of Cubism that focused on the use of pasted paper, what would in the "Cubism and Abstract Art" exhibition become the important phase of "Synthetic Cubism." Barr went on to comment that "Meanwhile outside of Paris, cubist tendency towards geometric form has been carried to an extreme by the suprematists. ... Abstract art flourishes in London. Davis and

---

29     Ibid., p. 4.

30     Alfred H. Barr, Jr., "Modern Works of Art," *Modern Works of Art,* exh cat., New York, The Museum of Modern Art, 1935, p. 15.

Gorki [sic] lead the cubists in New York. Bauer thrives in Berlin. Even futurism has won official recognition."[31] He spoke of "Post-War Painting" as having more "traditional" styles, "[which] to the extreme advance gardists ... seemed, as indeed they were, reactionary."[32] No longer does Barr embrace the idea that realistic currents were primary and Cubism finished; now he proposes that Cubism had led to abstraction, a vital tradition throughout the world. Barr still concluded, however, that there were many other tendencies in contemporary painting; they included Surrealism, Romanticism, and mural painting.

The essay for the *Modern Works of Art* catalogue was the last published prelude to the greatly expanded treatment of Cubism and abstract art in the 1936 exhibition, an exhibition that also included Dada and Surrealism as the descendants of Cubism. But there survives, in an undated and unsigned memorandum from the advisory committee to the trustees, one other interim draft proposal. In it Cubism was directly linked to industrial design: "The thesis might end at this climactic point or it might continue with an account of the various paths by which painters of abstractions emerged from their blind alley into other kinds of painting, dadaism, constructivism, counter-relief, purism, compressionism, architecture, photography, photomontage, typography, etc."[33] The argument was then made that the American public needed an exhibition of Cubist artists because commercial galleries rarely exhibited them. Although this memorandum did not issue from Barr himself, it did provide one interesting argument used to create the exhibition. One other archival document, an undated chart in Barr's handwriting, places Cubism at the top of a genealogical chart with three immediate descendants, Mondrian, Kandinsky, and Malevich. Several steps lead

---

31    Ibid.

32    Ibid., p. 16.

33    "Report to the Trustees from the Advisory Committee: An Exhibition 'Towards Abstraction.'" May 3, no year, prepared by Mrs. Russell. The proposed exhibition had five parts: Part I Tendency Toward Abstract Design in Painting 1850-1900; Part II Tendencies Toward Abstract Painting 1900-1910; Part III The Emergence of Abstract Design 1910-1914; Part IV The Cul de Sac of Pure Geometry 1914-1920; Archives (cited n. 10).

to Cubism's final progeny: typography, stage arts, and architecture.[34] Thus Cubism was not one stage of modern art that was concluded, but the linchpin of all aspects of early-twentieth-century art.

The catalogue for *Cubism and Abstract Art* began with a general statement that differed in character from those of Barr's earlier essays. Barr identified the nature of early modern art as an obsession with "a particular problem"; that of abstraction. Barr compared this obsession to the desire of Renaissance artists to achieve realism and linear perspective:

> In the early twentieth century the dominant interest was almost exactly the opposite. ... The more adventurous and original artists had grown bored with painting facts. By a common and powerful impulse they were driven to abandon the imitation of natural appearances. ... Resemblance to natural objects, while it does not necessarily destroy these esthetic values, may easily adulterate their purity.[35]

Even as he laid out these important principles that were to become the canon of contemporary art for many years, Barr suggested some ambivalence towards them by admitting that giving up references to nature led to impoverishment by "an elimination of the connotations of subject matter, the sentimental, documentary, political, sexual, religious, the pleasures of easy recognition and the enjoyment of technical dexterity ... but the abstract artist prefers impoverishment to adulteration."[36]

---

34      Archives (cited n. 10). Other proposed titles for the exhibition also in the Archives were "Out of Cubism," and "Abstract Design in Modern Art." The chart was probably prepared in conjunction with his teaching at Wellesley and probably dates from 1929, just after Barr's return from Russia. The fact that it appears in the archives in the middle of all the documents on the "Cubism and Abstract Art" exhibition, and is catalogued with them, suggests that Barr referred to it at that time. It appears to correspond to the first part of the lecture series of 1929, which, as was discussed above, was followed by many more chapters in 1929.

35      Alfred H. Barr, Jr., "Introduction," *Cubism and Abstract Art*, exh. cat., New York, The Museum of Modern Art, 1936, p. 11.

36      Ibid., p. 13.

In the section on Analytic Cubism, Barr reiterated some of the ideas of the *Modern Works of Art* catalogue. The new section on Synthetic Cubism expanded on the earlier explanation:

> Their texture ... adds to [the] independent reality so they may be, considered not a breaking down or analysis, but a building up or synthesis ... [p]asting strips of paper ... was a logical culmination of the interest in simulating textures and a further and complete repudiation of the convention that a painter was honor-bound to achieve the reproduction of a texture by means of paint rather than by the short cut of applying the texture itself to his canvas.[37]

This detailed discussion of individual Cubist works established with a new clarity the terminology of Cubist discussion and the idea of abstraction as a goal of twentieth-century artists. Barr's bias towards the post-Cubist return to realism, so clearly spelled out in earlier stages of his writings on Cubism, altered in 1936 to emphasize specific analysis of Cubist work, and the establishment of its legacy, abstraction, as a dominating aspect of the contemporary scene. Moreover, the catalogue and the exhibition specifically excluded realism, even when it was a logical aspect of a style, as in Dadaism and Surrealism.

The exhibition itself, as a comprehensive collection of loans, was also of a different type from all but one of the previous displays at the museum: it drew on the work from the artists' studios, private European collectors, Paris art dealers, and other new sources, rather than exclusively from the New York collections that had been the centerpiece of most of the previous exhibitions.[38] Thus Barr's show was a campaign and a carefully ordered strategy to present what he called in a letter to Jerome Klein, a young art historian, "an exercise in contemporary art history with particular reference to style." Yet in the same letter,

37    Ibid., p. 78.

38    The other major exhibition prior to "Cubism and Abstract Art" with a large group of loans from European collections was the Van Gogh exhibition of the previous fall. That exhibition had been a major change for the Museum, with its record breaking crowds and admission charges. Organized during the same summer as "Cubism and Abstract Art," some of its background is recounted in Margaret Scolari Barr, "Our Campaigns," *The New Criterion*, special issue (Summer 1987), pp. 40-43.

astonishingly, he went on to say: "I was very much interested in Cubism and abstract art ten years ago, but my interest in it has declined steadily since 1927."[39]

But if Barr had lost interest in Cubism, if he considered it a completed stage, why was he now claiming for it and its heirs a continued vitality? One possible explanation lies in Barr's plan of a series of exhibitions that would consider other aspects of modernism.[40] But that series of exhibitions does not explain the radical change in the nature of his support for Cubism and abstract art. Perhaps he himself offered the clearest answer:

> This essay and exhibition might well be dedicated to those painters of squares and circles (and the architects influenced by them) who have suffered at the hands of philistines with political power.[41]

In 1936, as Barr was writing the catalogue the forces of Stalinism and Nazism were becoming increasingly virulent in their attacks on avant-garde writers and artists.[42] More specifically, though, as early as

---

39     Alfred H. Barr, Jr. to Jerome Klein, July 19, 1936, Archives (cited n. 10).

40     The idea for a series has been mentioned in a number of places. One such is in A[lfred] H. Barr, Jr., "Preface," Fantastic Art, Dada and Surrealism, exh cat., New York, The Museum of Modern Art, 1936 p. 7, which characterizes that exhibition as second in a series of which "Cubism and Abstract Art" was the first. Margaret Barr (cited n. 38), p. 44, stated that the series included *Masters of Popular Painting* (1938), *American Realists and Magic Realists* (1943), and *Romantic Painting in America* (1943). This corresponds with Barr's early 1930s treatments of the complexity of realism, although none of these exhibitions were curated by Barr, nor stated at the time to be part of a series. Furthermore, Dorothy C. Miller, "Foreword and Acknowledgment," *American Realists and Magic Realists*, exh. cat., New York, The Museum of Modern Art, 1943, p. 5, states that that exhibition is part of a different series that began with *18 Artists from 9 States*, in 1942, a contemporary survey.

41     Barr (cited n. 35), p. 18.

42     See: *The Muses Flee Hitler*, ed. Jarrell Jackman and Carla Borden, eds., Washington, D.C., 1983, esp. pp. 29-44. The literature on the impact of politics on art in the 1930s is extensive. For an illuminating group of essays see: *Theories of Modern Art*, ed. Herschel Chipp, Berkeley, 1971, pp. 456-500.

1927, and again during his year in Germany in 1932-33, Barr himself had witnessed first hand the danger that totalitarianism posed to the avant-garde artist.

Barr's trip to Russia in the spring of 1928 took place shortly after Joseph Stalin had expelled Leon Trotsky from the Communist party. This act publicly repudiated Trotsky's commitment to avant-garde art as a part of the Revolution and replaced it with the Stalinist dictum that art was a propaganda tool that had to use realistic images to celebrate his economic policies. Barr experienced one blatant example of the suppression of avant-garde visual art when he attempted to visit the Museum of Abstract Art in Moscow and found it closed. Guides referred to the modern art that it contained as examples of bourgeois decadence.[43]

Even more disturbing was Barr's experience in 1932-33, when he lived in Stuttgart, while on leave from the Museum. There he was confronted with the early days of the rise of Hitler and its immediate effect on the visual arts. Margaret Barr described these early events with frightening clarity in her recently published memoir. The article details the sudden enthusiasm for Hitler among the residents of the pension where the Barrs were staying, primarily as a result of the power of the radio. It further recounts the sudden disappearance of a Schlemmer exhibition, the addition of gables to modern flat roofs, and the derogatory labeling of modern art works in art museums.[44] Alfred Barr, angered with these events, wrote a series of articles entitled "Hitler and the Nine Muses" in order to call the American public's attention to the then little-known events in Germany with respect to the dangers to the avant-garde. Only one of these articles was accepted for publication.[45]

---

43    Dwight Macdonald, "Profiles: Action on West Fifty-Third Street—I," *The New Yorker* (December 12, 1953), p. 82; see also: Vladimir Kemenov, "Aspects of Two Cultures," reprinted in Chipp (cited n. 42), pp. 490-96.

44    M. Barr (cited n. 38) pp. 31-32.

45    The article that was published appeared as "Notes on the Film: Nationalism in German Films." *The Hound and Horn,* 7 (January/ March 1934), pp. 278-83. The journal was edited by Lincoln Kirstein, a friend of Barr's. Even this article was published on a back page. The other articles were simply refused by the five publications to which they were submitted; see: Sandler and Newman (cited n. 18), p, 102. No archival documents on this incident are currently available.

Thus, Barr, sooner and more clearly than many other Americans, recognized the threat to avant-garde art that totalitarian regimes posed. On his return to America, in late 1933, he observed also in the United States the widespread resurgence of realistic styles. In December 1933 the Federal Arts Projects began to support realism.[46] In the fall of 1933, just as realism was emerging throughout Europe and America, Barr began increasingly to emphasize Cubism and abstract art, and to down-play realism. He promised a comprehensive exhibition.[47]

With the intervention of the Fifth Anniversary Exhibition—"Modern Works of Art"—in 1934-35 and the first major Van Gogh exhibition in late 1935, it took almost two years to assemble the exhibition "Cubism and Abstract Art." Barr arranged most of the loans in the summer of 1935 during a trip to Europe, in which he met with European collectors, critics, and writers, and visited Henry Moore, Miro, Mondrian, Giacometti, Léger, Braque, and Picasso, among others. Most dramatic was the emotional reunion with Larionov and Gontcharova: they had emigrated from Russia since Barr last saw them in Moscow in 1927,[48] another indication of the spreading repression during the early years of the Stalinist regime. Perhaps fueled by his anger at the situation for avant-garde artists in Europe, Barr approached many artists more directly than he had for any earlier exhibition. He frequently circumvented the dealers, who had been a considerable obstacle in earlier efforts

---

46    For examination of the art of the Public Works of Art Project, the Painting and Sculpture Division of the Treasury Department, and the Works Progress Administration see Richard D. McKinzie, *The New Deal for Artists,* Princeton, 1973. He summarized the attitude of one director; "The kind of art he sought gave him 'the same feeling I get when 1 smell a fresh ear of corn,' " p. 57. See also: Francis V. O'Connor, *WPA, Art for the Millions: Essays from the 1930s by Artists and Administrators of the WPA Federal Art Project,* Boston, 1973, based on a report first conceived in 1936. Greta Berman, *The Lost Years: Mural Painting in New York City under the WPA Federal Art Project, 1935-1943,* (New York University, Institute of Fine Arts, 1978), Garland. The type of art actually produced by the artists, although commissioned to present scenes of American life, varied widely stylistically, according to the training of the artists and the location of their work.

47    Barr (cited n. 28), p. 2.

48    M. Barr (cited n. 38), pp. 31-32.

to organize exhibitions of the established European modern artists, such as Picasso.[49]

"Cubism and Abstract Art" was finally assembled in the art season of 1935-36. Barr wrote the catalogue in only six weeks. He drew on his training in detached scholarship for his genealogical approach, anonymous treatment of style, and lucid connoisseurship of particular works. But he also drew on his concern for the threatened condition of the avant-garde. The combination of these circumstances gave the exhibition its breadth, universality, clarity, and permanence. More than just another exhibition of modern art, "Cubism and Abstract Art" was a vehicle for propaganda for a threatened cause.

Barr's sense of timing about the urgency of the situation was correct. Following its New York venue, the exhibition opened in San Francisco in the summer of 1936, just as the infamous display of Nazi power at the Berlin Olympics was taking place. In Moscow, on August 15, 1936, the Stalin trials began, trials that would last for two years and ultimately and systematically destroy all vestiges of the revolutionary generation in Russia, as well as its intellectual leaders. As the heroes of the Russian Revolution recanted their actions and declared themselves traitors to their country, American intellectuals, sympathizers with both the political and cultural programs of this revolutionary generation, were thrown in disarray. By 1936-37 both Hitler and Stalin had virtually completed the repression of avant-garde art and even the extermination of that art in favor of the more easily comprehensible Socialist Realist style. In the United States the massive Works Progress Administration spread American-scene realism across the country. The leftist *Art Front* called for an art that responded to conditions of life, while the regionalists demanded an art that reflected the American scene.

As documented by his articles written in Germany in 1932-33, Barr was acutely aware of economic, political, and artistic events and concerned about the preservation and protection of modern art and artists. One obvious instance of that concern in 1936 appeared in the publicity he gave to the holdup at customs of much of the abstract

---

49    Earlier in his career as Director, Barr had had much difficulty obtaining loans; see for example, documents relating to his effort to create a Picasso exhibition in 1930, when he was still a young director of a little-known museum, Archives (cited n. 10).

sculpture for "Cubism and Abstract Art." The *Museum Bulletin* prominently featured this event, and Barr also made a specific reference to it in the catalog.[50]

The full resources of the Museum of Modern Art promoted "Cubism and Abstract Art." The itinerary took the exhibition to San Francisco, Cincinnati, Minneapolis, Cleveland, Baltimore, Providence, and Grand Rapids. Paramount Pictures included it in the Movietone news. The sophistication of the Museum press apparatus by 1936 insured widespread coverage throughout the country. The critical response varied widely according to the predilections of the critics: the more-informed

---

50    T.D.M. "The Government Defines Art: The United States Government and Abstract Art," *The Bulletin of The Museum of Modern Art*, 3 (April 1936), pp. 2-6. The works held up at customs were by Jean Arp, Alberto Giacometti, Henri Laurens, Georges Vantongerloo, Raymond Duchamp-Villon, Julio Gonzales, Umberto Boccioni, Henry Moore, Ben Nicholson, and Joan Miro. See also: Barr (cited n. 35), p. 18. A record of some of these controversies is to be found in *Art Front*, the organ of the Artist's Union. See especially the issues of November 1934, January 1935, and April 1937. Barr's correspondence during these years contains occasional references to his concern for the economic situation resulting from the Depression, as well as the political situation of the mid thirties in the art world. He praised *Art Front* and ordered eight copies for the Museum of Modern Art Library, Alfred H. Barr Jr., to *Art Front*, February 19, 1935, Archives (cited n. 10). He was invited to attend meetings but apparently did not do so, Artists Coordination Committee to Alfred Barr, January 1, 1937, Archives, (cited n. 10). He refused to sign petitions even when in sympathy with the cause, because of his position at the Museum, Alfred Barr to Milton Horn, March 5, 1937. His correspondence contains only brief references to the economic exigencies resulting from the Depression, mainly in his efforts to obtain positions for close friends in art history. Barr, as conveyed in available archival letters from the 1930s, is removed from the day-to-day battles of the thirties, Archives (cited n. 10).

critics supported the show, the less-informed ridiculed it, just as they had ridiculed modern art exhibitions since the Armory show.[51]

More significant than the journalistic criticism, with respect to later developments, was its effect on artists and historians. Laying out a history of modernism was a significant educational resource for artists at all stages in their development. Such a mature artist as Hans Hofmann, for example, made many visits to the exhibition.[52] That the impact on his thinking was significant is documented by a comparative study of his lectures from the early 1930s and the late 1930s. Hofmann's heavy emphasis on Cubism and abstraction subsequently shaped Clement Greenberg's understanding of modernism and that critic's promotion of certain formalist issues. [53]

The astonishing omission from the exhibition of all twentieth-century American art with the exception of Alexander Calder and Man Ray had major consequences. Barr justified this omission by pointing out that the Whitney Museum had just exhibited American abstract art in 1935.[54] The reasons are, in fact, far more complex. Barr's believed

---


51    See, for example: Edward Alden Jewell, "Academicism on the Left," *The New York Times,* (March 8, 1936), n.p.; James W. Lane, "Current Exhibitions," *Parnassus,* 8 (1936), pp. 26-28; Balcomb Green, "Abstract Art at the Modern Museum," *Art Front,* 3 (April 1936), pp. 5-7; "Modern Museum Opens Show Despite Ignorance of U.S. Martinets," *The Art Digest,* March 15, 1936, p. 10. An example of conservative criticism is that of Royal Cortissoz in the *Herald Tribune*: "A Useful Book upon a Not at All Useful Phase of Painting," *Herald Tribune* (April 26, 1936), and "Why call the Results Art?" *Dayton Ohio Journal,* n.d. Frank Goodyear Scrapbooks, The Museum of Modern Art.

52    Lawrence Campbell in conversation with Susan Platt, Art Students' League, February 1987.

53    For Greenberg's well-known reference to the importance of Hofmann in his early development, see: Clement Greenberg, "Avant-Garde and Kitsch," *Art and Culture,* Boston, 1961, p. 7.

54    Barr (cited n. 35), p. 9. The exhibition at the Whitney was itself controversial for the compromised definition it gave to the term "Abstract." In fact, most of the artists were part of the Whitney Museum tradition of a type of compromise style between realism and abstraction. Whitney Museum of American Art, *Abstract Painting in America,* exh. cat., New York, Whitney Museum of American Art, 1935.

that the geometric abstract style of the American abstract artists was a played-out direction. He believed that non-geometric abstract art was a more significant development in the mid 1930s. Also influencing Barr's decision to omit American art was certainly the Museum's peculiar history with respect to the exhibition of contemporary American art, a history marked by much confusion and many confrontations.[55] The heated political situation in the American art world of the mid 1930s would have also deterred Barr from displaying American art, given his powerful plan to create a definitive statement that rose above politics.

Omitted American artists working abstractly, such as George L.K. Morris, who had even been involved in the creation of the exhibition as part of the Museum's advisory board, immediately began to show in other New York galleries. Albert E. Gallatin, Director of the Gallery of Living Art, organized an exhibition of five American abstract artists whom he called "concretionists," which appeared concurrently with "Cubism and Abstract Art."[56] Other exhibitions of abstract art held in April 1936 in New York featured the work of Hilaire Hiler, Carl Holty, and Joseph Albers, the last newly arrived from Germany.[57] In the fall of 1936 the American Abstract Artists group formed and began plans for a regular program of exhibitions.[58]

---

55    In 1951 The Museum of Modern Art finally filled part of this gap with Andrew Carnduff Ritchie, *Abstract Painting and Sculpture in America,* exh. cat., New York, The Museum of Modern Art, 1951.

56    The "concretionist" exhibition included Charles Shaw, Alexander Calder, George Morris, Charles Biederman, and John Ferren. Melinda Lorenz, *George Morris, Artist and Critic,* Ann Arbor, 1982, makes brief reference to Gallatin's exhibition as a "counter exhibition," p. 42. She also discusses some of the early stages of the American Abstract Artists Group, pp. 49-52. The role of Morris as an intermediary between the Museum and the American Abstract Artists Group is also briefly touched on by Lorenz, pp. 37-42. In the early 1930s Gallatin was an important competitor of Barr's and a much better known collector-artist; they were rivals but respected each other, Alfred Barr to A. E. Gallatin [1937], A. E. Gallatin Scrapbooks, Philadelphia Museum of Art, Philadelphia.

57    Lane (cited n. 51), p. 28.

58    The most complete source on the American Abstract Artists Group is Susan Larsen, "The American Abstract Artists Group: A History and Evaluation of Its Impact upon American Art," PhD diss., Northwestern University, 1975. Another response among American artists may be the writing and publication of John Graham's *Systems and Dialectics in Art,* New York, 1937.

The exhibition catalogue generated its own series of results. Barr mailed a copy to all the artists included in the exhibition, as well as to dealers, collectors, and libraries. Preserved in the Barr archives are various responses to the catalogue by contemporary artists and dealers. These letters range from precise corrections of dates and chronologies to sweeping analyses of Barr's methodology. Most comprehensive were Kandinsky's letters, and appropriately so, since he was misrepresented in the exhibition as simply a descendent of Gauguin and Cubism.

Kandinsky began by complimenting Barr on the "purely scientific" method of tracing the development of art but complained that he stressed outside influences at the expense of the more important inner influences.[59] He objected to being considered as part of a deterministic march to abstraction, since, in fact, he painted realistic and abstract paintings at the same time.[60] Kandinsky hit on crucial issues here. First, he questioned the validity of the idea of a common impulse towards abstraction. Second, he criticized the principle of an anonymous, purely formal, determination of art's development. By omitting any consideration of religious context, Barr radically misunderstood Kandinsky, as art historians now know.[61] Barr's idea of the outward, collective impulse towards abstraction was based on his understanding of the nature of style as he had studied it in his graduate work. Similarly his formalist bias resulted from the adaptation of his training in the connoisseurship of Renaissance art to the art of the twentieth century. These sources took him a long way from Kandinsky's reference points.

---

59    Wassily Kandinsky to Alfred H. Barr Jr., June 22, 1936, and July 16, 1936. Archives (cited n. 10). Quoted by permission. These and the other letters from Kandinsky are filled with poetically stated insights into the differences between his approach to art and Barr's interpretations.

60    Ibid., July 16, 1936.

61    There is some possibility that Philip Johnson influenced Barr in his underrating of Kandinsky. A critical letter (undated) from Johnson to Barr derides Kandinsky's sense of his own importance, Phillip Johnson to Alfred H Barr, Jr., Archives (cited n. 10). The literature on Kandinsky in the last decade has reinterpreted both his sources and his intentions; see: Rose-Carol Washton Long, "Expressionism, Abstraction, and the Search for Utopia in Germany," *The Spiritual in Art: Abstract Painting, 1890-1980*, exh. cat., Los Angeles, Los Angeles County Museum of Art, 1986. See also idem, *Kandinsky: The Development of an Abstract Style*, Oxford, 1980.

Moholy-Nagy corrected Barr's chronology of Constructivism, as well as the interpretation of his own sources, which, he emphatically stated, were more related to Cubism and Frank Lloyd Wright than to Constructivism. More pointedly though, Moholy-Nagy spoke, as did Kandinsky, to Barr's methodology, criticizing him for finding a single, central place for each style, when actually events occurred simultaneously throughout Europe. He therefore found fault with Barr's discussion of certain artists as eclectic.[62]

The letter of Daniel-Henry Kahnweiler, the dealer most intimately connected with the early events in Cubism, and author of his own book on its development, wrote to Barr respectfully, acknowledging Barr's book as the most serious study of modern art he had read, while adding that he himself saw "Cubism as a much more 'realistic' movement."[63] Other surviving letters, with corrections primarily to Barr's chronologies and terminologies, came from Hans Richter, Anton Pevsner, Auguste Herbin, Leonce Rosenberg, and Georges Vantongerloo.

One art historian, Meyer Schapiro, attacked the book for its reliance on an autonomous dynamic of style as the driving energy of art. Schapiro also sharply criticized the idea of the dialectic of realism and

---

62     Laszlo Moholy-Nagy to Alfred H. Barr Jr., May 23, 1939, Archives (cited n. 10). Although the letter is dated a few years later, the discussion is based on the *Cubism and Abstract Art* catalogue.

63     Daniel-Henry Kahnweiler to Alfred H. Barr, Jr., May 6, 1936, Archives (cited n. 10). See also: Gamwell (cited n. 3) pp. 86-88; Daniel-Henry Kahnweiler, *The Way of Cubism*, (New York, 1949) (English translation of *Der Weg Zum Kubismus*, Munich, 1920). Also interesting is the letter from Jay Leyda to Alfred H. Barr, Jr., May 23, 1936, Archives (cited n. 10) describing the excited response of Vladimir Tatlin to the exhibition catalogue.

abstraction as two purified absolutes separated from experience.[64] These letters and articles provide invaluable insights into the strengths and weaknesses of both the catalogue of the exhibition and Barr's methodology for the exhibition itself. They offer perspectives that in many cases have been only recently considered.

Barr, in response to these letters and others, wrote courteously and deferentially of his appreciation of their comments. He spoke of a proposed revision of the catalogue, something that never occurred.[65] The catalogue in all its reprintings up to the present time has continued to incorporate the original perspectives and errors of the 1936 edition.

Yet, despite criticism of the book and the exhibition, both had immense influence on later art history. The catalogue became a widely used source on the history of modernism for generations of students. Standard texts incorporated its interpretations of the significant artists and events as well as its impersonal approach to style that fit So easily with the methodologies of earlier periods of art history. The development of modern art, as it is widely taught, is still descended from the analysis of Barr, although later scholars have broadened and deepened those central outlines. For example, although the catalogue of a 1986 exhibition provided major new insights into the roles of symbolism and mysticism as central concerns of early-twentieth-century artists, the

---

64    Meyer Schapiro, "The Nature of Abstract Art," *Marxist Quarterly*, 1(January—March 1937), pp. 78-97, republished as "Cubism and Abstract Art," *Modern Art: Ninth and Twentieth Centuries*, New York, 1978, pp. 185-211. See also: idem, "The Social Bases of Art," *Artists against War and Fascism: Papers of the First American Artists' Congress*, ed. Matthew Baigell and Julia Williams, New Brunswick, NJ, 1986, pp. 103-13. Barr regarded Schapiro's perspective as also valid, Alfred Barr to Jerome Klein, July 19, 1936, Archives (cited n. 10). Schapiro and Barr respected each other. As their correspondence demonstrates Barr occasionally participated in a study group on the issues of modern art that Schapiro organized in the mid 1930s. See: Alfred H. Barr, Jr., to Meyer Schapiro, December 10, 1936, and Meyer Schapiro to Alfred H. Barr, Jr., December 17, 1936, Archives (cited n. 10). Schapiro has told me that the exhibition was of immense importance as the first time that all the modern movements were laid out for the New York art world, telephone conversation, Meyer Schapiro and Susan Platt, March 1987.

65    Alfred H. Barr to Moholy Nagy, May 26, 1939, Archives, (cited n. 10). See also: Alfred H. Barr, Jr., to Wassily Kandinsky, July 12, 1936.

exhibition's arbitrary title limiting those insights to the "abstract" owes its bias to the interpretations of "Cubism and Abstract Art."[66]

Although Barr established the traditions of Cubism and abstraction as timeless and universal, he himself viewed art as more than an autonomous stylistic event. In the midst of World War II, he wrote of Picasso's *Guernica*:

> Picasso employed these modern techniques not merely to express his mastery of form or some personal and private emotion but to proclaim through his art his horror and fury over the barbarous catastrophe which had destroyed his fellow countrymen in Guernica and which was soon to blast his fellow men in Warsaw, Rotterdam, London, Coventry, Chungking, Sebastopol, Pearl Harbor. … *Guernica* is a symbol, a visible symbol of the human spirit in its search, for truth, for freedom, for perfection.[67]

At that time, too, he expanded the options of art to include the plurality of styles obscured by the creation of the "Cubism and Abstract Art" exhibition and catalogue. Shortly after, Barr was asked to step down from the position of Director at The Museum of Modern Art for complex reasons.[68]

"Cubism and Abstract Art" immortalized one particular model for freedom in art. An accident of history caused the exhibition and the catalogue to fall on fertile ground, at a seminal moment in the political and artistic development of America. Ironically, the association of abstraction with freedom, progress, and purity was a concept taken up first by art critics, then adopted by politicians as an instrument

---

66    The chart from "Cubism and Abstract Art" is reproduced in the front of the catalogue (cited n. 61), p. 18.

67    Alfred H. Barr, Jr., *What is Modern Painting*, New York, The Museum of Modern Art, 1943, p. 41. Later editions of the book added a concluding section on postwar abstraction and more statements on the connection of abstraction and freedom; see: idem, *What is Modern Painting*, Boston, 1974, pp. 42-46; revised 1952, 1953, 1956.

68    Irving Sandler, "Introduction," in Sandler and Newman (cited n. 18), pp. 28-30. See also: Russell Lynes, *Good Old Modern*, New York, 1973, pp. 240-63

of propaganda in the Cold War of the 1950s.[69] Abstraction ultimately became a prison for contemporary artists and critics, from which they escaped only in the 1970s with the reestablishment of a plurality of styles.

Today, our perceptions are closer to Barr's of the late 1920s, in which Cubism was regarded as only one event. Historians no longer accept the model of a history of style and form that evolves neatly in an autonomous development. Barr's scientific order, based on nineteenth-century principles of evolution and the possibility of scientific objectivity, has broken down. The idea of confining a discussion of modern art to purely formal, linear, or even dialectical terms is now recognized as arbitrary, and limited. Furthermore, social, religious and political issues are no longer seen as extrinsic to Cubism and abstract art but as an integral part of them. Realism has regained validity; it has recovered from its association with Fascism and totalitarianism. References to the visual world are no longer considered simply as a monolithic regression from the progress of art.

In "Cubism and Abstract Art," and the book that accompanied it, Barr provided the first compelling model of formalist discussion and stylistic ordering for early-twentieth-century art. His contribution to the discourses of art history survives not only in his writings, but also, for many years, in the permanent display of the order and even many of the works from that exhibition in the Alfred H. Barr Galleries at The Museum of Modern Art.[70] Reproductions of many of the works have become the definitive examples for a particular phase of modern art in classrooms. We can do nothing less than honor the brilliant, analytical work and connoisseurship of Alfred Barr in creating such a durable model of the history of modernism and its major monuments, even as we alter, expand, and contradict it.

---

69    Serge Guilbaut, *How New York Stole the Idea of Modern Art*, trans, Arthur Goldhammer, Chicago, 1983. For articles on this subject, see: Max Kozloff, "American Painting during the Cold War," *Artforum*, 13 (May 1973), pp. 45-54; and Eva Cockcroft, "Abstract Expressionism: Weapon of the Cold War," *Artforum*, 12 (June 1974), pp. 39-41.

70    Since this article was written there have been numerous reinstallations of the permanent collection of the Museum of Modern Art, most recently in November 2019 but his core iconic works remain.

# Elizabeth McCausland: 1930s Essays on Georgia O'Keeffe, Kathe Kollwitz, Gertrude Stein, Martha Graham, and Berenice Abbott *(1998)*

*The critic is not supposed to be a partisan. He is not supposed to feel. To share the feelings of others, to suffer himself. His emotions are assumed to have been surgically removed, as perhaps his brains have been. I am glad I escaped the scalpel. I am glad I share the experience of my fellow human beings including that particularly intense and articulate expression called art.*

~Elizabeth McCausland, 1945[1]

ELIZABETH McCAUSLAND (1890-1965) WROTE emotionally charged articles on contemporary art during the 1930s that call for the modern artist to be immersed in society.[2] Coming to art from her own transgressive position as a lesbian feminist active in left-political causes. She intervened in both public affairs journalism and the domesticity of the art world to exhort all artists to belong to the world. She articulated a politically engaged avant-garde art that included both women and men. The separation of the public as political, activist, and male from the private as aesthetic, passive and female, with all artists positioned as the female Other (as June Wayne has pointed out),[3] is broken down

---

1    Elizabeth McCausland. 'A Critic Explains'. *American Contemporary Art*, 2:4 (1945), 3-4.

2    Previous articles on Elizabeth McCausland are Garnett McCoy, "Elizabeth McCausland, Critic and Idealist," *Journal of the Archives of American Art*, 6:2, (1966), 16-20; Susan Dodge Peters," Elizabeth McCausland on Photography" *Afterimage*, 1985,10-11 and *Eyewitness: The Rise of Modern Photography*, Horizon Press, 1982; See also: Susan Noyes Platt, *Art and Politics in the 1930s Modernism, Marxism, Americanism* (Midmarch Arts Press, 1999), chapter 5.

3    June Wayne in Judy Loeb. ed.. *Feminist Collage: Educating Women in the Visual Arts* (New York Columbia University Press, 1979), 129: "It appears to me that society unconsciously perceives the artist as a female."

by McCausland and replaced with an ongoing negotiation between those two positions. She further complicates her argument by polemics on gender politics and cloaked sexual games. In this essay I will look specifically at McCausland's reviews of women artists in terms of these shifting lenses of aesthetics, politics, sexuality and gender.

Elizabeth McCausland's criticism provides a stark contrast to the post-Second World War critical hegemony of modernist abstraction. The "American Action Painters," as characterised by Harold Rosenberg, were celebrated for being active only in terms of moving paint around a canvas.[4] In the modernist ideology, most famously perpetrated by Clement Greenberg, references to issues outside the artwork were seen as violating its 'purity'. Greenberg (and many others) returned the artist to the domestic sphere. The 'best' or most 'ambitious' modernist artist rejected politics and the world entirely.[5]

Under the sway of this ideology, the history of twentieth-century art has, until recently, been based on the paradigm of the isolated artist who rejected society. Such a perspective edited earlier art with an eye to locating a pedigree for post-Second World War abstract modernism. 'Ideological linkages constructed a narrative of a constant push towards abstraction.[6] All art that engaged politics, social concerns, and frequently even imagery at all, was excluded from this canon.

Many artists, critics and historians, particularly in the United States, still accept the simplistic idea that addressing political issues compromises art. One recent example of this position was seen in the critical response to the 1993 Whitney Biennial. Critics dismissed the first Biennial that had a significant representation of women and people of colour and, not coincidentally, politically engaged art. Arthur Danto, for example, declared that it was 'mawkish, frivolous, whining,

---

4

Harold Rosenberg. "The American Action Painter," *Art News*, 11:8 (1952), 22-23. 48-50.

5    Clement Greenberg, 'Modernist Painting', *Art and Literature*. 4 (1965). 193-201.

6    Cary Nelson, *Repression and Recovery: Modern American Poetry and the Politics of Cultural Memory*, (Madison, University of Wisconsin Press, 1989), 38; As far as I know the earliest formulation of this idea was by Alfred Barr, *Cubism and Abstract Art*, (New York, Museum of Modern Art, 1936.)

foolish, feckless, awful and thin.'[7] There was no analysis of the political issues presented or the legitimacy of the artists' relationship to those issues. This knee-jerk, canonical separation of art from politics basically forces artists to remain as part of the powerless 'Other,' while arbitrarily privileging some artists within that controlled place if they play the game 'successfully' (i.e. without any 'real' political concern). 'Apolitical' art is a political position that diminishes the power of art and artists.

Many revisionist historical studies, both feminist and Marxist, also suffer from this narrow historical template of an apolitical, formalist, modernist canon. *Modernism in Dispute*, for example, one effort at revisionism, is obsessed with the criticism of Clement Greenberg and the white male artists of abstract expressionism. It includes only brief token references to political art and art by women as the 'Other' to the dominant hegemony of abstraction.[8] The book purports to 'dispute' by means of the social and political contextualising of modernism, but it endlessly and repeatedly discusses the canonical Greenberg as the central reference point for everything else.

More oppositional writers wonder why modernism is even privileged at all. Houston Baker calls it 'an assumed supremacy of boorishly racist, indisputably sexist and unbelievably wealthy Anglo-Saxon males.'[9] Post-structuralist feminists see its definitions as 'constructions necessary to a highly political and successful cultural production of a highly privileged subject position. Modernist self-fashioning is accomplished ... over and against a feminized and devalued other, a space of not-self.'[10] A few literary historians look at that devalued space in political terms. They reject the dismissal of all communist writing as 'prescriptive'. In the women writers on the far left, for example, they

---

7     Arthur Danto, *Embodied Messages, Critical Essays and Aesthetic Meditations*, (New York, Strauss Giroux, 1994), 312-317.

8     Paul Wood, Francis Frascina, Jonathan Harris and Charles Harrison, *Modernism in Dispute, Art since the 1940s* (New Haven, Yale University Press, 1993).

9     Houston Baker, *Modernism and the Chicago Renaissance,* (Chicago, Chicago University Press, 1987,4. Rita Feiski, *The Gender of Modernity* (Cambridge, Harvard University Press, 1995),16.

10    Deborah Jacobs in Lisa Rado. ed. *Rereading Modernism, New Directions in Feminist Criticism,* (New York, Garland, 1994).

find not a useless wedding of art to communist orders, but an intersection of genre conventions, communism, sexuality and gender constructions that results in a rich and complicated literature.[11]

I argue here that Elizabeth McCausland can be grouped with these women. She intervened through writing to make a place for women artists within the politically engaged discourse of the 1930s. McCausland operated from a much marginalised place. Aside from the obvious factor of being a woman (that was not marginal in art writing) and working for a newspaper outside of New York, the genre of newspaper art criticism itself is regarded by front-page editors as much closer to society gossip than to hard news.

In function, journalistic art criticism is normally affirmative. enhancing the commodity value of the art on the market, and seen as irrelevant to more serious criticism published in art magazines and journals. Nonetheless, McCausland succeeded in redefining art criticism and becoming a widely respected presence.

Her art 'column' became an art 'page'. At the same time she was personal, subjective and obviously polemical, never even pretending to practice the 'objectivity' of traditional art criticism. And, finally, she linked art to public issues, political ideology and to women. Those linkages underwent constant revision in response to various pressures, many of which were the historical pressures of the 1930s as a whole. In many ways McCausland's positions were a product of those pressures.

As the Depression severely undermined both capitalism in general and the private patronage of art in particular, many middle-class artists moved to the left. They affiliated with communism, with workers and with the strategies of strikes and confrontation. The Federal Art Project relief programs as well as the United States Treasury mural programs responded with government support. As a result, the 'art world' expanded its boundaries from an elitist legitimising endeavour for the middle class to a dispersed activity often practiced by politically radical artists in communities throughout the United States. McCausland

---

11      Nelson. *Repression and Recovery*, Paula Rabinowitz. *Writing Red, An Anthology of Women Writers, 1930-1940* (New York Feminist Press, 1987); Barbara Foley. *Radical Representations*, (Durham, NC and London, Duke University Press, 1993).

was the critic who most clearly articulated the significance of this new expansion of the role, placement and practice of art.

From my own perspective as a feminist art historian who studies the history of twentieth-century art history and practices contemporary criticism,[12] I see Elizabeth McCausland's writing as emblematic of the politically engaged art discourse of the 1930s. as a feminist act of intervention and as a model for analysis of contemporary political art.

Coming from a pioneering family who helped develop Wichita, Kansas, in the late nineteenth century, McCausland seems an unlikely candidate to redefine art criticism and bear the epithet 'radical feminist'. Although a profound respect for the efforts of pioneers occasionally crops up in her writing, her effort is not to domesticate, but actually to undomesticate art, to get it out of the homestead and reposition it in the landscape of social issues.

It would seem to have been her sexuality that moved her to the activist left and gave her the confidence to intervene. Although never publicly identifying herself as a lesbian, her closest companions from 1930 until her death were other women who were politically on the left. Her leftist politics as well as her sexual orientation sparked deep compassion for the disadvantaged in society. This also made her profoundly aware of the limitations for women who were not playing the game according to the sexual rules of the male-dominated public arena. Her anger emerged in long, still unpublished poems that condemned the deep injustices and hypocrisies of American life at the same time that they celebrated the American land and its people. Later in life her anger turned to bitterness and alcoholism. But during the 1930s she achieved recognition and success as the most articulate art critic of her generation.

McCausland left Wichita, Kansas, in 1919 to attend Smith College, the year the national Woman's Suffrage Amendment was passed in the United States Congress (it was passed in Kansas in 1912). She

---

12     My first book *Modernism in the 1920s* (UMI research press, 1985) looked at the complexities of the roots of modernism.

received a master's degree in English in 1923.[13] Her master's thesis was on Chaucer, rather than her first choice, Emily Dickinson, or her second choice, Walt Whitman; McCausland started out by pressing the restraints of an academic tradition that regarded all American writers as less significant than British and other European writers.

She was immediately hired as a feature writer in the Sunday Department of the *Springfield* (Massachusetts) *Republican*. The newspaper had a long tradition of liberalism, dating back to the 1820s.[14] One editor, Waldo L. Cook, a member of the Sacco and Vanzetti defense committee, was to be a supporter of McCausland throughout her association with the newspaper.[15] As a result McCausland had an ever-increasing amount of space in the paper, and, even more unusually, freedom to say what she chose. Her correspondence records that she had an enthusiastic following that reached throughout New England and New York City and embraced different audiences. In the art world her articles were highly respected and frequently posted at museums and galleries.

McCausland identified, to some extent, with women workers. She saw herself quite literally as a 'worker' because of her demanding and exhausting job at the daily newspaper which frequently extended to seven days a week. At the same time, though, she was firmly linked to the middle class through her family and education.

---

13    In going east McCausland was following the example of her sister Helen who attended Simmons College. After earning her BA in 1920, McCausland returned to Wichita for one year of grueling teaching at Fairmount College, then went back for her Masters Degree. McCausland also had other relatives in the east, including an uncle, John Noble, who was an artist on Cape Cod. (Interview with Ross McCausland, 30 July 1996).

14    Richard Hooker, *The Story of an Independent Newspaper* (New York, Macmillan, 1924).

15    Richard Elizabeth McCausland, "Americans We Like, Waldo L. Cook," *The Nation*, 4 July 1928, 11-12. The Sacco and Vanzetti Committee attempted to reverse the decision that condemned two Italian anarchists to death. It was unsuccessful. They were put to death in 1927.

McCausland's affiliation with the political left was accelerated between 1930 and 1933 by her partner, Ruth Fisher. Fisher was a journalist specializing in industrial relations, and an activist for better labour laws for women.[16] This intersection of feminism and communism was a marginalized and difficult position.[17] While there is no evidence that McCausland herself was ever a member of the Communist Party, she felt the injustice of economic inequality deeply. She wrote lengthy newspaper articles analyzing, labour-capital relations in New England textile strikes. In a model of the type of intersection she would later advocate for artists, she incorporated her public political commitments into her private life. As she commented in a letter to her mother: 'pretty soon my daily life ought to embody all my economic and social beliefs. I think that people ought to do what they can to give their principles support. Recently we raked together a lot of old clothes to send to the striking mill workers in Gastonia.'[18]

Two years later she wrote to her mother that she and Ruth were 'waging battle practically single handed to maintain the labor laws for women.'[19] Such a close union of personal convictions and public issues

---

16    Fisher also spent much of her free time providing young factory workers with recreational activities. When her job was terminated, she emigrated to the Soviet Union in 1933 and is last referred to as writing for the *Moscow Daily News* in 1935. Information on Fisher is based on McCausland to Paul Strand, 1 September 1933 and 17 April 1935 Paul Strand Archives, Center for Creative Photography, Tucson.

17    Barbara Foley. 'Women and the Left in the 1930s, *American Literary History*, 2:1 (1990), 150-169; Debrorah Rosenbelt. 'From the Thirties: Tillie Olsen and the Radical Tradition', *Feminist Studies*, 7, 3 (1981), 371-406; Robert Shaffer. 'Women and the Communist Party. *USA Socialist Review*, 9:3 (1979), 73-118; Susan Ware. *Holding Their Own: American Women in the 1930s* (Boston, Twayne, 1982) especially chapter 5.

18    Elizabeth McCausland to Isabelle McCausland, May 1930 Elizabeth McCausland Papers, Archives of American Art). See her articles 'Capital-Labor in New Bedford I-III, *Springfield Republican*, 24,26 and 28 August 1928, and 'Easthampton Makes Denial,' 22 December 1928. Unless otherwise indicated all articles cited by McCausland are from the *Springfield Republican*. All the references here are from clippings with no page numbers in the McCausland Papers, but her articles frequently appeared on page 6.

19    Elizabeth McCausland to Isabelle McCausland, 5 December 1932 (McCausland Papers).

would become the foundation for her commitment to advocating a socially engaged art world.

In 1930 she described her early years as a feature writer for the Sunday Department with some irony: 'a newspaper man, there is no sex really in newspaper work is a permanently disenfranchised citizen of the world.' What she really knew was that there was only the male sex. She commented on her marginal status:

> I've never gone to Russia, I have never tracked Coolidge …
> There is no prospect that I will be sent to London to cover a
> disarmament conference.[20]

She wrote instead on 'almost anything from sports to philosophy'.[21]

Although all of her articles until 1932 were anonymous. McCausland was outspoken, and her work generated a lot of mail. In March 1928 under the pseudonym 'Libertas' she wrote a series of editorials objecting to the censorship activities of right-wing organizations and proudly reported to the Smith College alumnae magazine that she had been blacklisted.[22] She went after the hot-button issues of the day, including, as she enumerated them: 'Abolition of capital punishment. unemployment insurance, book censorship … minimum wage law enforcement; the right of married women to work in industry; birth control; free speech, and feminism.'

In preparing these articles she interviewed Jane Addams, Margaret Sanger, Felix Frankfurter, Bertrand Russell, Oliver Wendell Holmes and the Hungarian pacifist-feminist Rosika Schwimmer.[23] McCausland had an interest in almost everything. She wrote book reviews and drama reviews, as well as articles on construction, aeroplanes, dams, scientific processes and education.

---

20    Elizabeth McCausland. 'Behind the Front Page', *Purple Pastures, 1920 Reunion Booklet* (Northampton. Mass. Smith College 1930), 15, 16.

21    *Smith College Alumnae Quarterly* Class Notes. 1925, College Archives. Sophia Smith Collection. Northampton. Mass.

22    The articles were collected in a pamphlet. *The Blue Menace.* under her own name, and sold through the *Springfield Republican* 'To those interested in Free Speech and Liberal Opinion.'

23    'Experiences on Springfield Republican' (McCausland Papers): Smith College *Alumnae Quarterly Class Notes*, 1928.

It was a long way from exploited women workers in factories to the pampered visual artist. Initially the art world seemed to her a precious, self-indulgent sphere with little soul. Until the early 1930s, she wrote on it as a cloistered, although intriguing, manifestation of a small enclave, far from the powerful social forces with which she was principally pre-occupied. She found it disappointingly superficial, the artists were 'men of little faith, men who did not bleed their hearts', compared to Sacco and Vanzetti, for example.[24]

Her first signed art review was on Georgia O'Keeffe, already a somewhat defiant protest against the norms of objective criticism, since O'Keeffe was a close personal friend.[25] O'Keeffe's public persona as a reclusive woman artist immediately presented contradictions for McCausland to sort out as she examined the intersections of the politics of gender and art. McCausland first set aside the verbiage that had accrued to O'Keeffe's work, verbiage that created so many interpretations that she felt it made it 'impossible to see the artist and her work for words (not her own to be sure, for what she says about her paintings is modest and often merry)'. Such an aside, a personal interpolation that marks McCausland's friendship with the artist, intentionally interrupts the reporter's tone.

The exhibition had six skull paintings and several New Mexico landscapes. McCausland saw 'an O'Keeffe [who is]... sometimes almost too clever in her technical mastery, but still a pilgrim'. The pilgrimage to which she referred was the embrace of New Mexico as a place: 'There is another O'Keeffe present, who goes out and paints directly from Nature, who responds defiantly to the terrible majesty and fear that is New Mexico.'[26] Yet McCausland also felt that the profound emotion of that landscape was not yet part of O'Keeffe's work. She understood the effect of the landscape from personal experience; she herself had had a life-changing romantic encounter in New Mexico that had stimulated her to produce a huge outpouring of poetry and to turn more seriously to an identity as an art critic rather than as a general reporter.

---

24    'In Retrospect', 9 July 1930.

25    Georgia O'Keeffe to Elizabeth McCausland, 15 July 1935 and undated correspondence (McCausland Papers). The article was signed with an 'E'.

26    'Georgia O'Keeffe Exhibits Skulls and Roses of 1931', 10 January 1932.

McCausland defended O'Keeffe against those who saw her as only a 'precious' artist,[27] as well as those who sought 'proletarianism,' 'social significance' or the American scene.[28] She made space for the reclusive, but independent, O'Keeffe, an artist who would seem to be the antithesis of the engaged artistic practice that McCausland herself advocated.

As she defended O'Keeffe, she defended women artists in general. She felt that O'Keeffe had become

> a myth, as well as a symbol, of a withdrawn and esoteric state of blissful contemplation said to be peculiar to women (women artists perhaps one should say) which has done her no particular good and certainly has done the artist (feminine gender) no good at all.[29]

In overturning the stereotype of O'Keeffe as a recluse. McCausland sought to expand options for all women artists. O'Keeffe's notoriety was based on an already very public intersection of gender-construction and modernist aesthetics paired with sexuality through her early association with Alfred Stieglitz. This provided McCausland with an easy opportunity to polemicize about gender, but one full of ambiguity, as she endeavored to counter the contradictory construct of a public image of the woman artist as a private person. In working with these contradictions McCausland was working not only with the obvious dialectic of the public space and the private person, but also with the internal tensions within the artists themselves, particularly in the case of O'Keeffe.[30] O'Keeffe herself was bisexual, and by the mid-1930s she had shed the persona of the seductress and adopted an austere androgynous identity.

Kathe Kollwitz presented an entirely different challenge. In writing on Kollwitz in the United States, McCausland was a pioneer. Although

---

27    'Georgia O'Keeffe from 1919 to 1924',17 February 1935.

28    'Georgia O'Keeffe's Flower Paintings', 28 April 1935.

29    'Georgia O'Keeffe Shows Her Latest Paintings'. 2 January 1938.

30    Barbara Marshall, *Engendering Modernity: Feminism, Social Theory and Social Change* , Boston, Mass., Northeastern University Press, 1994), 114, analyses the tensions of public and private. See also Barbara Buhler Lynes, *O'Keeffe, Stieglitz and the Critics, 1916-1929* (Ann Arbor, UMI Research Press, 1989) on the construction of O'Keeffe's identity by earlier critics.

well known in Germany, she had been little seen in the United States; her art was the antithesis of the popular School of Paris modernism that had prevailed in New York since the Armory Show of 1913.[31] McCausland wrote the first major studies of the artist in the United States, mainly emphasizing the intersection of activism and aesthetics, with gender as a subsidiary theme. She struck the note throughout of Kollwitz's importance both as a profound social critic addressing a woman's perspective on war and as a profound artist in her handling of the print-making medium. She openly argued with the orthodox communist position that art was a tool of the working class in the class struggle. In Kollwitz she read the technique as part of the political message, both literally and metaphorically:

> At first sight the prints shown in the present exhibition exemplify, the Communist dictum 'Art is a 'weapon'; it is their social significance, their tremendous indictment of the needless waste of war of which one is immediately conscious. But these prints are more than propaganda ... Here is life wasted, violated, raped, needlessly offered up on the altar of war. Against this waste and this violence Kollwitz poses the etcher's plate. the lithographer's stone, the woodcutter's block, paper. ... ink and a few lines, a few dots ... the self-portraits become ... the portrait of all stricken and suffering women, bereaved and struck down by the violence of war. In the face of this aging woman may be read the history of her times. of her country ... the woodcuts ... are strong and violent in their contrasts, a use of black and white is emotionally consonant with the artist's mood of rebellion at the needless waste and sufferings of the era depicted.[32]

Kollwitz was paradigmatic for McCausland as an artist who intensely and personally addressed public issues. The politics are gendered in that Kollwitz speaks unequivocally of the mother's excruciating sense

---

31     Jean Owens Schaefer. 'Kollwitz in America: A Study of Reception 1900-1960', *Woman's Art Journal,* (1994) 29-34, examines McCausland's writings in comparison to the writings on Kollwitz during the hegemony of formalism.

32     'Kathe Kollwitz Work Being Shown at Museum Here', 11 December 1933.

of loss when her child dies in war, but they include the condemnation of all war as immoral. McCausland's own words also invoke the strong bite of Kollwitz's etched lines. McCausland here uses the written word as a means of political confrontation.

Gertrude Stein, a celebrated writer and publicly declared lesbian, fresh from the Left Bank in Paris, stimulated a different type of writing and polemic. McCausland here explored a more traditional model of modernist aesthetics as politically confrontational. At the same time, she inserted the surging energy of Stein's powerful sexual persona.[33] When Stein actually came to nearby Hartford, Connecticut, in conjunction with the opening of her opera 'Four Saints in Three Acts,' McCausland was euphoric. She attended three performances in Hartford and New York, then tackled the subject with a passion. The opera included music by Virgil Thomson, sets by Florine Stettheimer and a stunning all-black cast of dancers from Harlem. Notably, McCausland only briefly referred to the sets, dancing and music. Her main emphasis was on the text, which seemed to have washed over her physically, almost orgiastically:

> For the time being one may say that 'Four Saints' is about life, about reality, about the constant flow and flux of human experience … Moreover the opera is about experiences not solely and not chiefly in terms of volitioned and censored thought, but in terms of those deeper and more organic rhythms of existence, those buried sensory knowledges of sight and sound and kinesthetic sensation which explorers of the sub-conscious plumb and which the surrealists especially have invoked in their effort to translate the principle of automatic writing into many mediums.[34]

---

33    Her first review was 'Gertrude Stein's Reminiscences,' 3 September 1933.

34    'Super-Sense Applied to Twentieth Century Life', 4 March 1934. In November McCausland published an interview with Stein, following the poet's tour of the United States and spurred by the knowledge that Stein was scheduled to speak in Springfield in January 1935 at the Springfield Museum of Art ('Stein Sits Listening to America After Thirty-One Years 'Absence', 11 November 1934; 'Stein and Toklas Here', 8 January 1935).

McCausland identified Stein as the 'first' Surrealist and seemed to adopt the automatic process in her own writing. At the same time she clearly felt a deep attraction and even 'hero worship' for Stein which is contained within the intense words. She evoked personal physical feelings, while at the same time connecting the personal to the public:

> this matter of creating rhythms, cadences, concepts and con-notations and connections of words which echo ... Speed, broken rhythms, disconnected phrases, sentences without verbs, books without punctuation, these somehow seem con-sonant with the inner tempo of life as it beats through the western world today. This cadence, this beat, this irresistible pulse is the thing that Gertrude Stein (and her collaborators) have ... created in 'Four Saints,'[35]

Clearly, the opera forced McCausland to reach beyond her known boundaries in terms of her writing and her feelings, and she allowed those powerful feelings to emerge clearly. McCausland characterized Stein as a political activist. In her own terms: 'she has helped change the world insofar as an artist can with his intangible weapons of art.'[36] The gender switch in this sentence simply underscores the normative patriarchal language that even the feminist McCausland used without thinking in reference to 'the artist'. McCausland here, though, affirms the idea of aesthetic radicality as a type of confrontation that can be political. Aesthetics, politics and gender were in a powerful conjunction in Stein.

Martha Graham, like Stein, was obviously subverting tradition through the forms of her dance. But as Graham moved to the political left in the mid-1930s, she provided McCausland with the chance to elaborate on the relationship of aesthetics and social concerns. In her first lengthy account of Graham's work McCausland declared that 'The ideal of the dance today, not as an escape from life but as a means of putting one close to life, takes on an added importance in Martha Graham's

---

35    'Super-Sense Applied to Twentieth Century Life'.

36    'Stein Sits Listening to America After Thirty-One Years' Absence'; 'Stein and Toklas Here'.

eyes.' McCausland further saw the dance as a 'very powerful weapon of propaganda' in its correspondence 'to the society that produced it.'[37]

The particular model that McCausland had in mind in this article was native American dance.[38] In co-opting the rhythms of native dance, Graham was seemingly following the same course as Picasso in his use of African imagery. McCausland saw it more as an intervention in the traditions of classical European dance that brought it closer to 'life' in America.

Graham apparently wanted to be seen as a formalist. The following autumn, under the headline 'Insistence that Dance be Understood in Terms of Itself as Movement of the Body in Space.' McCausland spoke of Graham as declaring that her work was purely abstract: 'it is eternity the artist faces, not time.'[39] Two years later though, Graham modified her commitment to formalism. In 1935 McCausland, supported by the artist's program notes, stated that 'Panorama' expressed the harshness of fanaticism in the United States through the metaphor of dance. It culminated in a sense of liberation as people awakened to 'social consciousness' in the present:

> To be sure the fanatical intensity of our Puritan forefathers is in the American blood, as is the dreadful inheritance of slavery and sadism. There is also in the country's psyche the memory of the violence and brutality of the Western vigilante, the lust for power of the early empire builders … That is why we may speak of 'Panorama' as new and revolutionary. It is not a propaganda or proletarian work of art … it is to supply energy to mobilize the beholder as well as the dancer. Therefore the justice of the adjective 'revolutionary,' for motion is change and change is revolution.[40]

37    'American Dancer is Evolving a Typically American Rhythm', 30 April 1933; see also 'Study of Modern Dance in America: Pioneering Venture', 22 July 1934.

38    'Indian Dances Parallel Cycle of the Seasons', 1933 (no day or month given). Graham had a Guggenheim Fellowship to New Mexico to study southwestern Indian dances in 1931-32.

39    'Absolute and Abstract Art is Dance of Martha Graham', 9 September 1933.

40    'Modern Dance Takes Another Step Forward', 25 August 1935.

Here McCausland distinguishes Graham's work from the communist position on political art as the workers' art (proletarianism) and aligns it with the more generic principle of opposition to inequities and abuses of society.

In a characteristic intersection of public and private, the emotional intensity of the articles on Graham and Stein in 1934 and 1935 coincided with a new personal relationship for McCausland. In the autumn of 1934 she first met the photographer Berenice Abbott.[41] As she reviewed Abbott's photography, McCausland posited:

> the social muse and the artist can consort without either yielding position. the idea not subservient to the medium. the medium not the slave of communication ...[42]

The language signifies her personal feelings as much as the character of Abbott's work. The verb 'consort' points to a courtship within the article, a courtship that resulted in the most important relationship in McCausland's life. McCausland here again inserts sexuality itself into her theorizing on the relationship of art and society.

In the late winter of 1935 McCausland moved to New York City, propelled there by her new relationship with Abbott. She began to write for radical publications such as the *New Masses*, *Fight* and *Art Front* under the pseudonym 'Elizabeth Noble' (her grandmother's name), as well as writing sedate articles for the College Art Association Journal *Parnassus*. But her primary work continued to be as the main art writer for the *Springfield Republican*. Despite continued efforts over the next thirty years, McCausland never had a permanent position with the New York press.

On the other hand, her friendship with Abbott as well as her own reputation as a critic immediately brought McCausland into the center of the action in New York. In early 1936 feminism and modernism

---

41    Berenice Abbott to Elizabeth McCausland, 29 October 1934. A letter from Elizabeth McCausland to Berenice Abbott uses the word 'passion' eleven times: 5 November 1935, Abbott Archives, Commerce Graphics as cited in Bonnie Yochelson, *Berenice Abbott: Changing New York, The Complete WPA Project* (New York, New Press and Museum of City of New York. 1997), 19.

42    'New York City as Seen in Abbott Photographs', 14 October 1934.

were both subsumed by the specific anti-fascist agenda of the American Artists' Congress. McCausland's experience in reporting labour strikes was perfect to articulate the now widely confrontational and activist spirit of the art world. She wrote excited articles about the new 'world of reality' that the artists now occupied, in contrast to the 'ivory towers' of the past.[43]

The spirit of unified political purpose notwithstanding, McCausland continued frequently to feature women in her reviews. In 1936 she wrote on a Peruvian artist, Julia Codesido, in an article on the Latin American delegation to Congress. In the midst of the rhetoric of the American Artists' Congress, McCausland used a Marxist analysis to examine Codesido's art in relationship to the degree of capitalist exploitation in Peru.[44] She saw Peru as still intact compared to Mexico:

> such paintings as these are a standard by which we can judge a world in transition, passing from a primitive agrarian culture to a highly organized economy. Wait till the American metallurgical interests get their hands on the Andes and see what sort of art comes out of Lima then.[45]

McCausland now had more sophisticated theoretical tools. She could move beyond the unhistorical 'artist' looking at the 'world', to look at the production of art in the larger historical perspective of economic forces. In an article on the printmaking of Mabel Dwight, McCausland cited the 'social handicaps with which women even in this age of equal suffrage are still attended'. She saw the effects of 'this struggle' in formal terms, in a 'dryness and tightness of line'. The connection of aesthetics and politics here is a provocative parallel to her analysis of Kollwitz's work. But now the struggle is more gendered, more located in the art world, and more historical; it is the struggle of all women as artists in a hostile environment. She characterised Dwight's work as having

---

43    'Artists Thrown into World of Reality Present Their Case at Recent American Artists' Congress', 1 March 1936. McCausland covered the American Artists' Congress throughout its history in more detail than any other critic.

44    'Mexican Art with Social Message', 19 March 1936.

45    Ibid.

an emotion pressed back because the artist did not dare let herself go. Probably women will always show this last quality in their work until they are free from the beginning instead of having to fight bitterly for every opportunity and recognition. A quality in fact something like that of those pioneer workers for women's suffrage. who were not the most beautiful and seductive women of their age, but who were the true pioneers.[46]

McCausland hits here on both the struggle of the woman artist and the struggle of women in general. The reference to the pioneers of women's suffrage provides a historical reference that would have been familiar to most women at that time when suffrage had so recently been passed in the United States. At the same time McCausland again raises the ambiguity of women's position in the public sphere: the need to 'fight bitterly for every opportunity' speaks of the sexism encountered by women trying to make it in the public arena with a paying job and their consequent need to hold back their own opinions. In her own case, her ongoing effort to gain a position with a New York newspaper continued, and her frustration with the inequities of the world increased. The 'emotion pressed back' is clearly her own.

McCausland used a review of drawings of steelworkers by Elizabeth Olds to look at the position of women artists historically, giving a perspective that would not be repeated for many years.[47] She compares Olds to Berthe Morisot and Mary Cassatt, who had

no option except to glorify motherhood and children. In our time women have too often been driven back to a position of priestess or prophetess ... or at least [been]concerned with personal emotion as of comfort, love and narcissism.

In Olds McCausland saw someone who was moving out of the domestic and into the public arena, in her case in her subject of steelworkers: 'After the smell of hot damp earth from hothouses, [it is] a welcome relief.' But, McCausland firmly stated, the artist had not yet

---

46    'Mabel Dwight's Art in a Lithograph Showing', 9 January 1938.

47    Griselda Pollock. *Vision and Difference* (London, Routledge), 1988 finally again brings together Marxism and feminism.

made a 'full identification' with her subject, something which McCausland felt led to a loss of 'passion or emotional power' in the drawings. [48] She saw sympathy and support in Olds's drawings of steelworkers, not the kind of engagement that would realize social change. McCausland was not willing to settle for an art that was less than compelling as it negotiated with social and political concerns. She never hesitated to call on artists to engage more deeply in both aesthetic and social issues. She believed that artists collectively and individually, male and female, could make a difference in changing the world.

After 1938 McCausland wrote less frequently on women.[49] Feminism seems to have taken a back seat to fear for the survival of humanity as Hitler's army marched across Europe. McCausland became increasingly activist herself. She moved from her exhortatory role as a critic to become publicly involved in the American Artist's Congress. This bold act ran counter to the general tenor of the times. At the end of the 1930s artists were leaving the public arena and retreating to the more familiar studio as they were disillusioned by the Hitler—Stalin pact, the loss of the Spanish Civil War, and the increasing pressure within the United States from the House UnAmerican Activities Committee.

In 1946 the *Springfield Republican* closed and McCausland lost the freedom of writing long polemical articles. During the remaining years of her career she wrote commissioned books and monographs, all of them on men. Her feminism and even her commitment to social engagement was effectively silenced by the necessity of making a living and the atmosphere of the 1950s. But she remained an articulate writer who laced her writing with concerns that were equally threatening to the profit-oriented 1950s, such as the relationship of the artist to the market.[50]

At her death in 1966 McCausland had published only one book on a woman, an introduction to a portfolio of prints by Kathe Kollwitz

---

48    'Steel Mill Drawings by Elizabeth Olds,' December 1937.

49    Later articles include 'Lisette Model Show "Candid" Photographs', 27 May 1941; Irene Rice Pereira'. *American Magazine or Art*, December 1946, ;374-7.

50    'Must Artists Starve?' *New Masses*, 10 July 1945, 9, 10, and 'What is the Economic Future of the Artist?' *The Art Digest*, 1 November 1951, 22, 66.

in 1941.[51] Her major work on the social history of the artist in America remains in typescript to this day, and has not even been acquired by a public archive.[52] It is only in the *Springfield Republican* that her radical, feminist intervention in the staid tradition of art criticism survives. As a writer and a poet, as well as an art critic, Elizabeth McCausland can be grouped with other recently republished feminist writers of the 1930s like Tess Slesinger, Meridel Le Sueur, Josephine Herbst, Muriel Rukeyser, Genevieve Taggard and Agnes Smedley.[53] While less officially and publicly aligned with the far left than these women, McCausland, like them, successfully inserted herself as well as the concerns of women, into the male-dominated world of left politics, journalism and art. In the process. she formulated a model for a vanguard culture that was both politically and artistically engaged and negotiated the relationships between aesthetics, gender, sexuality, social concerns and politics.

---

51    Introductory Essay. *Kathe Kollwitz* (New York, Curt Valentin, 1941).

52    The incomplete manuscript entitled 'The Artist in America 1641-1941: A Social History' resided in a private collection in New Jersey at the time of writing.

53    Paula Rabinowitz. *Labor and Desire* (Chapel Hill, University of North Carolina Press, 1991) and *Writing Red.*

# From Immigration to Community: The Jersey Homesteads Mural by Ben Shahn and Bernarda Bryson *(1995)*

IN A MURAL FOR THE COMMUNITY OF Jersey Homesteads, (now Roosevelt), New Jersey, Ben Shahn, with the assistance of Bernarda Bryson,[1] redefined contemporary history painting by combining the difficult medium of true fresco with unusual historical themes, and a spatial order that dramatizes the psychological aspect of the scenes. Painted during 1937-1938 in a medium which demands rapid work in large simple forms, the mural nonetheless includes three detailed and interrelated historical episodes with many subordinate scenes and references. The primary themes are Jewish immigration, Union organizing, and the planning of a cooperative community in the early New Deal Resettlement Administration.[2] Spatially, the mural combines the traditional linear perspective of the Renaissance, the shallow space of some photographic portraits, the three dimensionality of theatrical sets, and the arrested action of film frames. These various devices serve to underline the contrasts between the dynamic and the static experiences depicted.

---

1    Bernarda Bryson Shahn has described her role as follows: "The conception was Ben's; I did a lot of the painting, of course, under his instructions and/or guidance." Letter to the author, July 5, 1992.

2    A previous study of this mural is by Frances K. Pohl, "Constructing History, A Mural by Ben Shahn," *Arts Magazine* (September 1987) pp 36-40. See also Frances K. Pohl, *Ben Shahn with Ben Shahn's Writings* (San Francisco Pomegranate 1993) 11- 21.

In narrating history, the mural departs from the tradition of the unified tableau, based in the theory of Diderot, which focuses on a single moment in which the action hangs in the balance, the peripateia. In the traditional tableau there is frequently a single identifiable heroic figure who with gesture and pose, implies the leadership of the moment in history depicted. This concept of history descends into still photography as the "decisive moment." Instead of the peripateia, the mural created in Jersey Homesteads, New Jersey presents groups of figures acting as part of an on-going process. The only suggestion of a "decisive moment" is provided by one central enlarged and isolated figure, but that figure, a union leader, is intentionally anonymous and emerges from a group. The decisive moment is replaced by historical process, a process based on economic and political forces. Although some identifiable portraits are included, these specific individuals act within a group, not as heroic individual leaders. At the same time, however, there is, in some of the individual scenes, the symbolism, if not the heroism, of the traditional tableaux. The tableau without heroism, but laden with symbols, is a common approach in New Deal murals. But usually history is depicted as static: the anonymous worker, farmer, or homesteader becomes the symbol of historical stability. In Shahn's mural workers in groups are a symbol of historical process and change.

In addition, there is a major element in the Jersey Homesteads mural of what Barthes calls the "obtuse" or "third" meaning that of emotion, beyond narrative discourse. In Barthes as developed in *Camera Lucida,* the element beyond narrative is personal memory. As elaborated on by Victor Burgin the third meaning is psychological, more than simple recollection it includes the idea of the fantastic and imaginary.[3] In the Jersey Homesteads mural Shahn's personal memories, as well as his autobiographical and psychological investment in the imagery that he is painting imbues it with this "third" meaning. For example, the depiction of the new arrivals hall at Ellis Island is both a symbol

---

3    Victor Burgin, *The End of Art Theory*, (Atlantic Highlands, NJ: Humanities Press International, Inc, 1986), pp.112-121, 129, Burgin argues for a separation of hieroglpyh and peripateia, but states that Barthes "conflates" them. Barthes approach is then more accurate for Shahn who also conflates them. See also Roland Barthes, "The Third Meaning," *A Barthes Reader* (New York: Hill and Wang, 1982), pp.317-333 and Roland Barthes, *Camera Lucida,* (New York: Hill and Wang, 1981).

of an historical event, and a personal memory of Shahn's own life experience.[4] The mural, in fact, coincides throughout with Ben Shahn's own memories and experiences as they intersect with historical events: he came to the United States from Lithuania as a Jewish immigrant in 1906 at the age of eight, participated in radical activities in the Artists Union in New York, then joined the New Deal.

The unusual approach to history painting in Jersey Homesteads is in part the product of the time in Shahn's career in which the mural was executed. Shahn turned to painting contemporary history painting shortly after the 1927 execution of Nicola Sacco and Bartolomeo Vanzetti for the murder of a postmaster in South Braintree, Massachusetts. Although the innocence of the accused became a widely adopted cause all over the United States and Europe, the judge refused to stay the execution. Shahn was deeply troubled by the profound injustice of the event and saw it as comparable to the Crucifixion itself. Individual sacrifice based on social injustice became a central subject of his work for several years.

*The Passion of Sacco-Vanzetti* of 1931-32 uses contemporary individuals as paradigms for the great tragic heroes of history. In early 1931 Shahn began clipping images and headlines from the newspapers as raw material for his contemporary history painting. Topics he researched, all widely popularized favorites of the left in the early 1930s, were the cases of Tom Moody, accused of throwing a bomb in 1916, and the Scottsboro boys, nine young blacks accused of attacking two white women in Chattanooga, Tennessee.[5] Although Shahn was dealing with popular causes, his style was more confrontational than other artists on the left. His images were simplified and flattened, based in part on the frontality of newspaper documentary photographs. One reviewer likened the Sacco and Vanzetti series to the history paintings of Emanuel Leutze and Baron Gros; he saw Shahn as a "valuable

---

4    For the artist's description of this process see Ben Shahn, *The Shape of Content* (Cambridge: Harvard University Press, 1957), pp. 29-30.

5    Gardner Jackson to Ben Shahn ( October 13, 1931, Shahn Papers (1991) Archives of American Art, Smithsonian Institution, Washington, D.C. (AAA) On Tom Mooney see file "Tom Mooney" Shahn Papers , AAA and Diego Rivera, "Forward" *The Mooney Case by Ben Shahn* ( New York, Downtown Gallery 1933); on Scottsboro Boys see file on "Scottsboro Boys" Shahn Papers AAA.

witness to our epoch."[6] Shortly after, Shahn enlarged three of the series as mural-scaled panels for an exhibition. Consequently, Shahn himself was drawn into contemporary political events: an effort was made to withhold his Sacco and Vanzetti mural study from the exhibition at the Museum of Modern Art in the fall of 1931.[7]

A more profound trauma resulted from his work with Diego Rivera at Rockefeller Center where Shahn assisted in the creation of the now infamous fresco *Man at the Crossroads*. As a result of the inclusion of a portrait of Lenin, the work was ordered suspended by the rental agents who feared, more than the Rockefellers, that the portrait would make it difficult to rent the building. Ten months later, the mural was destroyed. Shahn was a leader in organizing protests about the original work stoppage. He went on to assist Rivera from July to December 1933 with the creation of a cycle at the New Workers School based on the history of the United States according to the radical Marxist-Lovestonite analysis of class struggle, labor struggle and revolutionary rebellion. The murals were crowded with clusters of numerous identifiable portraits, a typical Rivera technique for the depiction of history. As first installed it partnered earlier and later historical figures on opposite walls, a dialectical technique that Shahn would later use.[8]

These events fundamentally altered Shahn's development as a history painter. He was at the very center of one of the major ruptures of the art world of the 1930s. The suspension of the work at Rockefeller

6    Jean Charlot, "Ben Shahn," *Hound and Horn*, 6,4 (July – September 1933) p. 633. Jean Charlot was a close friend of the Mexican mural painters and a participant in the mural renaissance in Mexico. Another reviewer referred to the works as part of our "modern revolutionary mythology "(Matthew Josephson" The Passion of Sacco and Vanzetti," *The New Republic* (April 20, 1932), p.275.

7    Lincoln Kirstein, *Mural Painting in America* (New York: Museum of Modern Art, 1932). On the censorship incident see Hugo Gellert, "We Capture the Walls!" *Art Front* (November 1934), p.8.

8    Diego Rivera, *Portrait of America,* with an explanatory note by Bertram Wolff (New York: Covici Friede, 1934). See especially panel XII, pp. 183-191 "The New Freedom," ill. p. 185. Lawrence Hurlburt, *The Mexican Muralists in the United States.* (Albuquerque: University of New Mexico Press, 1989), pp. 175-193. See also Ida Rodriguez-Prampolini, "Rivera's Concept of History," in *Diego Rivera, A Retrospective* (New York: Founders Society, Detroit Institute of Art and in conjunction with W.W. Norton and Company, 1986), pp. 131-137.

Center galvanized a broad spectrum of artists to protest in the streets. In addition, Shahn had an in-depth technical and theoretical apprenticeship under Rivera. Although according to Lucienne Bloch who also assisted Rivera, Shahn was mainly in charge of the historical research for the murals, he would also have learned by observation the complex process of fresco painting, as well as the idea of organizing large historical events in terms of groups that represent a revolutionary process.[9] In Rivera's mural at the New Workers School the structure of the paintings is entirely static. The figures pile up one above the other in a quotation of the type of space and time used in pre-Columbian art: history proceeds not in linear progression, but in repetitive events. Rivera's murals include numerous portraits of historically notable leaders, but those leaders do not stand out above the crowd, they are embedded within it.

Between 1933 and 1935 Shahn created two proposals for large scale murals, both related to historical issues that were less about individual martyrs and more about changing systems of injustice: the first focused on demonstrations both for and against Prohibition, the second on Prisons with a focus on contrasting old and new methods of correction. Both series were rejected for execution by the Municipal Arts Council in New York, but in their structural and pictorial differences they suggest the changes in Shahn's approach to history painting as a result of his contact with Rivera, changes that are central to the Roosevelt, New Jersey mural.

The Prohibition series of gouaches are, like the Sacco and Vanzetti, separate, static images. Frontal facing rows of demonstrators are the primary composition. The Prison series, created in collaboration with Lou Bloch and with the assistance of Lydia Nadajena, who drew the perspective, is far more complex. Intended for the Riker's Island Penitentiary, it was based on exhaustive research. The perspective used deep space projections in alternation with flat shallow spaces, in a way that would be adopted in a modified form at Jersey Homesteads. Shahn began to work in terms of a film-like sequencing of images connected with formal devices, particularly the alternation of the deep shot and the close up. The alternating deep and flat space suggested a pairing

---

9     Interview with Lucienne Bloch, November 2 and 3, 1992.

of old and new methods of penology on opposite sides of a narrow corridor.

At this time Shahn also began to use the Leica camera. As an instrument to record the depression in New York City streets it provided more intimate and personal views than newspaper mug shots. Although his photographs were primarily taken in public streets and parks, or as views of people through windows and on city stoops, they begin to confront the human face of deprivation, in contrast to large publicized examples of social injustice symbolized by such figures as the Scottsboro Boys. This more intimate look at deprivation may be in part a response to Bernarda's deep-seated concerns about individual deprivation. The Leica opened Shahn's perspective both psychologically and physically, allowing informal images (albeit often taken with a right angle lens without the subject's knowledge). In his early photography, he functioned without programmatic intent or a self-conscious, unified agenda, at a time of the dissolution of social mechanisms. Independent of a government ideology, he collected images of the Jewish ghetto, of poverty, of the life of the streets of New York, of artists' demonstrations.[10]

He first met Bryson in the summer of 1933 when she came from Ohio as a newspaper reporter to interview Diego Rivera. An active advocate of social causes in the early 1930s, Bryson was profoundly concerned with the injustices of the Depression. Bryson was such an articulate thinker and speaker that on moving to New York in the early fall of 1933 she immediately became a leader of radical causes in New York, particularly the Unemployed Artists Association and the Artists Union. Her contact with Shahn developed most prominently during the summer of 1934 when they began to work together on the newspaper *Art Front,* the newspaper of the Artist Union.[11] Ben Shahn provided

---

10    Laura Katzman "The Politics of Media-Painting and Photography in the Art of Ben Shahn," *American Art,* (Winter 1993), pp. 61-87 and Deborah Martin Kao, Jenna Webster and Laura Katzman *Ben Shahn's New York, The Photography of Modern Times,* (Yale University Press, 2000).

11    Interviews with Bernarda Bryson, August 2, 1991 and March 16, 1992. See also her interview with Lisa Kirwin, April 29, 1983 AAA. Bryson mentioned here that she was actually able to get her phoned-in reports included in the *New York Times* by knowing how to sound like one of their reporters.

layout, promotion, and editorial suggestions, such as filmic sequences of photographs of the artists' demonstrations. Both his involvement with Bernarda and the newspaper work deeply engaged him in the mass labor and economic issues of the Depression, as well as in the artists' particular plight. Bernarda has stated about the idea of collaboration with Ben Shahn that "our relationship went deep into theory. Both in art and in life. I am sure that I had great impact upon Ben's thinking—even upon his writing, but not upon his art."[12]

Such a statement underlines both Bryson's strong intellect as it worked in synergy with Shahn's throughout the rest of his life as well as her own social conditioning concerning Shahn as an autonomous artist. Yet, irrefutably, his work in conjunction with Bryson in the mid 1930s, demonstrates their strong interaction. Their intellectual and technical collaboration distinguishes their work from the New Deal American Scene mural movement. Their work encompasses concepts that are not simply programmatic responses to a government initiative.

In the fall of 1935 Bernarda Bryson and Ben Shahn both went to work for the Resettlement Administration of the New Deal in Washington, D.C. Through this program they created the Jersey Homesteads mural almost two years later. First developed under the leadership of Rex Tugwell, an idealistic economics professor from Columbia University, the Resettlement programs were intended to provide new housing and a better standard of living for impoverished workers in both urban and rural areas. The larger goals were relief of suffering, development of self-sufficiency, and maintenance of the family.[13] Shahn and Bryson were part of a close-knit group of radical thinkers that provided creative ideas for using art in the new programs.

---

12    Letter to the author, July 5, 1992.

13    Sidney Baldwin, *Poverty and Politics, The Rise and Decline of the Farm Security Administration* (Chapel Hill: University of North Carolina, 1968), pp. 107-118. See also Eleanor Roosevelt, *This I Remember* (New York: Harper Brothers, 1949), pp. 125-133. Eleanor Roosevelt was instrumental in urging help for these workers. The programs were also an outgrowth of activities first developed by the Quakers. (There were three programs: rural rehabilitation, land reform and the community program which was to combine industry with subsistence farming in a cooperative community.)

Initially, Ben Shahn was hired to publicize the programs of the Resettlement Administration with posters and graphics. As research for this activity, he began with the idea of visiting the mining areas of Pennsylvania and Appalachia. He and Bernarda Bryson took an epic two month driving trip (with Bryson doing all the driving) intended for the purpose of photographing resettlement clients. They ended up driving through Pennsylvania, West Virginia, Kentucky, Tennessee, Arkansas, Louisiana, and Mississippi. From September to October 1935, Shahn and Bryson approached impoverished rural workers. Bryson would often engage people in conversation, while Shahn would capture them informally with a right angle lens. Although they were working with the support of the government, their photographic journey was not made simply to create propaganda. Bryson and Shahn engaged serendipitously with the South and with the people they met.[14]

The pioneering images of Southern poverty that came out of the Shahns' mid-Depression journey laid the foundation for the more famous Farm Security Administration images. Shahn and Bryson were soon followed by Dorothea Lange, Walker Evans, and many others. Later Depression photographers were, however, more programmatic in their intentions and more edited by the ideology of the government to project a sense of the role of the government in creating a new stability out of desperate conditions.[15]

---

14    Interview July 16, 1993. Bryson spoke of going to towns simply because they liked their names, such as Freeze Fork, Kentucky and Sweet Home, Georgia.

15    F. Jack Hurley, *Portrait of a Decade, Roy Stryker and the Development of Documentary Photography in the Thirties* (Baton Rouge: Louisiana State University, 1972), p. 50. "In those early days, when Stryker was still groping for directions, talk, critique, endless sessions of looking at pictures, and personal growth were the order of the day. ... Shahn enjoyed these sessions and contributed to them as often as he could. Once he became involved in a discussion concerning a picture of eroded soil. Stryker liked the photograph. It was nice and sharp and it really did show what water could do to the land. Shahn was not so sure about the picture. "Look Roy," he said," You're not going to move anybody with this eroded soil—but the effect this eroded soil has on a kid who looks starved, this is going to move people." See also John Tagg. "The Currency of the Photograph: New Deal Reformism and Documentary Rhetoric," *The Burden of Representation* (London: MacMillan, 1988), pp. 153-183.

Although Shahn's photographs are often used in his murals, a film project in collaboration with Walker Evans reinforced the idea of cinematic scale and sequence. One film proposed by the Resettlement Administration promoted a new greenbelt community just outside Washington, D.C. The Shahn/Evans film was never created, but its form as well as its conceptualization is revealing:

> We propose to make a film, the subject matter of which will be people—the greater half of our nation. We want to show how they live now, and to show a way of life in planned communities such as the greenbelt town offers. To do this we will employ a device of flash-backs [sic] into the histories of five typical American workmen who apply for work on a greenbelt project. ... For some of the material we will rely upon stock or news shots. For the rest we will rely upon the actual conditions and people as we find them. ...

> Through such a film we hope, first to build up a public sympathy and understanding of the need of housing for some 40,000,000 Americans; second to popularize the idea of the planned community. We wish not only to awaken in our audience some feeling of responsibility and concern for the great segments of population shunted into the cast-off segments of our cities, the worked-out farms of our country; but we wish to articulate for our audience their own needs in housing, to spread some understanding of what housing can and ought to be for people of low income.[16]

Although the film addressed Greenbelt, Maryland, its techniques and concepts could also describe the program of Jersey Homesteads and its mural. The idea of history in flashback suggest the concept that probably underlay the immigration scene at Jersey Homesteads.

During these same months Bernarda Bryson was involved with creating historical images. She was asked to set up a lithography workshop as part of the Special Skills division of the Resettlement Administration which encouraged the idea of crafts such as furniture design, ceramics and printmaking. She began work on a "Frontier

---

16     "We are the People." typescript, Shahn Papers, 1991, AAA.

Book' inspired by a Roosevelt speech that the new frontier was that of the social frontier. The book was to have covered the importation of immigrants, the middle passage, as well as the movement west and the vanishing frontier. She also created lithographs and watercolors based on the history of the Underground Railroad, a topic in which she was intrigued not only because of her social principles, but also because her own grandparents' home was a stop on the Underground Railroad in Athens, Ohio.[17] Bernarda Bryson's historical images in these prints, though on a much smaller scale than murals, also mediated between memory, personal experience and the national narrative discourse.

It was at this point, following several years of working on a small scale with lithography and photography, as well as film and mural conceptions that Ben Shahn and Bernarda Bryson took on the commission to create a mural for Jersey Homesteads, their first executed mural-scaled fresco. According to Bernarda Bryson the community was funded as follows:

> … It began expressly with a group of New York workers in the garment trades. They discussed nostalgically how great it would be to have a factory in a rural area where—during off seasons for instance—they would not be languishing unemployed in teeming city areas, but could have a plot of land, a garden and so on. In pursuance of this dream, each of some eight to fifteen families raised five hundred dollars each. They had heard of Benjamin Brown who was noted for having instituted co-operative projects in the United States … and in Russia. They went to him. He located a tract of land contiguous to his own in New Jersey. Hearing of the oncoming New Deal projects, Mr. Brown took a delegation of the garment workers to Washington where they met with Harold Ickes, Secretary of the Interior, who immediately approved the project.[18]

---

17    Interview July 16, 1993.

18    Letter to the Author (September 7, 1993); Edwin Rosskam, *Roosevelt, New Jersey Big Dreams in a Small Town and What Time Did to Them* (New York: Grossman, 1972) pp 19–29. See also Memorandum Shahn Papers 1991 AAA.

The New Deal provided a huge infusion of funds for the building of the community, and renamed it Jersey Homesteads in order to invoke a reference to pioneers. After several calamitous events, the government hired Alfred Kastner, a German architect from the Bauhaus and student of Gropius, assisted by Louis Kahn, to build the town.[19] While the local residents might well have preferred a traditional style of architecture (as indicated by the transformations that have taken place in the houses over the decades since they were build), the utopian Bauhaus principles of functional architecture for workers dominated the entire planning. The government, although it provided the essential funds for the building of the community, also, in essence, took away the possibility of individual initiative from the residents.

Kastner invited Shahn, with Bryson as his assistant, to create a fresco in the town and designed what was originally the community building with the mural in mind. The dimensions of the wall and the lighting and viewing of the mural were all part of the original planning process.

> Mr. Shahn is to work out a script for the mural with a number of variations to same. The theme is to center about contemporary life to the Jewish emigrant, to touch on immigration and emigration, his assimilation into the country, industrialism and unionism with contrapointal adoption of programs elsewhere, and immigration to Palestine.[20]

Initially the mural was conceived by Shahn entirely as a narrative that invoked Jewish history, hopes, and memories. His narrative about the mural is filled with intimate characterizations of Jewish life, most of which do not emerge in the final mural. On the other hand, as a passionate narrative written at a time when Shahn was leaving Jewish life

---

19    "Two other architects preceded Kastner—one wanted to build tamped earth houses—he was let go. The second designed pre-fab houses and a huge factory was erected off the edge of town for the purpose of manufacturing the slabs. It was badly designed, was stopped and for a number of years stood at the edge of town, empty. Next a contractor made off with four million dollars worth of supplies." Letter to the author from Bernarda Bryson Shahn, September 7, 1993.

20    Inter-Office Communication to Mr. Adrian Dornbush from Alfred Kastner, March 2, 1936, Shahn Papers, 1991, AAA.

behind, it clearly demonstrates his personal relationship to the mural's subjects, particularly with respect to his place as a Jewish immigrant who aspired to be free of the bonds of tradition and to assimilate into the life of the United States:

> … The mural should begin with the life of the Jews in [a] Russian Ghetto. They are seen living in humbleness and fear, caring for their own as best they can, keeping up homes for their aged and schools for their young. They are deeply buried in their religion, finding there some compensation for their exclusion from the civil life about them. A fragment of a dream of return to the Holy Land is shown, and the nostalgic prayer: "On the coming year let us all hope that we will be reunited in Jerusalem."
>
> Around a table the Jews sit at the feast of the Passover. Behind them rages a pogrom. An inflammatory anti-Semitic myth often spread among the Russian peasants holds that at the Passover the Jews must have the blood of a Christian child. Because of this, pogroms sometimes begin at this time. The tragic conclusion of the pogrom is seen in a coffin, surrounded by a mournful family.
>
> The Passover symbolizes the departure of the Jews from Egypt, the land of bondage. So, with the feast of the Passover, and out of the background of Ghettos and pogroms comes a stream of immigrants to America with hope in their faces. Above them hovers the dream of America—a land of fruit and flowers, big cities with streets paved with gold, the Statue of Liberty—symbol of a new life to the immigrant.
>
> Looking away from the stream of immigrants is shown a dim loft in a New York sweatshop, where Jewish workers bend over long lines of machines straining to see in the dim lights. Other workers bend over gas irons smothered in clouds of steam. Others laboriously operate antiquated and back-breaking machinery. Here the Jews, disillusioned in their dream of America, again dream of the return to Zion. Or some think longingly of the open fields which they

have seen in America, and yearn for the soil and the ancient agricultural pursuits of their race. A scene in the New York ghetto is shown. The older immigrant Jews, cast in a mould by generations of fear, are found living in segregated groups, carrying on their traditional trades and customs, not venturing into fields which were forbidden.

Out of this scene of the New York ghetto and the older Jews surges a new generation—the young American Jews. Free from fear and oppression, they are now fully assimilated into their surroundings. They take part in the life of the country, its culture, its sports, its business, politics, and professions. Many of them work in the needle trades, but these are no longer sweatshop workers. They are meeting in unions of the needle trades, they are addressing crowds of workers, they picket in a strike. ...

A young Jewish worker stands with his two children where a pathway divides. Over him hangs a dark reddish cloud in which the horrors of Jewish persecution in Hitler's Germany are shown. The cloud hangs low with a suggestion of imminence. Before him one path leads toward the Holy Land, toward Tel Aviv, and the New Jewish settlements in Palestine. He looks longingly—shall he return to the homeland? But he seems rooted to the ground. He is an American, his children are Americans. ... A second branch of the path leads in the direction of another old dream of the Jews—a return to the land. Here is shown the co-operative community with its various aspects of communal living. ... There is seen here an adding to and an enriching of the group, without sacrifice of the racial and cultural treasures. The Jew is shown able to realize his potential growth ... practicing his trade and living on the land.[21]

As first characterized by Shahn in this narrative, in the spring of 1936, the entire Jersey Homesteads mural would have focused on Jewish oppression, immigration, and dreams. His narrative speaks of the

---

21    Shahn Papers, 1991 AAA

history of a generation of Jewish immigrants whose parents arrived in the early part of the twentieth century. The narrative could easily have been based not on research but on the conversations in his home of the conditions in Russia, and the hopes in the new country. The conflation of personal memory, personal experience, and received history parallels that of the images of the completed mural.

A directive of a year later significantly altered this original plan, upon which Shahn had based two sketches.[22] The memo of April 15, 1937 reflective of the ideology of the now well-established government art programs sponsored by the Treasury Departments and the Works Progress Administration read that:

> The theme of the picture may be described as the 'American Scene.' Its dominating composition shall show the arrival of the immigrants at the left, acclimatization and organization into the American community in the center and the revital-ized pursuit of human observations [sic] under the newly acquired democratic technique at the right.

> The time, dress and incidents used are characteristics of to-day and their application shall be without prejudice against race, creed, or color.[23]

The compromise for Jersey Homesteads was that Shahn was per-mitted to present a specifically ethnic history, as long as he showed it blending into the American scene and was not seen as disruptive or lacking in decorum. As finally completed, the mural met the approval of the authorities in Washington, D.C., all enthusiastic about Shahn personally in spite of his radical apprenticeship with Rivera, with only a few changes. The approval stressed the fact that

> the mural emphasized the human side of the story as against political or religious. Its presentation is quiet and it deliber-ately avoids the portrait of struggle or conflict or any other sensational matter as not befitting the dignity of the theme.[24]

---

22    These sketches are illustrated in Bernarda Bryson Shahn, *Ben Shahn* (New York: Abrams, 1972) pp 147-148.

23    Shahn Papers 1991 AAA.

24    Letter from Adrian Dornbush to Milo Perkins (January 1937, Shahn Papers, 1991) AAA.

On the left the mural is dominated by a large wedge shaped group of immigrants walking briskly toward the foreground across a red bridge with a portrait of Albert Einstein among the leaders. Also included in this group are portraits of Shahn's own parents. Next to Einstein and actually leading the group is a dominating female figure that is Shahn's mother,[25] as well as the archetypal Jewish matriarch; she wears a shawl covering her head, the traditional dress of a Jewish woman and borrows from images of Shahn's own great grandmother. To her right is Raphael Soyer, although his features also suggest Shahn's father. Further back, almost buried in the midst of the crowd is another famous scientist, Charles Steinmetz, the brilliant hunchbacked electrical engineer who became known as the "modern Jove" when he created lightning in his laboratory in 1922.[26] Many of the figures prominently wear badges that identify their number on the ship manifest, without which they could not enter the United States. Badges were also used during early pogroms to identify Jews, as well as in Nazi Germany.

The group purposely conflates several eras of immigration. Steinmetz and Shahn's own family came as political radicals to the United States fleeing late nineteenth and early twentieth century Jewish pogroms in Russia,[27] whereas Einstein came to escape from Hitler's repressive policies in 1933. Bernarda Bryson recently stated that emphasis on the large group of immigrants combined with specific individuals was intended to underline that immigrants made major contributions to the society to which they came.[28] Einstein was also living in nearby Princeton and a supporter of the Jersey Homesteads community.

Shahn used many approaches to suggest action and drama without utilizing heroic individuals or traditional gestures: several different

---

25    Bernarda Bryson Shahn letter to the author (July 5, 1992).

26    Ann Novotny, *Strangers at the Door* (Riverside, N.Y.: Chatham Press, 1971), p. 15. A photograph of Steinman with Einstein appears on this page.

27    Seldon Rodman, *Portrait of the Artist as an American, Ben Shahn, A Biography with Pictures* (New York: Harper and Bros, 1951), pp. 156-159. Photograph of Shahn's father, mother and great grandmother appear in this text.

28    Interview with Bernarda Bryson Shahn, July 16, 1993.

diagonal perspective constructions are based on Renaissance techniques. At the same time he punctuates the coherent mass of the immigrants by assertive portraits, photographs drawn from a combination of family albums, Lewis Hines's photographs, and anonymous newspaper images. These contradictory modes conflate the idea of memory and history, or in Roland Barthes' terms, the punctum, and the studium. They combine symbols of history, both spatial and figurative, drawn from Shahn's research in photographic files, with the hieroglyphs of his own imaginary and real personal history.

The mural is even further complicated by adoption of the Brechtian epic theatre technique of groups of workers as symbols of active social forces. Shahn also invokes the spatial and temporal collage of such films as Eisenstein's *Potemkin* in which long shots and close-ups, flashbacks, contemporary events, and even hallucinations, are combined: in the immigration segment smaller scenes refer to related developments. The violent actions of the Nazis appear in a ghetto scene in the upper left corner.

Prominently, in the lower left, is the Registry Hall at Ellis Island. It is shown starkly without benches as it was when Shahn arrived, but entirely empty except for one isolated family and a single man, an accurate depiction, since men frequently immigrated separately from their families. Above the immigrant group are families sleeping in a city park. These images all inhabited Shahn's memory. They replace the original plan of pogroms, ghettoes and the Jewish Passover.

The central section of the mural focuses on the history of unionization. It includes several types of garment workers compressed into tight spaces in contrast to the expanding wave of the arriving immigrants: assembly line workers with sewing machines, pressers bending over steam irons and home piece workers dominated by a maternal figure. In this section Shahn was combining photographic sources of sweat shop conditions, but he has a less personal connection to the scenes as his own family came from a tradition of skilled craftsmen and he apprenticed as a lithographer at a young age. The stasis of the sweatshops is countered by the line of the workers (among whom, significantly, is Bernarda Bryson) filing into a union hall with brick work that ties the mural to the brick of its setting, originally the community center of the town. Since Bryson was a key figure in encouraging Shahn's radicalism and participation in organized strikes, her placement is revealing.

At this point there is a sense of break (or scene change) in the sequencing of the mural as it shifts to the process of unionization and away from immigration. The last two parts of the mural are also distinguished by the fact that they have only one female, a traditional mother in the background; with the emergence of the Union the action is by men, although historically young girls played a dramatic role in the process of unionization.[29] The only dominant individual figure in the mural is the large speaker based on a "soap box orator" from Shahn's own photographs in New York on the Lower East Side, now metamorphosed into a union leader. Again the sense of a zoom close up against a film set is suggested: behind the speaker are the buildings that figured in the early tragic events of the garment workers that led to the creation of the union. Standing out clearly is the famous "Triangle Shirt Factory," scene of a horrific fire that killed 146 young girls in 1911 as a result of locked doors that were intended to give access to staircases.

The union organizer is the largest figure in the mural, and the closest to an heroic individual, but he is understated: he does not gesticulate except to point down to the workers below him, several of whom are also based on Shahn's own photographs. The words of the speech are written on a sign (suggesting a silent movie with captions). The leader resembles John Lewis, but is, as with most of Shahn's "portraits," a composite of several people.

Directly below the union leader is a pensive worker that emerges from the crowd, brooding on the speaker's message and pausing between the past turmoil of the milling workers and oppressed factory workers, and the future, represented by a sequence of ordered doorways that are replicas of the doorways of successive union halls, based again on photographs. This central part of the mural is by far the most complex. The process of unionization is an abstract idea, much less specific than the process of immigration, and Shahn had few visual references other

29    Shahn had a pamphlet on the history of the International Ladies Garment Workers Union that outlined the dramas of the early years of the union, dramas that frequently centered around young girls. Educational Department, *The Story of the I.L.G.W.U.* (New York: Abco Press, 1935). Shahn chose to focus on the more publicly recognizable male leaders.

than newspaper images from which to work. He himself was a part of the process only in the context of the artists' demonstrations of the mid 1930s, so he observed it as more of a commentator. On the other hand, the section also uses many of his own photographs as sources, rather than his remembered memories of immigration. The abrupt spatial and thematic segments seem to function as a metaphor of the difficult psychological transition that he himself was undergoing, from his roots in the restricted immigrant community of his youth, to the turbulent world of the activist mid1930s, and thence to the New Deal world of Washington, D.C. where he had a home with Bernarda Bryson for the first time.

The next section of the mural displays ordered and purposeful groups. It juxtaposes the benefits of unionization, a scene of education on the history of labor in a classroom,[30] and the cooperative construction of a factory building in an agricultural setting. The workers constructing a factory are a specific reference to the Jewish garment workers who originally founded Jersey Homesteads in 1932.

The New Deal concludes the mural. Seated around a table are the men who supported the utopian community that represented the ideals of the Resettlement Administration: Rexford Tugwell, leader of the Resettlement Administration, David Dubinsky of the International Ladies Garment Workers Union, Heywood Broun, head of the Newspaper Guild and a spokesman for labor, and Senator Robert Wagner, a sponsor of labor and housing legislation. A plan of the community refers to the planning of the town, and the planning process of the entire Resettlement Administration.

Although the individuals in the New Deal scene are more specific than in any other section of the mural, that specificity is paired with their activity as a group understood as part of a process, rather than an individual initiative. It was around this table, with the planners of the Resettlement Administration that Shahn could have placed himself and Bernarda Bryson, for they both were involved as artists in its early

---

30    The two unions AF of L and CIO, were still separated as indicated in a letter that documents Shahn being asked to avoid suggesting a sequential relationship between the two groups in his diagram in the background of the painting. Adrian Dornbush to Milo Perkins, n.d. Shahn Papers, 1991, AAA.

programs. Behind the prominent New Deal group is a small "flashback" of a young family leaving a poorly planned community to join the new cooperative. The spatial stasis of the segment of New Deal administrators contrasts with the dynamic processes of immigration and unionization. It invokes the ideals of the New Deal: re-establishing stability and traditional family units.

Without showing any sign of the extensive strife of the labor movement, Shahn, with great subtlety, made one theme a clear reference to the Marxist interpretation of history in terms of economic forces driving social change and the power of the worker. Shahn legitimizes his radical interpretation through devices that link the mural to traditional history painting. Not only does he structurally quote the spatial relationships of the Renaissance murals, he also invokes a biblical allegory of Moses leading the Jews into the Promised Land, with Einstein performing the sage role of Moses in the biblical emigration. The prominent female with covered head at the foreground of the painting may subtly refer to the Madonna. This conjunction of a Marxist view of historical process with traditional concepts, paired with Shahn's close rapport with the New Deal administrators provides the basis for Shahn's success in bypassing the potentially heavy censorship of the American Scene theme.

The themes themselves are not entirely unique among New Deal murals. Another example of sweatshops appears in George Biddle's murals for the Justice Department, completed in 1935.[31] In squares of space that structurally parallel Renaissance murals, Biddle creates static tableaux that become symbols of deprivation. Despite his deep concern for the subject, he makes whimsical errors: in the sweatshop he put himself at a sewing machine, although nothing could have been further from the experience of the wealthy scion of a Philadelphia family that dated back to before the revolution.

Shahn was closer to the subject matter. While his own family was not part of the textile sweat shops, his understanding of the psychological conditions gives his three sections of sweat shop workers an intensity

---

31     Illustrations of the murals by other artists discussed can be found in the following books: Francis O'Connor, ed., *The New Deal Art Projects, An Anthology of Memoirs,* (Washington D.C.:Smithsonian Institution Press, 1972) George Biddle, p. 33; Edward Laning, pp. 84-85;96-97; Francis V. O'Connor, *Art for the Millions* (Boston: New York Graphic Society, 1975), Philip Evergood, p. 46; Marion Greenwood, p. 51.

through his brilliant use of compressed space. The figures are physically jammed together or lined up on a long deep narrow table. As suggested in his outline, the narrowness of life and mind in New York was as oppressive as the ghetto of the Russian pale. Biddle's images suggest emotional despair and isolation from the rewards of society; Shahn's scenes project resignation and claustrophobia.

Another thematic comparison can be made with Edward Laning's Ellis Island cycle of murals completed in the spring of 1937, just before Shahn commenced work. Although the overall theme *The Role of the Immigrant in the Development of America* is entirely different, the arrival scene is similar. A close comparison reveals again the immediacy of Shahn's mural. In Shahn's work the arriving group faces us more directly and includes specific people. It suggests the tightness of a compact community, whereas Laning's immigrants are more isolated. Laning includes a reunion scene of husband and wife, rather than Shahn's accurate "holding pen" of the Registry Hall at Ellis Island. Laning suggests the symbol of the holy family with a mother/father/child as the prominent cluster in the foreground, whereas Shahn's central figure beside Einstein is a powerful mother figure without child, a reference to the fact that families were frequently separated in the immigration process. Last, Laning's large half naked figures draws not only from the academic tradition but also from the symbols of American work, as seen in the pioneering murals of Thomas Hart Benton. Benton's murals were, in fact, a fundamental reference point for many of the murals of the 1930s.

Benton's painting, above all *America Today* was accessible throughout the 1930s in the New School for Social Research in downtown New York.[32] In a series of nine active scenes that branched out from an energizing gyro engine he presented America from farm to city, including such industrial subjects as "Coal Mining" and "Steel." These panels were dominated and unified by huge foreground male bodies (often posed for by Jackson Pollock) with a background of smaller scaled details.

They interrelated in sequences based on the early Western sets that Benton himself had worked on in the teens. Significantly his film set

---

32    For illustrations of the mural see Henry Adams, *Thomas Hart Benton,* (New York:Knopf, 1989), pp. 157-167, 185-191.

source was more oriented toward the traditional tableau than those of Shahn who was familiar with the more avant-garde techniques of Eisenstein's *Potemkin*. Benton transformed the academic formula of the heroic leader by monumentalizing America with different types of workers and activities, in front of the "set," very much like the stars of early Hollywood movies. Benton's glorification of the worker links him to Marxism, but he emphasized specific activities and individuals, rather than groups and process.[33] In contrast, Shahn's dense communal groups invoke economic forces and link him to directly to Brecht's Marxism.

Although no other New Deal murals refer to union organizing, a mural by Marion Greenwood did address urban resettlement. Marion Greenwood's fresco *Blueprint for Living* in the Community Center of the Redhook Housing Project in Brooklyn, like Shahn's, addressed a New Deal Resettlement program. Completed in 1940, the mural also contrasts the old and new and like Shahn's, depicts the actual building of the new town. Greenwood had worked in Mexico as a fresco painter and was highly regarded by Diego Rivera. Her monumental workers are simplified and modernized, with the emphasis on the act of building. The image was integrated with the architecture of the room. She is also conforming to government ideology in showing the men working and the woman as a mother.[34]

The Jersey Homesteads mural was more autobiographic and oriented to Marxist theories and Jewish history than any of Shahn's own later mural cycles. During 1938-1939 Ben Shahn and Bernarda Bryson worked together on a second major mural cycle. *Resources of America* at the Bronx Post Office consisted of thirteen paintings created in egg tempera rather than fresco. Much less an integral part of a specific community than the Jersey Homesteads Project, and sponsored by the Treasury Section of Fine Arts, a more established group of art sponsors than the by-then defunct Resettlement Administration, the cycle of thirteen

---

33    Erica Doss, *Benton, Pollock and the Politics of Modernism* (Chicago: University of Chicago Press, 1991), has a useful discussion of Benton's murals.

34    On the theme of sexual stereotyping in New Deal murals see Barbara Melosh, *Engendering Culture: Manhood and Womanhood in New Deal Art and Theatre* (Washington: Smithsonian Institution Press, 1992). Melosh focuses only on the Treasury Section Post Office murals.

paintings was tied to the ideology of the New Deal and American workers as emblems, rather than to a narrative about the inhabitants of the community itself.

Bryson and Shahn won the commission jointly. Bryson's conception, as it survives in sketches was linked directly to New Deal programs, although her original plan was apparently to present a theme on the history of the post office, with a reference to women. Her surviving sketches include a mother and child in front of slum housing, a destitute city dweller, the building of new housing and parks; she also included a rancher, a miner, a farmer, a railroad foreman, and dam builders. The focal point of the cycle was Franklin Roosevelt, framed by an artist and a teacher (both women). The murals as executed for the Bronx Post Office followed Ben Shahn's proposals rather than Bryson's, as Bryson felt that "Either set of original designs would have been a complete concept in itself. To break up either would have been destructive to it. I chose to follow Ben's designs."[35] On the other hand, Shahn and Bryson were working so closely at this point that such a statement may be exaggerated. Some evidence shows that Bryson worked from Shahn's photographs in her sketches and that he embodied some of her approaches in his conception.

As installed, the mural has Walt Whitman as the focal figure instead of Roosevelt. Two large scaled single panels focused on workers who were cotton picking and bailing based on Shahn's photographs taken in 1935-1937. Other panels depict textile factory workers including a girl spooling and a man weaving, an electrical engineer holding a plan, an agricultural scene of a thresher and worker, and a hydroelectric dam. The connection to New Deal programs is looser than in Bryson's plan, but the overall theme is the same in terms of the building of society.

In both the sketches and completed mural, the imagery is segmented in many separate panels, the result of the post office design. The imagery is symbolic, rather than narrative. The relationship of the viewer in the Post Office to the murals' subject matter was remote, except in so far as the Bronx had a working class population and the mural depicted workers. As history painting, the Bronx imagery presents

---

35    Letter to the author, July 5, 1992. The finished mural does seem to use Bryson's design in the case of the workers.

isolated symbols of American industry, several of which are the same as those presented by Benton in his New School murals (agriculture, mining, hydroelectricity). Furthermore, the subjects are less connected to Shahn himself. His radical and complex approach to murals at Jersey Homesteads has now become a more programmatic and generalized image of the American scene.

In the following year, 1939, Shahn returned to the theme of immigration in a proposal for a post office in St. Louis. While these sketches also encompassed several other themes such as the "Four Freedoms," and the "History of the Frontier" and" River Life," the immigration images are a striking contrast to the subtle understatement of the Jersey Homestead painting. In the two immigration designs dramatic images of Nazi guns, concentration camps and desperately fleeing Jews unequivocally present the violent destruction of the compact Jewish community seen in the earlier painting. The murals were not accepted.[36]

Shahn's final mural painted in fresco in 1940-1942 was the *Meanings and Benefits of Social Security*. In this painting, he returned to Rivera's dialectical model by pairing images. In this case, one wall showed conditions before Social Security, and the other, after Social Security. Using several of his own earliest New York photographs as well as other sources, Shahn depicted no famous people, only ordinary people. He contrasted the handicapped, unemployed, old, young, mothers, children with, on the facing wall, people enjoying sports and building buildings. The images are clearly symbols of the conditions of life now presented in a more simplified color and space relationship. The *Meanings and Benefits of Social Security* is by a loyalist to the New Deal who avidly believes in the programs about which he is painting.

Shahn as a history painter, with the frequent assistance of Bernarda Bryson, created through his several murals a variety of images

---

36    One other unexecuted immigration series had been proposed earlier for Greenhills, Wisconsin that related to the history of the "progressive-liberal movement" and the "major immigrant groups, the Germans, refugees from the unsuccessful German Socialist uprising of 1848, bringing with them great social idealism; the Scandinavians with their fine farming tradition; the Irish, always politically gifted; the New Englanders with their rigid beliefs in personal liberty, free speech, and free education." Undated typescript, Shahn Papers, 1991, AAA.

that present both the history of the dreams of the New Deal and its specific programs. Yet, only in the Jersey Homestead murals, with its layered density of personal and political references, did he fully develop the many aspects of history that constantly interact and reinforce each other, particularly the intersection of the symbolic historical tableau and the hieroglyphs of his personal memory. In his innovative spatial relationships and his experiment with the intersection of narrative history and personal memory, he created one of the most complex images of the entire New Deal. Yet, Shahn presented, above all, the dreams and hopes of all people to have a better life. Such a dream was a central animating principle of life in the United States and the basis for the New Deal.

Yet, in the end, the mural depicts a myth. In spite of Shahn's optimistic image of stabilization, Jersey Homesteads, because of economic forces beyond its control, was already failing as an industrial and agricultural cooperative by the time that Shahn and Bryson completed the mural. In January of 1938 there was a tenant crises, problems with organized labor and the idea of the cooperatives, a lack of jobs, and a break with the Resettlement Administration. Anti-Semitism from nearby communities such as Hightstown, a center for the Ku Klux Klan, was also painfully isolating for the original Jewish residents. In addition, many of them found living in the country unpleasant and even frightening compared to the urban life to which they were accustomed.

The houses were put up for private occupancy. Ben Shahn and Bernarda Bryson moved into the community. Today, only a few descendants of the garment workers remain. The town is predominantly writers and artists, or academics from nearby institutions. Today, Jersey Homesteads, renamed Roosevelt, has no industry or cooperative agricultural programs supporting the community, the result certainly of current economic and political forces, as powerful as those that drove the creation of the community in the first place. Ben Shahn is not available to paint this contemporary chapter, but the economics that drive suburbia would probably not particularly inspire him.

# Gambling, Fencing and Camouflage, Homer Saint-Gaudens and the Carnegie International, 1922- 1950 *(1996)*

*This is not an age of a unified and glorious art on either side of the Atlantic, but it is an age of exciting exploration, adventure, and youth. Our Carnegie International will mirror that.*

~ Homer Saint-Gaudens [1]

HOMER SAINT-GAUDENS (1880-1958) WANTED TO believe that "aesthetics should be divorced and remain divorced from all the turmoil of the rest of the world."[2] Yet as director of the Carnegie Institute's Department of Fine Arts and organizer of the International Exhibition from 1922 to 1950 Saint-Gaudens knew well that the opposite was true. During the years that he directed the exhibition, he had to deal continually with chaotic political conditions abroad, and resistance and outrage at home.

Saint-Gaudens created the only annual exhibition in the United States that attempted a multi-national perspective on contemporary art, in a period when such an undertaking was problematic to say the least. In the 1920s and 1930s, it was hard to make artistic selections based on particular national characteristics as governments swiftly came and went, geographical boundaries shifted, dictators invaded and annexed their neighbors, and artists emigrated from one country to another. An additional challenge was posed by the city of Pittsburgh itself—a city marked by extremes of wealth and poverty. Culture, sponsored by the wealthy, was a Sunday-afternoon recreation. Related to that, the local

---

1     "Ten Nations will Exhibit Art Here," *New York Sun,* June 21, 1933.

2     Homer Saint-Gaudens to Arnold Palmer, October 24, 1945 (All cited correspondence from 1941 and later is in the archives of the Carnegie Museum of Art).

press was mainly interested in telling dramatic stories, not educating its audience and New York writers who could be lured to Pittsburgh were inclined to see the entire operation as provincial just because of its location.

Faced with this daunting combination of circumstances, Saint-Gaudens not only survived, he succeeded. He made the Carnegie International into a widely reviewed, albeit always controversial, exhibition. He increased its attendance and interest, its scope and importance. Amazingly, Saint-Gaudens accomplished all this without any previous training as either an art historian or a museum administrator. He succeeded because his skills were in gambling as a hobby, fencing as a sport, and camouflage as an art. As director of the International exhibition, Saint-Gaudens would "play the odds," parry and thrust with the many different constituencies that he needed to satisfy, and disguise radical styles in the midst of bland examples in order to avoid attacks.

Homer Saint-Gaudens arrived in Pittsburgh as Assistant Director of the Department of Fine Arts in the summer of 1921. His duties were immediately extensive. He had full responsibility for assisting in the formation of exhibitions, catalogues, educational work, shipping arrangements, publicity and even the architectural remodeling of the exhibition galleries of the Department of Fine Arts itself.[3] By the fall of 1921 he was already consumed with planning his first International Exhibition. A year later he was appointed director.

At first, his most useful attribute was his name. As the son of America's most famous sculptor, Augustus Saint-Gaudens (1848-1907), he was immediately able to command respect, particularly in Europe and among the conservative businessmen that served on the board of the Carnegie Institute. But more than that, Homer Saint-Gaudens grew up learning about the complex politics of art by observing his father's successful career during the late nineteenth century, the infamous Gilded Age. Perhaps for this reason Homer Saint-Gaudens believed that "there are no standards of art. Art must justify itself; must be measured by its effect on the social orders; both of its own particular day and all the

---

3    John Berry to Homer Saint-Gaudens, July 1, 1921 (All cited correspondence before 1941 is from the Carnegie Archives, Archives of American Art, Smithsonian Institution, Washington, D.C.

days in the past, not by conforming just to this or that rule or ideal."[4] He had good reason to feel this way. Augustus Saint-Gaudens' reputation, along with many artists of his generation, was rapidly eclipsed in the early twentieth century by the rise of modernism. Consequently, his son saw himself as a gambler that played the odds. As he put it "Picking favorites in the art world is like picking them on the Belmont Park track. Just when a painter reaches the peak of his career depends entirely on the judgment of your favorite critic."[5]

As a result, Saint-Gaudens believed that art required social approval. He looked as much at a given artist's status as at his style. Although he held firm opinions about which painting he wanted to show, those choices were based more on keeping everyone happy than an aesthetic philosophy. In his exhibitions, he tried to present a balance of different artistic positions and perspectives although his choices were heavily weighted to the conservative. In partnership with that he positioned himself near the top of the social ladder in the art world, working with well-heeled advisors, such as Arnold Palmer, the son of a Lord, in England, and Guillaume Lerolle, an academician's son in France. At the same time though he did not forget to invite the views and court the enthusiasms of the average person by, for example, establishing a Popular Prize voted on by visitors to the exhibition. He avoided radical confrontation in the social sense, and hence avoided radical work in the artistic arena. Social acceptance was crucial because it was directly linked to the exhibition's success in sales. The more acclaim he garnered, the more sales were generated.

## The Formative Years

Homer Saint-Gaudens had learned to be alert to social approval in art as a child and young adult. He once referred to himself as "virtually born in a studio."[6] He was actually born in Roxbury, Massachusetts at the home of his maternal grandparents, but he spent much time in his

---

4 Saint-Gaudens to Anne Stolzenbach, August 18, 1948.

5 Homer Saint-Gaudens, *The American Artist and His Times* (New York: Dodd Mead, 1941), 213.

6 Saint-Gaudens, *American Artist*, 303

early years in the company of artists, poets, and writers. His education for the future director of the Carnegie Institute was mainly provided by the milieu in which he spent his childhood.

His mother, Augusta Homer Saint-Gaudens (1848- 1926) was severely hearing impaired.[7] She had been an artist before she married, but painted little following Homer's birth. As a child, Homer spent many months each year travelling with her pursuing cures for her condition. When he was eight he met Robert Louis Stevenson, while his father was working on a sculpture relief of the writer. Stevenson wrote to the young Homer: "you were ... (to my European view) startlingly self-possessed."[8] The following year he was painted by Sargent (as an artist's exchange for a sculpture of Sargent's sister, Violet). In contrast to the languid brahmin children and elegant, self-assured women of Sargent's usual portraits, Homer sits at an angle on a chair, alone and bored, and dressed in ornate clothes, while his mother hovers in the darkness behind, reading to him.

The Saint-Gaudens family was not wealthy, but they provided their only son with the sophisticated education that Augustus Saint-Gaudens—an immigrant who had begun working for a living at age thirteen—never had. Homer attended Lawrenceville and Harvard, graduating in 1903. Although he was an indifferent student, one useful result of his Harvard years was that he became an accomplished fencer, even serving as captain of the school's team.

In 1905 he married his first wife, Carlota Dolley, a sculptor and painter, as well as suffragette.[9] There were also many other artists in the family. Homer's paternal uncle and aunt, Louis and Annette were sculptors. His cousin Louisa was an opera star. Practically all of Augustus Saint-Gaudens' friends were creative, some of them eminently so,

---

7    Frances Grimes, "Reminiscences," in *A Circle of Friends, Art Colonies of Cornish and Dublin* (Durham, N.H. University Art Galleries, University of New Hampshire, 1995) 70-71.

8    Louise Hall Tharp, *Saint-Gaudens and the Gilded Ara* (Boston: Little Brown, 1969) 215.

9    They had three children of whom one died at age three in 1910. See *A Circle of Friends,* 111-112. Carlota died in 1927 and Saint-Gaudens included one of her paintings in that year's International. See also Tharp, *Saint-Gaudens,* 327-328, 331-32 and 347. His second wife was Mary McBride, a Carnegie Institute secretary. They married in 1929.

such as the architect Stanford White, his father's closest friend. Their milieu was the Players Club on Gramercy Park, a quintessential turn of the century bohemian men's club.

Most formative of all for Homer Saint-Gaudens, though, as an example of art embedded in social life, was the community of the successful artists of the American Renaissance who gathered in Cornish, New Hampshire near his family's home. These artists, that included Abbott and Emma Thayer, Louise and Kenyon Cox, Thomas and Maria Dewing, and Everett and Florence Shinn, talked, read and created elaborate masques, according to the then fashionable invocation of Greek and Renaissance culture. It was by no means an avant-garde environment, but neither was it entirely an academic one. The classical was adulated, but in spirit, not as a formula. These artists were part of the genteel generation, that group against whom the more radical modernists would soon react. They were the bohemian fringe of the upper classes of the Gilded Age; they spoke with horror of Bolshevisim and its wild radical ideas. Saint-Gaudens would maintain a residence in Cornish for the rest of his life.

Saint-Gaudens also became familiar with a far less refined scene. He worked as a journalist and editor in New York. In 1903 as assistant editor of *The Critic* and in 1905 managing editor of the *Metropolitan Magazine,* he met many artists, including the urban realists who collectively came to be known as the Ash Can school. He wrote an article on Alfred Stieglitz and the Photo Secession.[10] At the same time, Homer spent several years editing his father's reminiscences after he died in 1907.[11]

In these same years he also embarked on a new career. Perhaps to escape the genteel world of his youth, perhaps to prolong its sense of freedom, he went on the road as a stage manager for the famous actress, Maude Adams. Maude Adams was a spectacular performer. Born to the stage, she was a child star who evolved into a much

---

10     Saint-Gaudens, *American Artist,* 271.

11     Augustus Saint-Gaudens, *Reminiscences of Augustus Saint-Gaudens,* edited and amplified by Homer Saint-Gaudens ( New York, Century, 1911).

adored adult performer.[12] Her most famous part was in the first stage version of James M. Barrie's *Peter Pan* in 1905, a role that served her for several seasons and that she later revived. Saint-Gaudens worked with her for fourteen seasons until her retirement in 1918.[13] In this job, he learned more about how the tides of critical fortune flowed and ebbed, as motion pictures began competing with the stage for public favor.[14] He learned how to promote a big public event, how to organize logistics while travelling, and how to reach an audience with what they wanted. It was grueling work. He has described travelling for weeks on a "broken-down old sleeping car … as we went through eight weeks of one-night stands."[15] It was the ideal apprenticeship for his annual trips to Europe to organize the Carnegie International exhibition.

During World War I Saint-Gaudens served in the United States Military as director of the first camouflage units. Camouflage, or protective coloration, is a familiar idea today, but at that time, it was just emerging. The idea developed from a study by a family friend and painter, Abbott Thayer, based on his observation of the ways that birds matched their coloring to their environment.[16] Following the Army, Saint-Gaudens managed Maude Adams' last season, and assisted his mother with the logistics of showing his father's sculpture. When he organized a display of his father's work for the 1921 Carnegie International, he was invited to direct the entire exhibition.

---

12      Acton Davies, *Maude Adams* (New York: Frederick A. Stokes Co, 1901).

13      Tharp, *Saint-Gaudens*, 369. Tharp states that he was Adams's assistant stage manager "for fourteen seasons (except for the interval of the First World War" but does not specify the years.

14      Homer Saint-Gaudens, "Other Days, Other Paintings," *Carnegie Magazine* 8(February 1935) 259.

15      Saint-Gaudens, *American Artist*, 210.

16      Thayer wrote and lectured widely on protective coloration before World War I, see *A Circle of Friends*, 120.

# The "Well-Oiled Machine"

He immediately set out to revise a cumbersome system. The Carnegie procedure that he inherited for the Annual Exhibition, as it was called for many years, included a complicated two-tiered system. Some artists received direct invitations to participate and others were invited to submit to a jury. The juried group from Europe was asked to send their work all the way to the United States to be judged, and then sometimes rejected. Understandably this process built up a considerable amount of ill-will. Consequently juries were set up in Europe for the 1922 International and Saint-Gaudens was authorized to go there himself—to establish personal and diplomatic relationships with both the jurors and the artists. He immediately urged the elimination of the jury system entirely, but without success.[17] By 1926 there was simply an advisory committee in Europe that drew up a list of recommended artists. European jurors were selected only to give awards at the exhibition itself.[18] The European agents and Saint-Gaudens visited as many of the recommended artists as possible in order to select specific work. They constantly juggled artists, according to who or what was available, to meet a quota already set for each country by the Carnegie Institute board.

On his first trip to London and Paris in the winter of 1921-1922, Saint-Gaudens encountered hostility on all sides from the artists who had been insulted by the Carnegie Institute juries in the United States. His immediate conclusion was that he needed to start appeasing people by telling the artists in each country that they should be making their own choices as to which artworks to send. His first International show had a small number of works from Europe, and even those he characterized, in line from a speech that he wisely canceled out, as an "expanse of mud."[19] He was referring to poor works, included in the interests of compromise and diplomacy, and to mediocre works that major artists had sent out of anger at the International. Nevertheless the new curator

17    Saint-Gaudens to John Beatty, December 14, 1921.

18    The system for American artists remained two-tiered, combining invitations and jurying.

19    "Speech from the Bridge," January 23, 1922. This was Saint-Gaudens annual opening lecture. Only a few typescripts of these speeches survive, and they are in the Carnegie Museum of Art archives.

stated hopefully, "Ten years from now what has struck us as mad and disrespectful will have produced a fresh and vital attitude which no assiduous carping of old masters could ever attain."[20]

Saint-Gaudens, it appears, was already beginning to understand the excitement of modern art, although, most of his arguments centered around the political need to be open to the recommendations of artists in Europe. As he wrote in a letter during his second trip in November 1923," We should not bring over a few pictures that represent our point of view and then call it that of the French. We must not fall into the popular modern sport of assuming knowledge of a situation that we have not got and then of resenting the truth when it comes in quite a different aspect."[21] With that virtual order to his recalcitrant board of directors, he introduced Picasso, Derain and Matisse.

To a certain extent Saint-Gaudens' lack of knowledge of contemporary art made him more willing to compromise with the various political factions with whom he had to work. On the other hand, his initial predisposition and loyalty to the turn of the century genteel figurative tradition or most radically, the "ash can" realists, made it difficult for him to understand modernism in his first years. Before judging him too harshly, however, it is necessary to note that no major museums were showing modernism in the early 1920s. The Metropolitan Museum of Art held a "modern" exhibition in 1920 that mainly included Impressionism, only to be greeted with great hostility. By 1929 the Museum of Modern Art inaugurated its new museum by showing the Post-Impressionists. During that decade only individual pioneers like Katherine Dreier and Jane Heap were sponsoring the German Expressionists, the Russian Constructivists, and the Surrealists.[22]

Saint-Gaudens included regular well-disguised forays into daring contemporary art. Disguise was accomplished by choosing the most innocuous examples of the work of a radical artist. In making such choices, he typically gravitated toward portraiture, for example Picasso's neoclassical portrait of *Mme Picasso,* correctly seeing it as a

---

20      Ibid.

21      Saint-Gaudens to Edward Duff Balken (acting director) November 11, 1923.

22      Susan Platt, *Modernism in the 1920s* (Ann Arbor: UMI Research Press, 1985) discusses the gradual acceptance of modernism.

more familiar format for viewers terrified of modernism. Through this procedure he gradually and subtly educated the Pittsburgh audience, as well as himself, to modern art.

This procedure, which could be seen as a type of camouflage, built on his real experience in camouflage in World War I. The art of camouflage was based on fooling the enemy into thinking there was nothing there. At the Carnegie, Saint-Gaudens camouflaged not only radical art, but the political balancing act he was playing by saying blandly, year after year, that his exhibition was simply "a report on contemporary picture-making, its immediate past, its present, and its possible future; a report devoid of bias or special pleading for young or old, conservative or advanced."[23] He wanted to speak to as many audiences as possible. By placing the responsibility for judgement in the hands of the audience, he side-stepped responsibility when critics complained that the show was either too boring or too radical.

He was, needless to say, acutely aware of the "battleground of modernistic and academic ideas." He referred to the idea of sheeps (conservatives) and goats (radicals) in art throughout his career, although from the beginning he saw the contrast as amusingly murky:

> The trouble was that the public ... could never tell whether they were looking at old sheep and new goats or old goats and new sheep. Nor did the sheep, or perhaps it was the goats, know which way to go once they hopped their fences; for in the increasing turmoil the dust of loose conversation effectually shrouded this ever-growing battleground of modernistic and academic ideas.[24]

He learned to effectively exploit this ambiguity in organizing the Carnegie exhibition. In addition to juggling artists, according to their willingness to participate and the availability of particular works, he also tried to constantly keep in mind a balance between conservative, "medium" and "advanced" or what he called in the early years "wild" works. Saint-Gaudens wrote to Edward Balken, Acting Director, in

---

23    As quoted in "Report of Gordon Bailey Washburn Director, "Sixty-Second Annual Report of the Department of Fine Arts", (Pittsburgh, Carnegie Institute, 1958) 3.

24    Saint-Gaudens, *American Artist*, 213.

1923 that he had included 21 per cent "wild" in the British and French sections, "higher than our committee wants. We will try to soften it somewhat ??"[25]

A key issue was, of course, what was his starting point, from whom did he obtain his advice? Saint-Gaudens gathered recommendations from artists and curators in the United States, as well as well-established (usually academic) artists in Europe. In addition, however, he planned his trip to attend the large regular European exhibitions such as the Salon d'Automne in Paris, the Venice Biennale (most comparable to the Pittsburgh exhibition), and the Royal Academy exhibition in London.

Perhaps his most pivotal act and one that would determine the conservative bias of the International exhibition throughout his tenure at the Carnegie Institute, was the appointment of Guillaume Lerolle, an academic painter, as the "European Representative" starting in 1923. He would continue with Saint-Gaudens to the end, in 1950. Lerolle was apparently an excellent diplomat, much needed when Saint-Gaudens took the reins, but he was also firmly entrenched in the conservative side of the French art world and detested modernism. Fortunately Saint-Gaudens' philosophy of presenting all aspects of the art world led to the inclusion of artists such as Picasso and Matisse that balanced Lerolle's position.

The situation in Germany was exactly the reverse. Whereas in France, Saint-Gaudens insisted on including modernists, in Germany, he had to be convinced to include German Expressionism by his representative, Charlotte Weidler. Weidler was an accomplished and established art critic; in this she was unique among his European advisers.[26] She immediately realized how conservative Saint-Gaudens was, but did succeed in persuading him to include several German Expressionists in 1925, the first year that the director visited Germany and created a German section. Saint-Gaudens' response was characteristically diplomatic.

---

25     Saint-Gaudens to Balken, November 13, 1923.

26     Garnett McCoy, ed, "Letters from Germany," *Archives of American Art Journal* 25, nos 1 and 2(1985) 3-4, 13-26.

Schmidt-Rottluff was included as an advanced artist, but with a painting of a woman combing her hair.[27]

In England Saint-Gaudens seems to have come closest to his ideal of representing a wide spectrum of work. Organized by Arnold Palmer, the English section contained a cross section of contemporary art, ranging from the work of the Royal Academician William Orpen, to the eccentric but now acceptable Augustus John, and the cubist-influenced Duncan Grant and Vanessa Bell. It was William Nicholson, Ben Nicholson's father who was the juror, along with Laura Knight, a well-respected painter who was not yet permitted to join the Royal Academy because she was a woman.

Saint-Gaudens first travelled to Spain in 1923. Margaret Palmer, a well-heeled American ex-patriot who moved in embassy circles, had been the Carnegie's representative there for a year. She encouraged the selection of artists best known among the social elite, such as Ignacio Zuloaga and Hermenegildo Anglada Camarasa, both of whom proved difficult people.[28] The preeminent Spanish-born modernists of Spain, Picasso and Miro, had already moved to Paris. Picasso showed primarily with the French section. Intriguingly artists in Spain themselves recommended that the International include José Guttierez Solana. While Solana was not receiving the approbation of the embassy set, he made extraordinary and haunting works that appeared in several exhibitions at the Carnegie Institute. He had a one-person exhibition in 1936, the year that the Civil War broke out.

Saint-Gaudens also went to Italy,[29] Austria, and as early as 1923, Czechoslavakia, created only in 1918. In 1925 he added Poland, also newly independent, Germany, fraught with complexity because of German hostility from the war, Sweden and Holland. In 1926 Hungary

---

27    Penny Beale, "Obstacles and Advocates, Factors Influencing the Introduction of Modern Art from Germany to New York City, 1912-33: Major Promoters and Exhibitions," Ph.D. diss Cornell University, 1990. See Chapter 3, "The Carnegie versus Weimar's Liberal Attitudes: German-American Art Politics, 1924-1928."

28    Garnett McCoy, ed, "Letters from Spain," *Archives of American Art Journal* 26 nos 2 and 3 (1986): 2-20.

29    The agent in Italy from 1922 to 1950 was Ilario Neri, first identified as "Secretary of the Cerclo Artistico" (Homer Saint-Gaudens to Balken, December 12, 1922) Saint-Gaudens held him in high regard. For reasons of space his role is not detailed in this essay.

and Rumania were included. Predictably, given the upper-class bias of the Carnegie Institute, the radical Soviet Union was represented by Russian émigrés in Paris except in the early 1930s when Lerolle briefly braved the USSR (about which more below).

The percentage of American works relative to the total number of works in the exhibition began decreasing. In 1925 the exhibition opened for the first time in the fall, mainly to avoid logistical conflicts with major spring exhibitions in Europe.

By 1925 Saint-Gaudens letters from abroad began to be filled with characterizations of the different cultures, a factor that he saw as vital to appreciating their art. In this respect, Saint-Gaudens lack of art training was again an advantage, because he saw the art in a cultural context. This was an unusual perspective to take at a time when the dominant emphasis in art criticism was formalism or intuition. He often characterized cultures in a way that revealed his down-to earth method of analysis. For instance, he commented on the Italians that they had "a disregard for death and suffering all mixed in an extraordinary mixture that makes you think of their food—it's vital—and you admire it— even the vitality of death. It's so different from our endless tepid evasion of the uncomfortable and the unfortunate."[30]

Saint-Gaudens wrote that he preferred the French to the English because in France he could eat in a cafe in Montmartre "where everyone is talking too much in order to choke off the blows of thought. ..."[31] He wrote amusingly from England, " I have seen the soul of England. It sat under the umbrellas round a bowl of beautifully mown grass sprinkled with crimson and gold uniforms so well turned out you know."[32]

He contrasted the Spanish and Italian approaches to religion:

The Italian churches are not as inspiring as Spanish ones. You feel that now they are mortuary enclosures used to fleece Cook tourists—successfully! You don't get the feeling of their being used, of a permeating faith in a gorgeous, agonizing soul

---

30    Saint-Gaudens to Balken, December 10, 1932.

31    Saint-Gaudens to Balken, June 5, 1925.

32    Saint-Gaudens to Balken, May 22, 1925.

stirring legend, such as you have in Spain, that really inspires my agnostic spirit.[33]

The following year though he was more inspired in Italy.

It was never like this at the First Presbyterian Church of Winsor, Vermont. … It had none of the aridity. Obviously there were styles of faith and somewhere I felt in a stumbling way that there must be a parallel between that and styles in art.[34]

Only rarely, as in a 1925 comment about Constantin Brancusi, does Saint-Gaudens analyze an artist's work. He described one of the artist's sculptures as an "egg shaped as would be the egg if the hen had lived on the seeds of violets, and yet, who, by tender care, had grown to the size of an ostrich."[35]

By the fourth exhibition in 1925 Saint-Gaudens had what he later referred to as a "well-oiled machine" already in place; he had selected permanent agents in England, France, Spain, Italy and Germany. He added what he called minor agents in other countries who selected smaller groups of works. The agents all overseen by Lerolle, organized Saint-Gaudens' travels, the local juries, the shipping of all works through designated central agents, the invitation of prize juries to come to the United States, and all last minute questions as to which works to send. In 1923 the Carnegie began to hang the galleries by countries. The number of works from each country, the political balance of the work (radical to conservative), the political balance of the jurors who would come to the United States to give awards, the personality of the jurors, the transportation of the jurors to Pittsburgh, the official connections that needed to be cultivated to get the works out of the country, all were on-going topics of intense discussion in the voluminous correspondence that the Carnegie agents carried on with each other and with the Museum in Pittsburgh. In addition to all of these political issues, there were logistical questions about shipping to and from the United States, questions of availability of particular works and finally, the obvious need to keep all the artists happy.

---

33    Saint-Gaudens to Balken, May 4, 1925.

34    Saint-Gaudens to Balken, April 10, 1926.

35    Saint-Gaudens to Balken, June 5, 1925.

The procedures that Saint-Gaudens put in place lasted until 1939 and then, after World War II, were re-activated once, in 1950. The calendar was set in a yearly rhythm: advisory groups recommended artists in the winter, Saint-Gaudens travelled in the early spring often with his agents to visit studios, the works were shipped in July, and the jurors (usually two from Europe) arrived in late August to award prizes. The show opened in October. In November the cycle immediately began again, with the schedule for Saint-Gaudens tour set in December. While this schedule was established in the 1920s, the difficulties created by political upheaval in Europe often altered the procedure in the 1930s. Moreover, beneath the surface of this structure roiled a day-to-day chaos and complexity that Homer Saint-Gaudens chronicled in his many letters back to the Carnegie Museum. He sometimes wrote letters up to ten pages long as often as half-a dozen times in one day. The lynchpins of the operation were his agents. At one point he declared "You know we have an extraordinary set of persons working for us. I have not the faintest notion where we could find their like again."[36]

Along with this organization, Saint-Gaudens orchestrated and courted the press, the public, the artists, and the Museum board. He redesigned and enlarged the size of the innocuous catalog, putting a more contemporary image by Rockwell Kent on the cover, and expanding it with essays and many more photographs. In 1924 he ambitiously commissioned essays from eleven critics including writers from Poland, Czechoslovakia, Belgium, Holland, Spain, and Sweden.[37] He also began to send the International segment of the exhibition to other American cities (nine cities in 1924) and to send press clippings and catalogues back to the participating artists in Europe. The local support staff in Pittsburgh, particularly John O'Connor, orchestrated the local and national press as well as the American section of the exhibition.[38] He also arranged a lecture series by visiting critics included his old friend, the arch conservative critic Royal Cortissoz, and the moderate Forbes

---

36    Saint-Gaudens to John O'Connor, April 9, 1937.

37    He produced a catalog of comparable scope for only one other International in 1927.

38    The American section was a major part of the exhibition every year, but for reasons of space it is not discussed in this essay.

Watson, who supported modernism. The press and the invited lecturers created dramatic arguments about the exhibition.[39]

His early experience as a journalist undoubtedly helped him in his dealings with the press. In 1924 the New York newspapers already began to increase their coverage of the International. That year Homer Saint-Gaudens appeared on the cover of *Time* Magazine.[40] Each year he created a news item—a change in the format of the exhibition or a highlighted event, for example the arrival of celebrity jurors such as Matisse in 1930—that the press could publicize. In addition, his curatorial proclivity to present a broad sampling routinely sparked controversy among the critics. Complaints were frequent and praise was rare.[41]

Saint-Gaudens was also adept at using the press in his effort to adapt to the volatile realities of Europe in the 1920s. Rather than avoiding powerful political forces that affected his endeavor, he dealt with them subtly and diplomatically. Indeed, he needed to be on good terms with whoever ruled a given country in order to continue exporting works from the country. One such ruler was Benito Mussolini. In the first years of the fascist dictator's reign, Saint-Gaudens felt that Mussolini's leadership had stimulated the production of contemporary art in Italy. "Art in Italy," he stated, "is passing through a new Renaissance under the inspiration that Mussolini has given to the whole national life."[42]

In 1927 Saint-Gaudens was granted an interview with Il Duce, after which the curator issued a widely published press release in which he quoted Mussolini as supporting the policy of including various styles and schools in the International. According to Saint-Gaudens, Mussolini asserted:

39   "Editor Defends Prize Pictures, Critic Assailed," *Pittsburgh Press,* October 31, 1930. See also "Thirty Fifth Annual Report of the Department of Fine Arts" (Pittsburgh: Carnegie Institute, 1931).

40   *Time* 3, no 19 (May 12, 1914) cover and p. 13.

41   For example, "Cortissoz Assails 'Stupid Jury," *Pittsburgh Press,* October 18, 1930 and "Editor Defends Prize Pictures, Critic Assailed, *Pittsburgh Press,* October 31, 1930.

42   "St. Gaudens (sic) Is Back after Tour abroad," *Pittsburgh Press,* October 31, 1930.

All these men that you have chosen are important, each in his own way. Art is one thing for one man, another thing for another. Nowadays everyone fights and misunderstands, but there is no harm in that, providing art is genuine and stirs someone's emotions. Art is just as important as it ever was. It is always basically essential because the fruit of our imaginations is the only thing worthwhile in life.[43]

Saint-Gaudens' ability to generate and effectively disseminate such publicity evidently had an effect. The same year as the Mussolini interview he was able to report that the European leaders were all "taking an extraordinary interest in the coming international."[44]

## Art Meets Politics

In the 1930 International Saint-Gaudens for the first time included works from the Soviet Union. Guillaume Lerolle went to Moscow to choose the works. He first attended large museum exhibitions to determine which artists he liked, then visited them in their studios. The situation was in flux as Stalin was increasingly assuming control. Lerolle reported to Saint-Gaudens of several groups "which I told you about don't exist anymore." Not surprisingly, Lerolle, the bourgeois academic, was utterly bewildered by what was designated as revolutionary in Soviet Russia: "a cashier at his desk is not revolutionary, but a mechanic hammering on a piece of steel is revolutionary. A man playing golf is anti-revolutionary, but a man playing football is revolutionary."[45] He nonetheless braved his confusions and the bureaucratic obstacles of the Soviet State to come up with a small group of works.

In 1931, in the depths of the Depression, the Carnegie International hit a peak of attendance, sales, and publicity. That peak can be largely attributed to the controversy stirred when the First Prize went to

---

43    Quoted in *Magazine of the Art World, Chicago Evening Post*, August 30, 1927. Mussolini gave a second interview in 1931. See Saint-Gaudens to O'Connor, March 23, 1931.

44    *Pittsburgh Post-Gazette*, September 3, 1927.

45    Guillaume Lerolle to Saint-Gaudens, March 26, 1930.

a little-known American artist, Franklin Watkins. His work provocatively titled, *Suicide in Costume*, depicted a dead clown, symbolizing, as Watkins said, the world-wide Depression.[46] Saint-Gaudens many years later, in writing a history of American art, celebrated the controversy saying (rather melodramatically and self-servingly) that the Carnegie Institute was "the laboratory wherein was touched off the fuse that exploded the charge that within the last two decades blew up the illusions of self-contented ignorance."[47]

Despite the success of the 1931 exhibition, Saint-Gaudens was already keenly feeling the pressure of international economic conditions. He began trying to get the European governments to contribute to the costs, or to hire out his team to other museums, with little success. The 1932 exhibition was cancelled for financial reasons. In that year the College Art Association attempted to mount its own International, but the effort was disastrously disorganized.[48] The College Art Association experience underlined Saint-Gaudens' superb organization.

The necessity of working with European governments and receiving their support was to be the major source of tension for Homer Saint-Gaudens during his second decade as director of the International. As the rule of fascism tightened in Italy, Hitler took control of Germany, and the Civil War erupted in Spain, it was increasingly difficult for Saint-Gaudens to achieve his ends through good public relations and personal diplomacy.

---

46     "It's Ugly, But Is It Art," *Pittsburgh Press*, October 17, 1931. Watkins was quoted as saying that the "clown in costume is our civilization."

47     *American Artist* 311. A second bombshell was Peter Blume's *South of Scranton* awarded First Prize in 1934, the year Alfred Barr Jr, founding director of the Museum of Modern art, sat on the jury. Barr and Blume were friends.

48     See "Carnegie Again," *The Art Digest*, vol 8, n.11 (March 1, 1933),5. Entitled *International – 1933*, the exhibition was apparently seen as competing with Carnegie Institute's monopoly in this area. Saint-Gaudens wrote the next year of the "remains of the College Art Association show. ... The pictures that the German artists sent have not been returned, nor have the artists' letters been answered." Saint-Gaudens to O'Connor, April 24, 1934.

In 1933, the year Hitler came to power, Saint-Gaudens had to negotiate with the Nazis to protect Charlotte Weidler from harassment.[49] In that year, when the new government's policy on the arts was still in flux with respect to German Expressionism, he included several avowed Nazi artists in the International and was able to show works by Jewish artists as well. His letters to the Museum expressed shock and disgust with Germany which he saw as being in "just as bad shape as it can possibly be."[50]

In 1934 Saint-Gaudens again was able to see his principles honored. He agreed to Weidler's plan to include Nazi artists in order "to placate the powers that be," despite the fact that he found these artists' work unacceptable. But once more he insisted on including work by Jewish artists, too. "If they stop the German Section on that point," he stated, "why there it stops."[51] German nationalist pride paired with the prestige of the exhibition led the government to accede to Saint-Gaudens demand for the last time.

In 1935 economic constraints kept Saint-Gaudens from travelling in Europe. The exhibition was arranged entirely through correspondence with his agents. Mexican artists were shown by arrangement with the United States Embassy in Mexico City as well as artists from Argentina, Brazil, Chile, and Canada.

In 1936 Homer again set out to brave the difficult conditions in Europe. His letters from abroad during the next three years document the march of the Nazism across the continent. In 1936 he reduced the European representation to only eight countries, but the first prize went to Jewish artist, Leon Kroll, perhaps in explicit refutation of Hitler's policies. The Third Reich responded by terming the International a "Jewish propaganda show."[52] In 1937 the Nazis prevailed; thirty government

---

49    Samuel Harden Church's vehemently anti-Nazi articles "Hitler and the German people," *Carnegie Magazine* 7 (April 1933), 28,29, "Are the German People Culpable?" *Carnegie Magazine* 12 (November 1938) 189-90 created problems for Weidler. Her files were ransacked and her room repeatedly searched. Church was president of Carnegie Institute and editor of *Carnegie Magazine*.

50    Saint-Gaudens to O'Connor, March 19, 1933.

51    Saint-Gaudens to O'Connor, April 24, 1934.

52    Saint-Gaudens to O'Connor, April 13, 1937.

sanctioned pictures were shown. However, Saint-Gaudens also featured work by officially unacceptable artists like Otto Dix and Oscar Kokoschka, and diplomatically dismissed the majority of works from Germany by stating that "the Nazi regime is pushing [the German painters] more and more into what might be called a heroic style."[53]

The following year, Weidler took Saint-Gaudens to the "Degenerate Art Exhibition" in Berlin. The German government had mounted this large-scale show in order to cast its official ridicule on modernism, and by extension, Jewish artists. An exhibition of "approved" German art was on view at the same time. The former show proved far more popular, and was met with long lines and crowds for the length of its run. Saint-Gaudens attended the "Degenerate" exhibition mainly because there was virtually nothing else to see. Even the German academy had closed down. Of the "Exhibition of Forbidden Art" as it was also known, he wrote:

> I see no reason for taking the exponents of these various expressions of colour and sound by the scruff of the neck and throwing them into a ditch, especially when the painting or music that replaces their efforts isn't only utterly dreadful of its sort, but lacks the backing of any aesthetically intelligent social order. The only way art can advance is to fight out the situation on its own. Art is certainly not going to develop in any kind of prison.[54]

Saint-Gaudens' belief that art expressed the society in which it was embedded meant that, in his mind, the Nazi's official art was automatically invalidated.

That same year Saint-Gaudens visited Austria shortly after the Anschluss, and commented on its effects on the country:

> From the moment we stepped off the train we were surrounded by Nazi flags and German troops; ... The Ring was full of parades, soldiers, brown shirts, school boys, labour

---

53    *Pittsburgh Post-Gazette,* April 22, 1937, See also "Saint-Gaudens says Nazi Painters are Showing Romantic Touch," *Pittsburgh Post-Gazette,* April 21, 1937.

54    Saint-Gaudens to O'Connor, April 23, 1938.

battalions ... Heels clicked, medals flashed, hands made Nazi salutes.[55]

Realizing that he could not have a separate Austrian section, he took the Austrian quota and divided it between Italy and Germany. Saint-Gaudens looked at the two dictators bordering Austria and carefully added the same number to each in order to keep the numbers even and the nationalist pride in balance. In his annual report he pointedly mentioned having included the work of "what had been Austria" in the exhibition.[56]

Despite the bleak German situation, Saint-Gaudens strove to stay positive:

> in these difficult times German art needs every ounce of encouragement we can give it. We are working not only for the present exhibition, but for artists and art lovers as a whole. That is why in these dark days we should plug along to keep alive an understanding of and a discussion of visual aesthetics.[57]

In December 1939 having worked heroically to represent the International in Germany, Charlotte Weidler left for the United States and Saint-Gaudens helped her to get there.[58] After receiving a warm reception in Pittsburgh, she went on to settle in New York where she continued her efforts to help artists in Germany.

In Spain Margaret Palmer confronted equally challenging problems although in different political circumstances. During the early 1930s as the king was toppled in Spain and the Republic began to emerge as a coalition of Socialists, Communists, and Democrats, both Saint-Gaudens and Palmer regretted the passing of the familiar old order within which they had worked. Yet, their need to rely on the given power structure was reflected by the fact that they soon adjusted to the new Republican government. Indeed, Palmer became an avid

---

55    Saint-Gaudens to O'Connor, April 9, 1938.

56    *Forty-Second Annual Report of Department of Fine Arts,* (Pittsburgh:Carnegie Institute, 1939),11.

57    Saint-Gaudens to O'Connor, April 23, 1938.

58    Charlotte Wiedler to Saint-Gaudens, October 30, 1936, and November 16, 1936.

partisan. She continued assembling work for the International, even in the midst of the Civil War which broke out in July 1936. Through miraculous luck, Palmer managed to get the paintings she had chosen out of Spain.[59]

In 1937 Palmer returned to Spain from Paris to arrange the paintings for the next International. In Madrid she stayed at the American Embassy where she supervised the loading of the canvases for the Spanish section. Dramatically, she discovered that the same truck was secretly also carrying the Prado Museum's most valuable treasures, to be stored out of harm's way. As the truck bearing the precious cargo departed Madrid in the dark of the night, a driver declared:

> Never in your lives have you carried so rich a burden as tonight—you have with you no less that Don Francisco Goya, the honor and dignity of Spain.[60]

Palmer also continued in valiant service to the Carnegie Institute for the duration of the Civil War, although she was forced to base her work from Paris.

By the end of the decade, the military and political chaos into which Europe had fallen had wreaked havoc with Saint-Gaudens' usual practice of presenting the International in neatly defined national sections. So many artists were now émigrés that he agreed to set up a section in the 1939 exhibition devoted to their work as a whole. The section included twenty-six artists from as many countries, including Germany, the Soviet Union, Italy, Poland, Czechoslovakia and the Netherlands. That same year most of the awards went to American artists, with the First Prize going to Alexander Brook, for a somber depiction of a desolate share cropping scene called *Georgia Jungle*. The International could no longer celebrate an international art scene. Brook's somber painting seemed to capture the mood of the day.

The exhibition as it appeared in Pittsburgh, only subtly reflected the on-going drama behind-the-scenes. Continuity, in fact, became increasingly important as a statement of opposition to the political repression of artists in Europe. While during the 1920s Saint-Gaudens

---

59     McCoy "Letters from Spain," 6 – 14.

60     Ibid.

had worked to strike a balance among styles, in the late 1930s he was increasingly forced to figure political and even racial factors into his equation. The complexity of this problem is pointed up in a letter Margaret Palmer wrote to Saint-Gaudens in 1937:

> You spoke of not showing political partiality for one group of painters above another. The Spanish painters are not divided into well-defined groups, such as Nazis and Jews, or as Russian proletariat and expatriated aristocrat. This is not a class war, pure and simple, as in Russia, or a racial antagonism as in Germany. I know Spaniards of wealth ... who are "red"; I know servants who are "white". If we send the same painters as have always gone to Pittsburgh, and are to be expected, I cannot see why the question of politics should come up. For the most part, they have kept out of politics, and they would be the last to wish to be labeled as belonging to any political party. With but one or two exceptions, I do not myself know their political views, though I am quite sure that not many are fascists, and not many are communists. I think most of them would like to live in a mildly liberal Republic, and to be allowed to paint.[61]

The exhibitions perhaps said more than was intended. The 1930s shows cumulatively mirrored the anguish experienced by the artists who were included—a quality that only rarely appears in the prizes. This anguish particularly pervades the works from Italy, Spain, and Germany, irrespective of their stylistic, political, or social position. Whether Saint-Gaudens sensed this quality himself is difficult to determine, but its presence is unmistakable.

## The 1940s

In 1940 with World War II raging and cutting off the possibility of organizing true Internationals, Saint-Gaudens bowed to the inevitable and mounted a survey of American art. As ambitious as the Internationals, the American Art survey proved much more difficult to assemble

---

61    Margaret Palmer to Saint-Gaudens, January 21, 1937.

without his hard working agents doing all the preliminary work for him. The survey was predictable. A contemporary section ranged from the elderly artists that Saint-Gaudens had first known as a child such as George de Forest Bush to the well-established modernists Charles Sheeler and Georgia O'Keeffe. For the accompanying catalogue, Saint-Gaudens wrote a lengthy autobiographical introduction, which developed into a book on the history of American art laced with personal anecdotes.[62]

From January 1941 until late 1945 Saint-Gaudens was in the Army as Chief of the Camouflage Section in Europe. The fortunes of his faithful European agents varied. During World War II and its aftermath, Saint-Gaudens followed up on their loyalty by assistance both financial and logistical. At the outset of World War II, he continued their salaries even when the show had to be cancelled. Guillaume Lerolle wrote to Saint-Gaudens that he used his pay to buy food to give to refugees.[63] Weidler, as noted, emigrated to the United States in 1939, the same year Margaret Palmer returned home to America. Following the fall of Paris, Guillaume Lerolle was imprisoned briefly then released, but endured the deprivations of occupied France for five years. Ilario Neri, the Italian agent, narrowly escaped being sent to a death camp, and his son spent two years in a concentration camp.[64] The Carnegie Institute stored the paintings from the 1939 International at its own expense throughout the war.

During the director's wartime absence, John O. Connor organized annual exhibitions of Contemporary American Art. But these shows did not have the luster of the International. On his return to the museum in 1945, Saint-Gaudens put together four more American art surveys between 1946 and 1949. He gradually increased the expressionist and even abstract work. He kept hoping to resume the International. In those years he also considered, but never realized, an exhibition of war-related paintings and a show of Augustus Johns' works in American collections. As anti-Communism heated up in the postwar year, it

---

62    Homer Saint-Gaudens Introduction to *Survey of American Painting* (Pittsburgh: Department of Fine Arts, Carnegie Institute, 1940 and Saint-Gaudens, *American Artists.*

63    Guillaume Lerolle to Saint-Gaudens, May 19, 1940.

64    Ilario Neri to Saint-Gaudens, May 31, and August 12, 1945, January 20, 1946.

began to encroach on his American art exhibitions. Accusations from viewers declared that too many of his artists were "red" or "pink." He longed each year to return to Europe.

Finally in 1950 his wish came true. With renewed funding from the Andrew Carnegie Foundation, he put together one more International with his old team. Lerolle almost refused to work for him because of the tiny salary he was offered. Weidler, still in New York, went to Germany for the summer to assist in the preparations, and Palmer, also living in New York, likewise returned to Spain. The new exhibition included a higher than usual proportion of abstract modernist work.

Gordon Bailey Washburn, who became director of the Museum in 1950, accompanied Homer Saint-Gaudens, now director emeritus, as an observer in order to see what sort of organization was in place for the exhibition. Although Washburn would shift its focus toward the Abstract Expressionists, he retained some of the veteran agents, notably Charlotte Weidler for Germany and Ilario Neri in Italy. John O'Connor continued as associate director until 1952. Saint-Gaudens retired in 1950. He was to live only eight more years, dying unexpectedly in 1958 in Miami, Florida.

Although Saint-Gaudens rarely admitted it, he found the Byzantine intricacies of the political shoals of exhibition preparation extremely difficult. His clearest statement of that was shortly after he left the U.S. Army following World War II when he said that he preferred the military to his job at the Carnegie Institute because he always knew where he stood in the Army.[65] On another occasion he said that a battlefield was like a Quaker meeting when compared to the running of an art gallery.[66] He warned his successor, Gordon Washburn: "You may think life has treated you rough, but just wait. You don't even know what trouble is."[67]

The difficulties of the exhibition were, of course, a product of a world vastly different from the turn-of-the-century art colony in which

---

65      Saint-Gaudens to Arnold Palmer, November 16, 1945.

66      Saint-Gaudens, "Other Days, Other Paintings," 268.

67      Saint-Gaudens to Gordon Bailey Washburn, December 28, 1949.

Homer Saint-Gaudens had grown up. In one essay he summarized that world in terms of

> the radio, Boulder Dam, thirty-one million automobiles, the American Scene, Leopold and Loeb, abstract photography, Gertrude Stein, setback skyscrapers, bombing planes, modernism, and this terrific military and social struggle [that] have all been thrown pell mell into the news of the day.[68]

He understood that he lived in an age of accelerated social change, of political upheaval. He saw artistic experiments conducted in response to that change and upheaval that he could not fully explain or justify.

But above all, Saint-Gaudens saw the forum of the Carnegie International exhibition as a means to promote understanding and communication between the United States and Europe. His vision was very much in tune with the purpose of the International as Andrew Carnegie first conceived it. At a time when America was obsessed with isolationism and with nationalism, and when Europe was collapsing into strife, Saint-Gaudens provided a model through art of international cooperation.

---

68     Saint-Gaudens, *American Artist,* 235.

# Franz Kafka, T.S. Eliot and Hans Hofmann: The Formation of Clement Greenberg in the late 1930s *(1989)*

> *Kafka sees life as sealed off and governed by unknowable powers who permit us the liberty only to repeat ourselves until we succumb.*
>
> ~Clement Greenberg (1946)

IN CLEMENT GREENBERG'S UNSETTLING COMMENT on Franz Kafka, he unwittingly described his own career as an art critic. Greenberg established his permanent criteria for significant art during the same months that the armies of Hitler were engulfing Europe. As he witnessed the disintegration of European civilization, he declared that abstract art, conceived in terms of a purified aesthetic appropriate to the medium in which it was made (i.e., in the case of painting, the art must be flat and concerned with surface), and characterized by unity, immediacy, and authority, was the only art which had a lasting value. This aesthetic, and its accompanying negative value judgments of art that was not in this category, remained the cornerstone of his criticism throughout his career.

For almost fifty years, through drastic social, political, and economic changes, and with the mounting opposition of artists, critics and historians, Greenberg continued to reiterate the importance of the autonomous aesthetic experience of abstract art above all others, and to denigrate art that he saw as engaging with lesser issues. His astonishing consistency, paired with a repetitive and assertive dogmatism, created an aura of absolute verity about his proclamations concerning the nature of art. Almost hypnotically, the art world used his premises as a reference point, both positive and negative, for discussions on art and aesthetics in contemporary art up until the 1980s.[1] Yet, in spite of Greenberg's obvious centrality to the mid twentieth-century dialogue on art, much confusion remains as to exactly how to place Greenberg's contribution in the history of twentieth-century art criticism.

To accurately assess Greenberg's contribution, he must be seen in the larger perspective of twentieth-century political and aesthetic history in Europe and America, rather than simply in the limited arena of the post World War II art world.[2] Greenberg wrote the two most seminal essays of his career as the entire fabric of European civilization was threatened by totalitarianism. Also directly affecting Greenberg was the type of art that was sponsored by the totalitarian governments of Hitler and Stalin and the threat such sponsorship posed to the avant-garde artists who opposed it. These apocalyptic confrontations, in both the political and aesthetic sphere, as well as the particular environment in New York, determined the nature of Greenberg's formulations.

In this article I will examine Clement Greenberg's formative years in the late 1930s, when he had his first contacts with art, aesthetics and politics. My purpose in elucidating the political and cultural context of Greenberg's early work will be to explain why and how he chose the particular stance that he did as well as to suggest why he adhered so rigidly to the same position for five decades.

---

1     The bibliography on Clement Greenberg is extensive: Donald Kuspit, *Clement Greenberg, Art Critic*, (Madison, 1979). Cited in this article are *Clement Greenberg, The Collected Essays and Criticism, vol. i. Perceptions and Judgments, 1939-1940*, and *vol. ii. Arrogant Purpose, 1945-1949*, ed. John O'Brian (Chicago, 1986. Page numbers and titles from these anthologies are identified as "reprint." The best recent study is Caroline Jones, *Eyesight Alone: Clement Greenberg's Modernism and the Bureaucratization of the Senses.* Chicago: Chicago University Press, 2006.

2     Fred Orton and Griselda Pollock, "Avant-Gardes and Partisans Reviewed," *Art History*, vol. 4, no. 3 (September 1981): 305-327 examines his career from a political perspective.

# Part I Root Sources

In his early essays, Greenberg drew eclectically and arbitrarily on political ideology, art, art theory, and critical practices, filtered through specific cultural references. The combination of all these aspects led directly to the startling, dogmatic, dialectical argument in his influential essay "Avant-Garde and Kitsch"(1939), as well as to the aesthetic proclaimed in "Towards a Newer Laocoon"(1940). Taken together these two essays contain the core of his thinking. Their principles, generalities, values and language created for Greenberg the bedrock of his later art criticism.[3] They forge an alliance between formalist methodologies and political metaphors that created a new type of dialogue about art after World War II.[4]

Greenberg transformed the general principles of his early essays into a simplified and absolute norm, a norm that initially defined a new generation of artists in the 1940s, but was not flexible enough to respond to the issues raised by later developments in contemporary art. Despite its inadequacies, this norm and the terms and concepts that accompanied it, have been the source of his astonishing influence.[5]

Clement Greenberg was born in 1909 in the Bronx, New York, the oldest son of three brothers. His parents were Lithuanian Jews who

3    Clement Greenberg, "Avant-Garde and Kitsch," *Partisan Review*, vol. 6, no. 5 (Fall 1939), reprint (cited n. 1), vol. I, pp. 5-22, and "Towards a Newer Laocoon," *Partisan Review*, vol. 7, no. 4 (July-August 1940), reprint (cited n. 1), vol. I, pp. 23-38.

4    For a general survey of some aspects of the thirties' alliances of art and politics see Serge Guilbaut, *How New York Stole the Idea of Modem Art* (Chicago, 1983), chap. 1. Susan Noyes Platt, *Art and Politics in the 1930s, Modernism, Marxism, Americanism* (Midmarch Arts Press, 1999) Chap 13 "Modernism and Marxism: Clement Greenberg and the *Partisan Review*," looks in detail at Greenberg's relationship to the writers of the *Partisan Review*.

5    The concept of what constitutes an avant-garde has been the focus of major reconsideration in theoretical studies. A reference to Greenberg's early essays is usually included. See for example Renato Poggioli, *The Theory of the Avant-Garde* (Cambridge, 1968), pp. 80-81; Peter Burger, *Theory of the Avant-Garde* (Minneapolis, 1984) and Andreas Huyssen, *After the Great Divide, Modernism, Mass Culture, Postmodernism* (Bloomington, 1986). Huyssen makes a parallel between Greenberg and the theory of Theodor Adorno, p. 9.

had come to the United States separately as children from Russia and Poland. While they were not orthodox in their religious practices, they did speak Yiddish at home. The family moved from the Bronx to Norfolk, Virginia in 1914, then to Brooklyn in 1920. Greenberg attended Syracuse University from 1926 to 1930, majoring in foreign languages. After college Greenberg worked sporadically for his father at variously successful business ventures in dry goods manufacturing. In 1934-1935 he married and had a son. At that time Greenberg obtained a few jobs as a translator for Knight Publications,[6] but from 1936 until 1942 he primarily supported himself by a job in the federal government with the Appraiser's Division of the United States Customs Division, the Department of Wines and Liquors, an intriguing parallel to his developing stance as an appraiser of culture. Unlike many other second generation Jews in the 1930s, he did not work for the Works Progress Administration, but rather obtained a more traditional and economically secure employment. His background places him between the working class roots of some Jewish intellectuals of this era and the Ivy League credentials of others.[7]

Greenberg's Jewish heritage shaped his responses to both art and politics. He emphasized the importance of that heritage by including an essay on Kafka, "The Jewishness of Kafka," in his *Art and Culture* collection of 1961, the book which, for many years, was the only collection of his published writings.[8] In the Kafka essay

---

6    Greenberg's first translation was of the report by the World Committee for the Victims of German Fascism, *The Brown Network, The Activities of the Nazis in Foreign Countries* (New York, 1936). The book focused on political infiltration and activities such as the kidnapping of Berthold Jacob. Anti-semitism was discussed only occasionally. His second translation, in collaboration with Emma Ashton and Jay Chatter, was Manfred Schneider, *Goya: A Portrait of the Artist as a Man* (New York, 1936). The first book introduced Greenberg to urgent contemporary political issues, the second to art history.

7    Alfred Kazin, *Starting Out in the Thirties* (Boston, 1962, 1965) exemplifies the working class branch. The Ivy League background of writers such as Lionel Trilling and Sidney Hook is discussed in Alan M. Wald, *The New York Intellectuals* (Chapel Hill, 1987), pp. 33-47 and pp. 50-52 and Terry A. Cooney, *The Rise of the New York Intellectuals Partisan Review and Its Circle* (Madison, 1986) pp. 100, 101.

8    Clement Greenberg, *Art and Culture* (Boston, 1961), pp. 266-273. The book has a subtle art historical order in terms of the

and elsewhere, Greenberg provides a fascinating perspective on his own work.[9] One of Greenberg's early reviews suggested that the tendency to conceptualize, to think abstractly, was a mode of self-protection for the Jew from the excruciating realities of the ghetto.[10] This inclination toward abstraction and the channeling of emotion into a logical framework was a central characteristic of Greenberg's own writings.

In the two articles that Greenberg devoted specifically to Kafka, he transposed those issues into the character and content of the writing and compared them to the Orthodox Jewish experience:

> Kafka's fiction is composed of parables and cases and deals with the paradigm, the patterns or habits of individual existence, not its originality or unicity (sic).

> Kafka's static, treadmill … world bears many resemblances to the one presented in the Halacha, the legal part of the

---

artists discussed, indicating Greenberg's leanings at that time. On Greenberg's liaison with art historians in his later career see the insightful articles by Barbara Reise, "Greenberg and the group: a retrospective view," *Studio International*, vol. 175, no. 900 (May, 1968), pp. 254-257 and vol. 175, no. 901 (June, 19681, pp. 314-315. Kuspit (cited n. 1), pp. 21-22, makes the important point that Greenberg heavily revised his essays when they were published in *Art and Culture* into an "oracular" style. This type of revision is strongly in evidence in the case of the Kafka essay, which first appeared as "The Jewishness of Franz Kafka: Some Sources of His Particular Vision," *Commentary*, vol. 19 (April, 1955), pp. 320-324. At that time it generated some discussion; see F.R. Leavis, "How Good is Kafka," *Commentary*, vol. 19 (June, 1955), pp. 595-596 and Greenberg's reply, ibid., pp. 595-596; F.R. Leavis;"A Critical Exchange': *Commentary*, vol. 19 (August, 1955, pp. 178-179. Leavis complained about Greenberg's unfounded assertions as well as his separation of art and life which "would lead to a doctrine of aestheticism and Pure Art Value. …(which) no one seriously interested in literature has ever readily held." Curiously, unlike the other revisions, Greenberg does not acknowledge these in *Art and Culture.*

9     He stated "I believe that a quality of Jewishness is present in every word I write." "Under Forty: A Symposium on American Literature and the Younger Generation of American Jews." *Contemporary Jewish Record*, vol. vii, no. 1 (February 1944, reprint (cited n. 1), vol. 1, p. 177.

10    "The Jewish Dickens: review of The *World of Shalom Aleichem* by Maurice Samuel," *The Nation*, 16 October 1943, reprint (cited n. 1), vol. 1, pp. 156-157.

post-Biblical Jewish religious tradition ... the Law ... But whereas Halacha arrests and systemizes life into case history for the sake of relating every jot and tittle of it to God, ... Kafka with his Westernized sensibility, finds the world static ... and experiences, not only alienation, but also its lack of drama, resolution, and history, as a nightmare paralyzing us in the face of a doom that wells up out of its very orderliness.[11]

Greenberg's criticism bears a strange resemblance to this description. From the perspective of the Jewish tradition of the Halacha or Law, his rigid aesthetic stance, based on the reiteration of a few concrete aspects of an artwork, assume the character of a new Halacha. Greenberg transposed, rigid and by then historical, Jewish law into the fabric of his thinking and writing. He can be seen as the prophet of a new type of Messianic event. Such an absolute faith shielded him from that sense of meaninglessness and impending doom that was so prevalent in the 1940s and so prominent in Kafka.

Greenberg returned to the theme of the Halacha in the 1955 article on Kafka that he included in *Art and Culture*. There he stated the role it played in Jewish secular culture, with its "petty concerns, its parochial absorption in the here and now and its conformism. Routine, prudence, sobriety are enjoined for their own sake, as ends in themselves and for the sake purely of security. ... The emancipated Jew longs for history more deeply and at the same time more immediately than the Orthodox Jew."

The concern for the "Halachic sensibility" in the work of Kafka, according to Greenberg, made it "difficult to charge their matter with dramatic movement." Likewise, Greenberg was unable to significantly modify or alter his original ideas, to display any movement or development in his own thinking. Last, Greenberg suggested that Kafka "wanted more than anything else to be an artist, a writer of fiction, not of oracles." This too can apply to Greenberg, who was a writer of oracles.[12] The emancipated Greenberg himself clearly deeply longed for his own history.

---

11    "Introduction to 'The Great Wall of China' by Franz Kafka," *Commentary*, vol. 2, (October, 1946), reprint (cited n. 1), vol.2, pp. 101-102.

12    *Art and Culture*, [cited n. 8), p. 269.

# Part II Aesthetic Opportunism

Greenberg selected a purified, abstract art as the law of his aesthetic. That choice related directly to the artists he first came in contact with just before World War II when he began to involve himself in the art world. In 1938-1939 he attended three lectures by Hans Hofmann and first met the group of writers centered around the *Partisan Review.*[13] These two events were fundamental to the development of his criticism and his aesthetic predilections.

At the time that Greenberg attended the Hofmann lectures (half of the complete series of six lectures Hofmann gave that winter), he had only a cursory knowledge of art and even less of modem art. Except for a single art class in high school at the Art Student's League, Greenberg had been entirely immersed in the study of literature and language.[14] Thus in approaching the Hofmann lectures, he was almost entirely unfamiliar with the principles that Hofmann presented. Greenberg has frequently acknowledged that these lectures were fundamental to his aesthetic ideas.[15] They apparently enabled Greenberg to make a rapid leap from a traditional view of art to a conception of the abstract principles governing modern art. Certainly Greenberg's inclination to think in terms of abstract ideas as well as his need for a reference point in understanding art increased the impact of Hofmann's ideas.

Hofmann's own interpretation of modernism came out of Paris and Germany before World War I. He began teaching American students in

---

13 The literature on the *Partisan Review* is extensive. See for example, James B. Gilbert, *Writers and Partisans: A History of Literary Radicalism in America* (London, 1968, chap. 4-8 and Cooney (cited n. 7), 1986.

14 Clement Greenberg to Susan Platt, June 1, 1984, San Francisco. In this conversation, Greenberg stated that he had read Sheldon Cheney's book on modern art [probably *The Story of Modern Art*, New York, 1941, see essay in this collection] around this time, also reinforcing the idea that he was not at all versed in modern art. See "The Late Thirties in New York," *Art and Culture* (cited n. 8), p. 230 where he states he knew little about modern art then.

15 Clement Greenberg, "Avant-Garde and Kitsch," reprint(cited n, 1), vol. 1, p. 9, note; "Review of an Exhibition of Hans Hofmann...." reprint (cited n. 1), vol.2, p. 18; "The Late Thirties in New York," (cited, n. 8), p. 230. See also "Hans Hofmann," ibid., pp. 189.

Germany in 1915. Coming to America with their support in 1930, he settled in New York the following year. He thus had little contact with the continuing European avant-garde of the 1920s and 1930s. After 1936 and particularly the large exhibition of "Cubism and Abstract Art" at the Museum of Modern Art, his lectures contained more examples from recent art, particularly Matisse, Miro and Mondrian. But he continued to discuss space in a way that exactly corresponded to the type of low relief/deep space, flat surface tension apparent in the work of Cézanne and the early Cubism of Braque and Picasso.

In the 1938-1939 lecture series Hofmann spoke of the dynamic of the picture plane. After almost twenty years of teaching American art students, he had an acute awareness of their particular academic perspective; all of his teaching was aimed at breaking through that limited understanding. He contrasted the concept of the plane to the traditional one-point perspective of earlier art. He spoke of the importance of the given reality of the surface on which the artist worked and the role of the medium. These two issues, planar surface, which Greenberg later simplified to flatness, and the important role of medium and surface, became the cornerstone of Greenberg's aesthetics.

But there is a crucial difference between Hofmann and Greenberg. Hofmann spoke of surface and flatness in terms of space. He demonstrated planar relationships (the famous "push and pull"). The surface was given, but the artist created, by means of formal shapes, tension in it. This planar tension effected a sense of depth, it was a central issue in his teaching. Greenberg heard the lecture in which Hofmann stated:

> ... the real problem in planes creation is just this—to destroy this two dimensionality and recreate with three dimensionality this two dimensionality. In other words, there is a fundamental difference between flatness and flatness.

> There can be a flatness which is meaningless and there can be a flatness that is a highest experience of life—from infinite depth and up to the surface—restoring ultimately the two dimensionality. This is what plastic creation means. Otherwise it is decoration.

... Naturally we cannot create actual depth—we can only create the illusion of depth as opposed to movement on the surface. Many of the so-called abstract artists today are not clear about this.[16]

Hofmann's entire teaching hinged on this crucial issue: space was "something concrete," not just the surroundings of an image and not just two dimensional surface. Depth was necessary, and it was based on a relationship with the given space. For Greenberg, this subtle idea and distinction would ultimately become simply flatness and the two dimensional surface, a "premise" that Hofmann was carefully avoiding.

Hofmann linked spatial tensions to a conflict or struggle with the medium, a crucial point in lecture 2 of his 1938-1939 series:

Nobody can make a hole in his picture to go into the picture and come out again. No—the depth is here and must be created with the understanding of the medium with which we create. ... Richness, fullness, vitality—these are all things that must be experienced in a direct or indirect way ... in the conflict with the medium with which I struggle. So when an artist works by heart he takes the nature of his medium as the basis for his creation.[17]

The idea of a struggle with the medium would also be fundamental to Greenberg.

Hofmann went on to explain the importance of purity, particularly with respect to color and color relationships. Another constant theme was unity of the picture plane. He accompanied his lectures with diagrams that demonstrated his theories. On the issue of abstraction, Hofmann felt it was not absolutely necessary in 1938-1939, but that abstract ways of thinking about the creation of a work of art were fundamental. (Hofmann himself did not begin to paint completely abstract works until the early 1940s.) Greenberg's focus on abstraction came from other sources initially.

---

16    Transcription by Lenib Manry, "Hans Hofmann Lectures, Winter 1938-1939," Lecture 1, p. 5, Lenita Manry Papers, Microfilm Roll 151, Archives of American Art, Smithsonian Institution.

17    Hofmann (cited n. 16), pp. 4, 6.

The first essay in which Greenberg fully embraced Hofmann's ideas on the importance of unity, purity, and formalism in art was "Towards a Newer Laocoon," which appeared in the *Partisan Review* of July-August 1940. Greenberg combined Hofmann's emphasis on the importance of purity in the use of the elements and medium of art with the idea of purity in terms of content:

> from the point of view of the artist engrossed in the problems of his medium…purism is the terminus of a salutary reaction against the mistakes of painting and sculpture in the past several centuries which were due to such a confusion (of the arts).[18]

In developing the idea of purity, Greenberg also borrowed from a conservative theorist. He cited *A New Laocoon: An Essay on the Confusion of the Arts* (1910) by Irving Babbitt. Babbitt, in turn, relied on the ideas of an eighteenth-century writer, Gotthold Lessing. Babbitt favored formal classicism and opposed Romanticism as impure because of its narrative elements. Romanticism was also a regression for Greenberg. In Greenberg's article, the turning point in the purification of the medium was Courbet, in whose painting "flatness" explicitly emerged. Thus Greenberg arrived at the avant-garde ghetto of purity:

> … the avant-garde arts have in the last fifty years achieved a purity and a radical delimitation of their fields of activity for which there is no previous example in the history of culture. The arts lie safe now, each within its "legitimate" boundaries and free trade has been replaced by autarchy. Purity in art consists in the acceptance, willing acceptance of the limitations of the medium of the specific art. … The arts, then, have been hunted back to their mediums.[19]

The peculiar territorial note to this remark may well have been a subconscious parallel to the European losses of territorial integrity in the spring of 1939. As Greenberg wrote his theory of pure art, Paris was surrendering to the Nazis, the perpetrators of the idea of racial purity.

---

18    "Towards a Newer Laocoon," (cited, n. 1), vol. 1, p. 23, 32.

19    Ibid, p.32.

In "Towards A Newer Laocoon," Greenberg defined purified art in terms of Hofmann's formalist aesthetic, explaining what was specifically happening in purified painting. He elaborated on the denial of perspective space and the importance of the "square" of canvas and its "actual surface." He tackled the Hofmann concepts of planar complexity, but subtly transformed them into a progressive development from a type of struggle between volume and plane into a "further stage" in which the "realistic space cracks and splinters into flat planes which come forward, parallel to the plane surface."

The culmination of this development appeared, according to Greenberg, in the work of the recent "abstract purism" of the Dutch, Germans, English and Americans. These artists were contrasted on the one hand to the "orthodox surrealists" who "turned back to the confusion of literature with painting," and, on the other hand, the "mock surrealists" like Miro, Klee, and Arp, "whose work, despite its apparent intention only contributed to the further deployment of abstract painting pure and simple." Greenberg suggested that these artists intended to be expressive but "so inexorable was the logic of the development that in the end their work constituted but another step towards abstract art." Greenberg added here to his sequence of avant-gardism, purism, and abstraction, a deterministic "imperative."[20]

Greenberg directly reflected, in the specific artists cited above, not simply Hofmann's preferences, but also the environment of the *Partisan Review*, the magazine for which he was writing. George L.K. Morris, an editor and backer of the *Partisan Review*, was their official art critic as well as an abstract artist and leader of the large group known as the American Abstract Artists. Morris's reviews of abstract art in the *Partisan Review* from 1937 to 1943 stand out, amidst the political complexity of the rest of the magazine, as an Olympian statement of an ideal. In addition to an interview with Jean Hélion, reviews of the English abstract artist Ben Nicholson and French artists such as Jean Arp, Hans Hartung and Joan Miro, Morris wrote "On the Mechanics of Abstract Painting" and the "Relations of Painting and Sculpture."[21] Greenberg

---

20      Ibid., pp. 35-38. Greenberg's determinism has already been widely discussed and will not be treated here. See Kuspit (cited n. 1), chap 2.

21      George L.K. Morris, "Modernism, in England," book review of *Circle, Partisan Review*, vol. 4, no. 1 (December 1937), pp. 69-70; "Art Chronicle: Hans Arp," *Partisan Review*, vol. 4, no. 2 (January 1938),

cited this review in one of his own reviews, although the article does not at all correspond to Greenberg's own theory of medium purity.[22] Morris wrote with a sophisticated formal vocabulary; he emphasized the "decisive properties" of the medium and he introduced Greenberg to the abstract artists working from 1939-1943.

Greenberg was not aware in 1940 that Morris based his writing on principles developed by Roger Fry and Clive Bell in the teens and twenties. Nor was he aware of the full scope of twentieth-century art. This lack of perspective led him to cling to Hofmann's emphasis on Cubism as well as Morris's formalist advocacy of abstraction with the ardent belief of a new disciple who had received a revelation. That revelation remained his credo throughout his career.

At one point in "Towards a Newer Laocoon," Greenberg linked the early stages of the avant-garde to "opposition to bourgeois society," an act of "self-preservation … responsible to … only the values of art"[23] Here he was utilizing Leon Trotsky's analysis of the role of art in a revolutionary society. Greenberg simply transformed aesthetic purism into a radical act of social revolution. Under the pressure of the era, Greenberg declared abstraction, inseparable from radical politics, as the last hope for the survival of culture.[24]

---

p. 32-33, "Miro and the Spanish Civil War," *Partisan Review*, vol. 4 no. 3 (February 1938), pp. 32-33; "Interview with Jean Hélion," *Partisan Review*, vol. 4, no. 5 (April 1938), pp. 33-40; "Art Chronicle: Recent Tendencies in Europe," *Partisan Review*, vol. 4, no. 5 (Fall, 1939), pp. 31-33; "On the Mechanics of Abstract Painting," *Partisan Review*," vol. 8. no. 5 (December 1941), pp. 403-417; "Relations of Painting and Sculpture," *Partisan Review*, vol. 10, no. 1 (January-February 1943), pp. 63-71. For a helpful comparison of Morris and Greenberg see Melinda Lorenz, *George LK. Morris, Artist and Critic* (Ann Arbor, 1982), pp. 95-103.

22    Greenberg, "Review of the Exhibition 'American Sculpture of Our Time,'" *The Nation*, January 23, 1943, reprint (cited n. 1), vol. 1, p. 140.

23    Ibid., p. 28.

24    Two poignant examples of the apocalyptic atmosphere of those years and the *Partisan Review's* concern are an article of January-February 1941(immediately following Morris's "Art Chronicle") titled "What Has Become of Them? A Checklist of European Artists, Writers and Musicians," *Partisan Review*, vol. 8, no. 1 (January-February 1941), pp. 59-62. Photographs labelled as "the only photographs ever

# Part III Political Opportunism

The underpinning for this position appears in "Avant-Garde and Kitsch." Its main focus was the linkage of aesthetics and politics. It was the direct result of Greenberg's contact, in 1938-1939, with Dwight Macdonald, an editor at the *Partisan Review*. When Greenberg met Macdonald, his contact with politics, apart from the generally socialistic orientation in which he had grown up, was almost as slight as his contact with visual art.[25] His interests had been intellectual rather than activist. As in the case of formalism, Greenberg engaged with radical politics in the cultural sphere when it was already an acknowledged, serious influence on American intellectuals. In fact, by the late 1930s, the political/cultural nexus had reached a peak of tension and complexity.

The linkage of radical art and radical politics began early in America. It existed already in the teens, in the Greenwich Village activities of Floyd Dell, John Reed, Randolph Bourne, and others.[26] By the time Greenberg joined the influential intellectual group around the *Partisan Review* in late 1938, it had already gone through several stages of Marxism. *Partisan Review* writers included Meyer Schapiro, Edmund Wilson, Mary McCarthy, Sidney Hook, Lionel Trilling, and Harold Rosenberg, as well as Philip Rahv and William Phillips, the original founders, and Dwight Macdonald, Frederick Dupee and George Morris, who helped reorganize the magazine in late 1937. They made a brave anti-Communist stand in late 1937, after the news from Russia of the Moscow purges and the persecution of the intellectuals reached

---

taken of murals by Joan Miro ... According to reports, the walls of the house were knocked out when the Germans recently converted it into a stable. Thus, Miro's only mural work has presumably been destroyed" Miro's photograph appeared in *Partisan Review*, vol. 8, no. 3 (May-June 1941) inside front cover. The photograph was by Suzy Frelingheusen, another member of the Abstract American Artists. Gilbert (cited n. 13), p. 194 also discusses some of the activities of the *Partisan Review* to save the writers and artists.

25    Cooney (cited n. 7), p. 21 treats the role of socialism for the young Jewish intellectual. See also Alfred Kazin, (cited n. 7).

26    Daniel Aaron, *Writers on the Left* (New York, 1961) and Donald Drew Egbert and Stow Persons, *Socialism and American Life*, 2 vols. (Princeton, 1952) offer comprehensive accounts of socialism, communism and Marxism in America. See also Gilbert (cited n. 17).

America. In lieu of Stalin and Communism, the editors embraced a more traditional Marxist-Socialism that called for workers' revolutions to overturn the ruling class.

They also actively sought a solution to the dilemma of creating culture in a revolutionary society. They turned to gleanings from early Marxist writings and to Leon Trotsky.[27] Trotsky's ideas about the role of the intellectual, and the current status of revolutionary art, appeared in the *Partisan Review* in two articles in the summer and fall of 1938.

Trotsky claimed that the masses did not create revolutionary ideas, but were led by the cultural sphere. That sphere maintained its separate activity yet provided the central inspiration for revolution, because

> the artist cannot serve the struggle for freedom unless he subjectively assimilates its social content, unless he feels in his very nerves its meaning and drama and freely seeks to give his own inner world incarnation in his art.

At the same time, Trotsky was opposed to purism: "It is far from our wish to revive a so-called pure art."[28]

Greenberg would have read these articles about the time he met Dwight Macdonald in late 1938. In his own writing, however, he ignored the fact that Trotsky was opposed to purism and aestheticism in art, and adopted the model of art he learned from Hofmann and Morris as the only acceptable radical art. For Greenberg, new to the art world, abstraction and purity appeared to be sufficiently radical tools in the cultural struggle.

His basic theoretical accomplishment was to change the idea of the artist as a subconscious participant in the revolution working in a separate sphere, into the notion that abstract art, through its struggle with the medium and pursuit of purity can function as the emblem of

---

27    William Phillips, "The Esthetic of the Founding Fathers," *Partisan Review*, vol. 4, no. 4 (March 1938), pp. 11-21.

28    Leon Trotsky and André Breton, "Manifesto: Toward a Free Revolutionary Art," *Partisan Review,* vol. v, no. 4 (Fall 1938), pp. 51, 52. Although signed by Andre Bréton and Diego Rivera, the article is by Trotsky and Breton; see Herschel Chipp,ed. *Theories of Modern Art* (Berkeley, 1971), p. 457, n. 1. See also Leon Trotsky, "Art and Politics In Our Epoch," *Partisan Review*, vol. v, no. 3 (August 1938), pp. 3-10.

the revolution. That was how Greenberg himself turned "Trotskyism…
into art for art's sake, and thereby cleared the way, heroically, for what
was to come," as he proclaimed with the hindsight of the 1950s.[29]

In 1939 Greenberg published a short study of Bertolt Brecht,
establishing his Marxist credentials.[30] He was in Europe from April to
June of 1939, a tense time to travel there. He interviewed Ignazio Silone
in exile in Zurich who was an important figure to the *Partisan Review*.
An anti-Stalinist, he balanced art and politics, ideas and reality.[31]

Greenberg's interview appeared in the *Partisan Review* in the fall
of 1939, in the same issue with his first major article, "Avant-Garde and
Kitsch." The published interview provided several constructs Greenberg
used in his own article. Silone spoke of a "third front," which would
be politically independent, and to which writers would belong: "The
third front, existing as yet only in an ideal state, must be kept pure as
an ideal. And for that too, courage was required." Silone opposed the
*ersatz,* conservative solutions of Fascism, asserting that socialism was
crucial to "a regime of real freedom." He then went on to oppose the
role that writers played under Stalinism, saying that they "risk nothing." Finally, he spoke of the work of art as "beautiful, quite apart from
the intentions of the artist."[32] Silone's language—"courage," "idealism,"
"risk," "beauty"—easily found its way into Greenberg's youthful aesthetic and political vocabulary.

His short article on Bertolt Brecht had opened the door of *Partisan Review* for him by its display—however short lived—of the correct political credentials, Greenberg's second article "Avant-Garde and
Kitsch" established him as an influential critic. As a theoretical statement it picked up on Silone's ideas about the importance of an absolute

---

29     "The Late Thirties," (cited n. 8), p. 230.

30     "The Beggar's Opera-After Marx: Review of *A Penny for the Poor* by
       Bertolt Brecht" *Partisan Review*, vol. 4 no. 4 (Winter 1939), reprint
       (cited n. 1), vol. 1, pp. 3-4. A Marxist interpretation is briefly alluded
       to in certain class references, almost unavoidable in Brecht, but the
       bulk of the article is not Marxist.

31     Cooney (cited., n. 7), pp. 148-149.

32     An Interview with Ignazio Silone," *Partisan Review*, vol. 6, no. 3
       (Fall 1939), pp. 23, 26, 28. According to the introductory note, the
       interview was written by Silone based on Greenberg's notes.

or ideal realm of art. Greenberg linked that ideal realm to Hofmann's aesthetic of "spaces, surfaces, shapes, colors etc., to the exclusion of whatever is not necessarily implicated in these factors."[33]

Greenberg contrasted such pure art, specified by sweeping general examples, to "kitsch," the term he adopted to describe mass culture. Mass culture, in Greenberg's definition, was mechanically reproduced, and "draws its life blood" from real culture. Greenberg equated this type of mass culture with resentment of avant-garde culture, and to the type of realism supported by fascism:

> Most often this resentment toward culture is to be found where the dissatisfaction with society is a reactionary dissat-isfaction which expresses itself in revivalism and puritanism, and latest of all, in fascism. Here revolvers and torches begin to be mentioned in the same breath as culture. In the name of godliness or the blood's health, in the name of simple ways and solid virtues, the statue-smashing commences.[34]

Greenberg saw these regimes as responding to mass taste and uti-lizing that taste as an effective tool of propaganda. Greenberg was more elitist than either Trotsky or Silone, for he utterly disdained the mass taste of the worker:

> There has always been on one side the minority of the powerful—and therefore the cultivated—and on the other the great mass of the exploited and poor—and therefore ignorant. Formal culture has always belonged to the first, while the last have had to content themselves with folk or rudimentary culture, or kitsch.[35]

Thus, Greenberg expanded his category of kitsch, adding folk art to realism and to mass produced imitations of the avant-garde. Greenberg derived his notion of the nature of working class taste, or kitsch from an article by Dwight Macdonald on Soviet Cinema, in which Mac-donald connected the decline of avant-garde Soviet Cinema with the government's desire to use film as understandable propaganda directed

---

33    "Avant-Garde and Kitsch," (cited n. 3), p. 9.

34    Ibid., p. 17.

35    Ibid., p. 17.

to the working class. The Soviet Government supported popular style, in some cases basing it on Hollywood movies, in order to communicate the Government's socialist message to a large public.[36]

Greenberg combined mass culture, folk art, and realism into a single negative. In viewing realism as a regression to an easy art, Greenberg adopted the model of Hofmann, who regarded realism (and surrealism, especially as used by Dali) as less modern than art that utilized abstract formal principles. Abstraction became the radical alternative to realism (and by extension mass culture) that would preserve the revolution, if not bring it about. The obvious contradiction that the working class didn't like abstraction, that it was in fact an elite art, and that it required the support of the powerful class that was supposed to be overthrown, did not trouble Greenberg.

In his fundamentally elitist definition and privileging of a realm of culture, Greenberg borrowed more from T.S. Eliot than Trotsky and Silone.[37] In the 1930s, Eliot pursued a "reactionary" direction: he converted to Catholicism, and was considered a fascist. But Eliot's dicta for writing, and his model of the development of art echoed in Greenberg's work. Indeed, it fit seamlessly together with his other intellectual frameworks.

Eliot, in his 1923 essay "The Function of Criticism," spoke of the "problem of order." He regarded the critic's responsibility to be the making of order, that is, providing a system as a context for individual works of art:

There is accordingly something outside of the artist to which he owes allegiance, a devotion to which he must surrender

---

36    "Dwight Macdonald, "Soviet Society and Its Cinema," *Partisan Review*, vol. 6, no. 2 (Winter, 1939), pp. 80-95. Greenberg made several direct references to ideas in the article in his own essay. The term "kitsch" appears to be Greenberg's own choice of terminology for the mass culture. Since he knew German, it is probable that tie simply knew the word and its meaning, "trash, sappy stuff."

37    Clement Greenberg to Susan Platt (cited n. 14). In this conversation he stated emphatically (speaking as he writes) that Eliot was the principle inspiration for his criticism. Greenberg did not acknowledge his debt to Eliot until he included an article about him in *Art and Culture*.

and sacrifice himself in order to earn and to obtain his unique position.

The idea of an issue larger than art itself, which Eliot at one point said "may provisionally be called truth," dominated individual artists.[38]

Eliot offered a more hierarchical model of art than Trotsky. For Trotsky, the artist led the uninformed masses to revolution by reason of his intellectual superiority. For Eliot, the artist followed a higher concept, which had nothing to do with the masses. For Greenberg, the issue of art was this independent ideal. By focusing on this great abstract absolute—seemingly fortuitously represented by abstract art—, Greenberg justified a privileged realm of art and artist. This led to a narrow view of culture (and indirectly of politics). It precluded engagement with political or social change. In fact, it encouraged maintenance of the established system, the ideological *status quo.* Indeed, art had no social necessity in this view.

Socialism, then, was a mere dusting on Greenberg's vocabulary, designed to give him access to the politicized pages of the *Partisan Review.*[39] He also adopted the magazine's embattled tone, its call-to-arms chic. The *Partisan Review* regarded itself as preserving and identifying the only authentic radical culture of the late 1930s. It thought of itself as the only hope for the future of culture. Greenberg aggressively asserted, in true *Partisan Review* style: "Since the avant-garde forms the only living culture we now have, the survival in the near future of culture in general is thus threatened."[40]

---

38    T.S. Eliot, "The Function of Criticism," *Selected Essays, 1917-1932* (London 1933), pp. 12-13, 22.

39    Two analysis of "Avant-Garde and Kitsch," that point out its weaknesses as an ideological document, are in Cooney (cited, n. 7), pp. 211-212 and Andrew Higgins, "Clement Greenberg and the Idea of the Avant-Garde," *Studio International* 182 (October 1971), pp. 144-147. Greenberg's contact with Macdonald, a highly politicized writer, would have required him to engage in political stances. Macdonald's sponsorship of Greenberg provided the budding writer with his rapidly developing position within the magazine. His closeness to Macdonald is suggested by their collaboration on "Ten Propositions on the War," *Partisan Review*, vol. 8, no. 4 (July-August 1941), pp. 271-278.

40    "Avant-Garde and Kitsch," reprint (cited n. 1), vol. 1 p. 11.

Fundamental to the year 1939 was a sense of combat and confrontation—struggle between opposing forces. Greenberg's dogmatic certainty and polarities reflect anxiety about the future of culture, and by implication of humanity, during the bleak hours immediately before and just after the start of World War II. It was a time when hundreds of European artists faced a choice of exile or death. The Zeitgeist did not allow for petty quibbling and precious subtleties. Ultimately, Greenberg's formulation of an artistic/political avant-garde, with a shallow link to socialism, sought—for all its conservative aspects—to create an atmosphere of hope. He, in effect, attempted to save high culture from social catastrophe. Ironically, it could only be saved if it voluntarily went into the ghetto of abstraction.

## Part IV The Art Critic

Greenberg did not actually work as an art critic—as opposed to a theoretician of culture—until 1941, when he began to write for *The Nation* in two inches of space at the end of the magazine. After a brief stint in the military in the Spring and Summer of 1943, he became a regular reviewer. His criticism of the early and mid forties continues to utilize the instruments of aesthetic critical taste he developed from 1938-40. This remained the case even as he was confronted by the increasingly varied styles of the artworld itself. To his frustration and surprise, Greenberg discovered that much art—particularly Surrealism—did not correspond to his aesthetic.

While, at the end of "Towards a Newer Laocoon," he had written that he did not know which way art would develop, in his first exhibition review he was in fact dogmatic about what was "necessary" in art: "Shows of the works of three great, or once great abstract painters held in New York recently afforded an opportunity to consider the present condition of our most advanced painting ... It is my opinion that the fate of our particular tradition of art depends upon that into which abstract art develops."[41] This statement initiated the strategy of prediction—in effect an attempt to predetermine significance—Greenberg avoided in his earlier essay.

By 1944 Greenberg wrote, emphatically, that "the most ambitious and effective pictorial art of these times is abstract or goes in that direction." He justified his statement with a passing dialectical allusion to history. By 1946 Greenberg declared, with assurance, that "Gorky, Hare, Roszak, Tobey, Maclver, Price and even Motherwell have to be taken seriously, whether for good or bad ... they are among the relatively few people upon whom the fate of American art depends."[42] This little ghetto of abstract artists, with their supposed avant-garde idealism, had nothing less than the fate of art in their hands. The presumably only hope of culture in the dark forties was a delusion of abstract grandeur.

Greenberg developed the metaphor of the artist struggling to avoid surrendering in a fight, a theme readymade for war time: "How arduous is the career of the abstract painter, how difficult it is to sustain his freshness and growth. ... When the abstract artist grows tired, he becomes an interior decorator."[43] For Greenberg's aesthetic of theoretically autonomous abstract art, the wartime struggle was transformed into—reduced to—that between artist and medium, rather than Nazi and Jew, or socialist and bourgeois.

At the same time, he was confronted—surrounded—by Surrealism. Initially he thought it represented "the world on the point of dissolution." This telling metaphor suggests the reason for his uneasiness with the style.[44] In 1944 he was "worried" about such artists as Dali, Blume, Tchelitchew, Berman, Tanguy, among others: "The extreme eclecticism now prevailing in art is unhealthy and it should be counteracted, even at

---

41     "Review of Exhibitions of Joan Miro, Fernand Léger, and Wassily Kandinsky," *The Nation*, April 19, 1941, reprint (cited n. 1), vol. 1, p. 62.

42     "Review of the Pepsi-Cola Annual; the Exhibition 'Fourteen Americans'; and the Exhibition 'Advancing American Art'," reprint (cited n. 1), vol. 2, p. 113.

43     Miro, Léger, Kandinsky," reprint (cited n. 1), vol. 1, pp. 63-64.

44     "Walter Quirt," *The Nation*, 7 March 1942, p. 294 (Not included in reprint).

the risk of dogmatism and intolerance."[45] Finally, he wrote a long essay opposing Surrealism, referring to it contemptuously as "vicarious wish fulfillment."[46]

Shortly after his attack on Surrealism he reviewed an exhibition at Peggy Guggenheim's Art of this Century Gallery. He declared that "Jackson Pollock and William Baziotes… [were] among the six or seven best young painters we possess. … Baziotes is unadulterated talent … deflected by nothing extraneous to painting." Greenberg said that if Motherwell, "Only let himself stop watching himself, let him stop thinking. … Let him forget his personal 'subject matter' … But he has already done enough to make it no exaggeration to say the future of American painting depends on what he, Baziotes, Pollock and only a comparatively few others do from now on."[47]

The Abstract Expressionists, interpreted strictly in terms of their articulation of surface seemed to prove Greenberg's aesthetic. Lauded as the critic who discovered the Abstract Expressionists, Greenberg did no more than interpret them in the voice he had created for himself, editing out their extensive interest in symbolism and content. He castrated them for the sake of his limp aestheticism.

Through his simplification of Abstract Expressionism Greenberg perpetuated his 1939-1940 polarized aesthetic of abstraction based on surface, flatness, and purity. He spoke of the "dangerous and exciting abstract," as "ambitious" and "serious." The terms of his dialectic changed slightly, but his grand distinction between avant-garde and kitsch

---

45     "A New Installation at the Metropolitan Museum of Art, and a Review of the Exhibition 'Art in Progress' " The Nation, 10 June 1944, reprint (cited n. 1), vol. 1, p.213.

46     "Surrealist Painting," *The Nation* 19 August 1944, reprint (cited n. 1), vol. 1, p. 231. Piri Halasz, "Art Criticism (and Art History) in New York: The 1940s vs. the 1980s; Part Three: Clement Greenberg," *Arts Magazine,* vol. 57 (April 1983), pp. 80-89, discusses Greenberg's writings on Surrealism, taking issue with the idea that Greenberg opposed it.

47     Review of Exhibitions of William Baziotes and Robert Motherwell," *The Nation,*11, November 1944, reprint (cited n. 1), vol. I, pp. 239, 240, 241. The challenges raised by Pollock's work for Greenberg's criticism are material for a separate study. See for example, "Review of Exhibitions of Marc Chagall, Lyonel Feininger, and Jackson Pollock," Ibid., pp. 165-166.

persisted. Greenberg set the difficulties of avant-garde art over against the facile and the decorative, "merely pleasing" and "naturalistic."[48]

In the forties Greenberg began to speak of taste as the deciding factor in the polarized art situation. Good taste, rather than good politics, became the key issue.[49] In spite of his embellishment with fresh metaphors and adjectives, his writing continued to be based—redundantly—on a post-Cubist aesthetic.

In the late 1940s, Greenberg made a grand aesthetic stand in several long *Partisan Review* articles.[50] Now a powerful intellectual force in New York, after writing for many years in *The Nation*, he aroused strong objections to his criticism. The first attack came from his former colleague at *Partisan Review*, George L.K. Morris. He found Greenberg a disgrace to the profession:

> So deftly and inaccurately are the appraisals contrived that one suspects the thesis of having been the starting point—especially as several names that do not follow the pattern get left off the lists entirely. The field of contemporary art is given the semblance of a tournament. Umpire Greenberg charts the last rounds.[51]

Morris's skepticism, and his sense of Greenberg as a manipulator of reputations, seemed, at the time, to be related to his apparent conservatism as a critic. In fact, Morris forecasts what became some of the

---

48    Reprint (cited n. 1), vol. II, pp. 211, 131, 153, 287. Stephen C. Foster, *The Critics of Abstract Expressionism* (Ann Arbor, 1980), chap. 3-4; Foster makes a helpful comparison between Greenberg and Walter Pater, pp. 20-21.

49    Kuspit (cited n. 1), chap. 6 amusingly discussed this issue at length.

50    "The Situation at the Moment," *Partisan Review*, vol. 15, no. 1 (January 1948) reprint (cited n. 1), pp. 192-196. "The Decline of Cubism," *Partisan Review*, vol. 15, no. 3 (March 1948), reprint (cited n. 1), vol. II pp. 211-215. "The Crises of the Easel Picture," *Partisan Review*, vol. 15, no. 4 (April 1948,) reprint (cited n. 1), vol. II, pp. 221-225. "Irrelevance and Irresponsibility," *Partisan Review*, vol. 15, no. 5 (May1948), reprint (cited n. 1), vol. II, pp. 573-579; for other *Partisan Review* articles see Kuspit (cited n. 1), p. 207.

51    "On Critics and Greenberg: A Communication," *Partisan Review*, June 1948, p. 682.

terms of objection to Greenberg which became universal in the fifties and sixties.

Other critics with more complex criteria recognized the Abstract Expressionists,[52] but Greenberg got all the credit. In the 1950s, the New York art world lionized him. The domination of his simplistic dialectical formalism, based on a facile antithesis of good and bad, avant-garde and kitsch, acceptable and unacceptable, in or out, matched the debilitating polarities of the McCarthy Era and the Cold War.

But even as abstract painters—products of Hofmann's teaching and Greenberg's preaching—began to dominate the New York art world in the late 1940s and 1950s, the banned aesthetics of realism, decorative art, narrative art, and even mass culture itself developed vigorously, proliferating until it could no longer be ignored nor matter-of-factly dismissed as trivial and irrelevant. By the 1970s, Greenberg's clear dialectic of good and bad taste dissolved in a new environment of ambiguity and pluralism.

Greenberg's tragedy was his inability to modify his ideas on art to respond to changing circumstances. He rigidly adhered to an aesthetic of abstraction, defined in terms of flatness and purity. He had latched onto those ideas, borrowed from Hofmann, and promoted by Morris. For Greenberg, they became a security blanket against the threatened obliteration of all culture. That sense of threat remained alive in Greenberg's writing to the end of his career. Perhaps if he had allowed himself a more difficult, sustained struggle with his own medium of art criticism his thinking would have had more depth. But in the desperate atmosphere of the late thirties, extended theoretical explorations were not possible. Decisions, including art decisions, had to be made quickly. Greenberg needed the certainty of a fixed point of reference. Carefully dissected, the conservativism of his criticism—in the original sense of that term—becomes evident. Related to his Jewish heritage, described by Greenberg himself, was his emphasis on logic, abstraction, and the

---

52　　The criticism of James Johnson Sweeney stands out as more subtle and sophisticated, than Greenberg's in its engagement with elements other than form. See for example James Johnson Sweeney, "Art Chronicle," *Partisan Review,* vol. 12, no. 2 (Spring 1945), pp. 240-242 and "An Interview with Jacques Lipchitz," *Partisan Review,* vol.12, no. 1 (Winter 1945), pp. 83-89.

belief in an absolute. Greenberg brought these predispositions to bear on an early twentieth-century version of aesthetic significance, clothing it in a forceful style of writing, and giving it a political flair.

His repetitive, increasingly mechanical dialectic of art contrasts sharply with his subtle analysis of literature, especially in the first ten years of his career. He never settled for an absolute norm in his analysis of Franz Kafka, Bertolt Brecht, and the Victorian novel.[53] His literary criticism is at times more daring than his art criticism. Although he adopted, particularly in his later writing, some of the same notions, such as medium purity, he did not use them as uncompromisingly. The dogmatism of his art criticism, his whole program of formalism in visual art seems, in retrospect, Kafkaesque. It reflects Greenberg's fear of impending doom as well as his own insecurities as an art critic. This fear forced him to maintain an absolute—religious—belief in a utopian sphere of aesthetic activity, in order to avoid surrender to despair.

*Kafka sees life as sealed off and governed by unknowable powers who permit us the liberty only to repeat ourselves until we succumb.*[54] ~Clement Greenberg (1946)

---

53    The best example of the subtlety of his arguments about literature is the essay "Bertold Brecht's Poetry," *Partisan Review,* vol, 8, no. 2 (March-April 1941), reprint (cited n. 1), vol. I, pp. 49-62. Also published in *Art and Culture* (cited n. 8), pp. 252-265; and "A Victorian Novel," *Partisan Review,* vol. 2, no. 2 (Spring 1944) reprint (cited n. 1), vol. I, pp. 193-198. Also published in *Art and Culture* (cited n. 8), pp. 245-251. The inclusion of these early, lengthy essays, much less revised than those on art, suggests that Greenberg felt they were among his best works.

54    "Introduction to 'The Great Wall of China' by Franz Kafka," (cited n. 11), p. 101.

A native of New York City, SUSAN NOYES PLATT is currently a freelance art historian and art critic based in Seattle, Washington. She has published three books on art and criticism, *Modernism in the 1920s* (1985) *Art and Politics in the 1930s* (1999) and *Art and Politics Now* (2010). She was an assistant professor of Art History at Mills College, and a tenured professor at Washington State University and The University of North Texas. In 1999-2000 she taught at Yıldız Technical University, Istanbul, Turkey supported by a Fulbright Fellowship. As a critic she has written for numerous publications both national and international, as well as locally in a monthly newspaper column and bimonthly art magazine. She also writes a blog on her website www.artandpoliticsnow.com.